Mometrix
TEST PREPARATION

Secrets of the

CFP Exam
Study Guide

DEAR FUTURE EXAM SUCCESS STORY

First of all, **THANK YOU** for purchasing Mometrix study materials!

Second, congratulations! You are one of the few determined test-takers who are committed to doing whatever it takes to excel on your exam. **You have come to the right place.** We developed these study materials with one goal in mind: to deliver you the information you need in a format that's concise and easy to use.

In addition to optimizing your guide for the content of the test, we've outlined our recommended steps for breaking down the preparation process into small, attainable goals so you can make sure you stay on track.

We've also analyzed the entire test-taking process, identifying the most common pitfalls and showing how you can overcome them and be ready for any curveball the test throws you.

Standardized testing is one of the biggest obstacles on your road to success, which only increases the importance of doing well in the high-pressure, high-stakes environment of test day. Your results on this test could have a significant impact on your future, and this guide provides the information and practical advice to help you achieve your full potential on test day.

Your success is our success

We would love to hear from you! If you would like to share the story of your exam success or if you have any questions or comments in regard to our products, please contact us at **800-673-8175** or **support@mometrix.com**.

Thanks again for your business and we wish you continued success!

Sincerely,
The Mometrix Test Preparation Team

Need more help? Check out our flashcards at:
http://MometrixFlashcards.com/CFP

TABLE OF CONTENTS

Introduction

Thank you for purchasing this resource! You have made the choice to prepare yourself for a test that could have a huge impact on your future, and this guide is designed to help you be fully ready for test day. Obviously, it's important to have a solid understanding of the test material, but you also need to be prepared for the unique environment and stressors of the test, so that you can perform to the best of your abilities.

For this purpose, the first section that appears in this guide is the **Secret Keys**. We've devoted countless hours to meticulously researching what works and what doesn't, and we've boiled down our findings to the five most impactful steps you can take to improve your performance on the test. We start at the beginning with study planning and move through the preparation process, all the way to the testing strategies that will help you get the most out of what you know when you're finally sitting in front of the test.

We recommend that you start preparing for your test as far in advance as possible. However, if you've bought this guide as a last-minute study resource and only have a few days before your test, we recommend that you skip over the first two Secret Keys since they address a long-term study plan.

If you struggle with **test anxiety**, we strongly encourage you to check out our recommendations for how you can overcome it. Test anxiety is a formidable foe, but it can be beaten, and we want to make sure you have the tools you need to defeat it.

1

Secret Key #1 – Plan Big, Study Small

There's a lot riding on your performance. If you want to ace this test, you're going to need to keep your skills sharp and the material fresh in your mind. You need a plan that lets you review everything you need to know while still fitting in your schedule. We'll break this strategy down into three categories.

Information Organization

Start with the information you already have: the official test outline. From this, you can make a complete list of all the concepts you need to cover before the test. Organize these concepts into groups that can be studied together, and create a list of any related vocabulary you need to learn so you can brush up on any difficult terms. You'll want to keep this vocabulary list handy once you actually start studying since you may need to add to it along the way.

Time Management

Once you have your set of study concepts, decide how to spread them out over the time you have left before the test. Break your study plan into small, clear goals so you have a manageable task for each day and know exactly what you're doing. Then just focus on one small step at a time. When you manage your time this way, you don't need to spend hours at a time studying. Studying a small block of content for a short period each day helps you retain information better and avoid stressing over how much you have left to do. You can relax knowing that you have a plan to cover everything in time. In order for this strategy to be effective though, you have to start studying early and stick to your schedule. Avoid the exhaustion and futility that comes from last-minute cramming!

Study Environment

The environment you study in has a big impact on your learning. Studying in a coffee shop, while probably more enjoyable, is not likely to be as fruitful as studying in a quiet room. It's important to keep distractions to a minimum. You're only planning to study for a short block of time, so make the most of it. Don't pause to check your phone or get up to find a snack. It's also important to **avoid multitasking**. Research has consistently shown that multitasking will make your studying dramatically less effective. Your study area should also be comfortable and well-lit so you don't have the distraction of straining your eyes or sitting on an uncomfortable chair.

 The time of day you study is also important. You want to be rested and alert. Don't wait until just before bedtime. Study when you'll be most likely to comprehend and remember. Even better, if you know what time of day your test will be, set that time aside for study. That way your brain will be used to working on that subject at that specific time and you'll have a better chance of recalling information.

Finally, it can be helpful to team up with others who are studying for the same test. Your actual studying should be done in as isolated an environment as possible, but the work of organizing the information and setting up the study plan can be divided up. In between study sessions, you can discuss with your teammates the concepts that you're all studying and quiz each other on the details. Just be sure that your teammates are as serious about the test as you are. If you find that your study time is being replaced with social time, you might need to find a new team.

2

Secret Key #2 – Make Your Studying Count

You're devoting a lot of time and effort to preparing for this test, so you want to be absolutely certain it will pay off. This means doing more than just reading the content and hoping you can remember it on test day. It's important to make every minute of study count. There are two main areas you can focus on to make your studying count.

Retention

It doesn't matter how much time you study if you can't remember the material. You need to make sure you are retaining the concepts. To check your retention of the information you're learning, try recalling it at later times with minimal prompting. Try carrying around flashcards and glance at one or two from time to time or ask a friend who's also studying for the test to quiz you.

To enhance your retention, look for ways to put the information into practice so that you can apply it rather than simply recalling it. If you're using the information in practical ways, it will be much easier to remember. Similarly, it helps to solidify a concept in your mind if you're not only reading it to yourself but also explaining it to someone else. Ask a friend to let you teach them about a concept you're a little shaky on (or speak aloud to an imaginary audience if necessary). As you try to summarize, define, give examples, and answer your friend's questions, you'll understand the concepts better and they will stay with you longer. Finally, step back for a big picture view and ask yourself how each piece of information fits with the whole subject. When you link the different concepts together and see them working together as a whole, it's easier to remember the individual components.

Finally, practice showing your work on any multi-step problems, even if you're just studying. Writing out each step you take to solve a problem will help solidify the process in your mind, and you'll be more likely to remember it during the test.

Modality

Modality simply refers to the means or method by which you study. Choosing a study modality that fits your own individual learning style is crucial. No two people learn best in exactly the same way, so it's important to know your strengths and use them to your advantage.

For example, if you learn best by visualization, focus on visualizing a concept in your mind and draw an image or a diagram. Try color-coding your notes, illustrating them, or creating symbols that will trigger your mind to recall a learned concept. If you learn best by hearing or discussing information, find a study partner who learns the same way or read aloud to yourself. Think about how to put the information in your own words. Imagine that you are giving a lecture on the topic and record yourself so you can listen to it later.

For any learning style, flashcards can be helpful. Organize the information so you can take advantage of spare moments to review. Underline key words or phrases. Use different colors for different categories. Mnemonic devices (such as creating a short list in which every item starts with the same letter) can also help with retention. Find what works best for you and use it to store the information in your mind most effectively and easily.

3

Secret Key #3 – Practice the Right Way

Your success on test day depends not only on how many hours you put into preparing, but also on whether you prepared the right way. It's good to check along the way to see if your studying is paying off. One of the most effective ways to do this is by taking practice tests to evaluate your progress. Practice tests are useful because they show exactly where you need to improve. Every time you take a practice test, pay special attention to these three groups of questions:

- The questions you got wrong
- The questions you had to guess on, even if you guessed right
- The questions you found difficult or slow to work through

This will show you exactly what your weak areas are, and where you need to devote more study time. Ask yourself why each of these questions gave you trouble. Was it because you didn't understand the material? Was it because you didn't remember the vocabulary? Do you need more repetitions on this type of question to build speed and confidence? Dig into those questions and figure out how you can strengthen your weak areas as you go back to review the material.

 Additionally, many practice tests have a section explaining the answer choices. It can be tempting to read the explanation and think that you now have a good understanding of the concept. However, an explanation likely only covers part of the question's broader context. Even if the explanation makes perfect sense, **go back and investigate** every concept related to the question until you're positive you have a thorough understanding.

As you go along, keep in mind that the practice test is just that: practice. Memorizing these questions and answers will not be very helpful on the actual test because it is unlikely to have any of the same exact questions. If you only know the right answers to the sample questions, you won't be prepared for the real thing. **Study the concepts** until you understand them fully, and then you'll be able to answer any question that shows up on the test.

It's important to wait on the practice tests until you're ready. If you take a test on your first day of study, you may be overwhelmed by the amount of material covered and how much you need to learn. Work up to it gradually.

On test day, you'll need to be prepared for answering questions, managing your time, and using the test-taking strategies you've learned. It's a lot to balance, like a mental marathon that will have a big impact on your future. Like training for a marathon, you'll need to start slowly and work your way up. When test day arrives, you'll be ready.

Start with the strategies you've read in the first two Secret Keys—plan your course and study in the way that works best for you. If you have time, consider using multiple study resources to get different approaches to the same concepts. It can be helpful to see difficult concepts from more than one angle. Then find a good source for practice tests. Many times, the test website will suggest potential study resources or provide sample tests.

Practice Test Strategy

If you're able to find at least three practice tests, we recommend this strategy:

UNTIMED AND OPEN-BOOK PRACTICE

Take the first test with no time constraints and with your notes and study guide handy. Take your time and focus on applying the strategies you've learned.

TIMED AND OPEN-BOOK PRACTICE

Take the second practice test open-book as well, but set a timer and practice pacing yourself to finish in time.

TIMED AND CLOSED-BOOK PRACTICE

Take any other practice tests as if it were test day. Set a timer and put away your study materials. Sit at a table or desk in a quiet room, imagine yourself at the testing center, and answer questions as quickly and accurately as possible.

Keep repeating timed and closed-book tests on a regular basis until you run out of practice tests or it's time for the actual test. Your mind will be ready for the schedule and stress of test day, and you'll be able to focus on recalling the material you've learned.

Secret Key #4 – Pace Yourself

Once you're fully prepared for the material on the test, your biggest challenge on test day will be managing your time. Just knowing that the clock is ticking can make you panic even if you have plenty of time left. Work on pacing yourself so you can build confidence against the time constraints of the exam. Pacing is a difficult skill to master, especially in a high-pressure environment, so **practice is vital**.

Set time expectations for your pace based on how much time is available. For example, if a section has 60 questions and the time limit is 30 minutes, you know you have to average 30 seconds or less per question in order to answer them all. Although 30 seconds is the hard limit, set 25 seconds per question as your goal, so you reserve extra time to spend on harder questions. When you budget extra time for the harder questions, you no longer have any reason to stress when those questions take longer to answer.

Don't let this time expectation distract you from working through the test at a calm, steady pace, but keep it in mind so you don't spend too much time on any one question. Recognize that taking extra time on one question you don't understand may keep you from answering two that you do understand later in the test. If your time limit for a question is up and you're still not sure of the answer, mark it and move on, and come back to it later if the time and the test format allow. If the testing format doesn't allow you to return to earlier questions, just make an educated guess; then put it out of your mind and move on.

On the easier questions, be careful not to rush. It may seem wise to hurry through them so you have more time for the challenging ones, but it's not worth missing one if you know the concept and just didn't take the time to read the question fully. Work efficiently but make sure you understand the question and have looked at all of the answer choices, since more than one may seem right at first.

Even if you're paying attention to the time, you may find yourself a little behind at some point. You should speed up to get back on track, but do so wisely. Don't panic; just take a few seconds less on each question until you're caught up. Don't guess without thinking, but do look through the answer choices and eliminate any you know are wrong. If you can get down to two choices, it is often worthwhile to guess from those. Once you've chosen an answer, move on and don't dwell on any that you skipped or had to hurry through. If a question was taking too long, chances are it was one of the harder ones, so you weren't as likely to get it right anyway.

On the other hand, if you find yourself getting ahead of schedule, it may be beneficial to slow down a little. The more quickly you work, the more likely you are to make a careless mistake that will affect your score. You've budgeted time for each question, so don't be afraid to spend that time. Practice an efficient but careful pace to get the most out of the time you have.

Secret Key #5 – Have a Plan for Guessing

When you're taking the test, you may find yourself stuck on a question. Some of the answer choices seem better than others, but you don't see the one answer choice that is obviously correct. What do you do?

The scenario described above is very common, yet most test takers have not effectively prepared for it. Developing and practicing a plan for guessing may be one of the single most effective uses of your time as you get ready for the exam.

In developing your plan for guessing, there are three questions to address:

- When should you start the guessing process?
- How should you narrow down the choices?
- Which answer should you choose?

When to Start the Guessing Process

Unless your plan for guessing is to select C every time (which, despite its merits, is not what we recommend), you need to leave yourself enough time to apply your answer elimination strategies. Since you have a limited amount of time for each question, that means that if you're going to give yourself the best shot at guessing correctly, you have to decide quickly whether or not you will guess.

Of course, the best-case scenario is that you don't have to guess at all, so first, see if you can answer the question based on your knowledge of the subject and basic reasoning skills. Focus on the key words in the question and try to jog your memory of related topics. Give yourself a chance to bring the knowledge to mind, but once you realize that you don't have (or you can't access) the knowledge you need to answer the question, it's time to start the guessing process.

It's almost always better to start the guessing process too early than too late. It only takes a few seconds to remember something and answer the question from knowledge. Carefully eliminating wrong answer choices takes longer. Plus, going through the process of eliminating answer choices can actually help jog your memory.

Summary: Start the guessing process as soon as you decide that you can't answer the question based on your knowledge.

How to Narrow Down the Choices

The next chapter in this book (**Test-Taking Strategies**) includes a wide range of strategies for how to approach questions and how to look for answer choices to eliminate. You will definitely want to read those carefully, practice them, and figure out which ones work best for you. Here though, we're going to address a mindset rather than a particular strategy.

Your odds of guessing an answer correctly depend on how many options you are choosing from.

Number of options left	5	4	3	2	1
Odds of guessing correctly	20%	25%	33%	50%	100%

You can see from this chart just how valuable it is to be able to eliminate incorrect answers and make an educated guess, but there are two things that many test takers do that cause them to miss out on the benefits of guessing:

- Accidentally eliminating the correct answer
- Selecting an answer based on an impression

We'll look at the first one here, and the second one in the next section.

To avoid accidentally eliminating the correct answer, we recommend a thought exercise called **the $5 challenge**. In this challenge, you only eliminate an answer choice from contention if you are willing to bet $5 on it being wrong. Why $5? Five dollars is a small but not insignificant amount of money. It's an amount you could afford to lose but wouldn't want to throw away. And while losing

$5 once might not hurt too much, doing it twenty times will set you back $100. In the same way, each small decision you make—eliminating a choice here, guessing on a question there—won't by itself impact your score very much, but when you put them all together, they can make a big difference. By holding each answer choice elimination decision to a higher standard, you can reduce the risk of accidentally eliminating the correct answer.

The $5 challenge can also be applied in a positive sense: If you are willing to bet $5 that an answer choice *is* correct, go ahead and mark it as correct.

Summary: Only eliminate an answer choice if you are willing to bet $5 that it is wrong.

8

Which Answer to Choose

You're taking the test. You've run into a hard question and decided you'll have to guess. You've eliminated all the answer choices you're willing to bet $5 on. Now you have to pick an answer. Why do we even need to talk about this? Why can't you just pick whichever one you feel like when the time comes?

The answer to these questions is that if you don't come into the test with a plan, you'll rely on your impression to select an answer choice, and if you do that, you risk falling into a trap. The test writers know that everyone who takes their test will be guessing on some of the questions, so they intentionally write wrong answer choices to seem plausible. You still have to pick an answer though, and if the wrong answer choices are designed to look right, how can you ever be sure that you're not falling for their trap? The best solution we've found to this dilemma is to take the decision out of your hands entirely. Here is the process we recommend:

Once you've eliminated any choices that you are confident (willing to bet $5) are wrong, select the first remaining choice as your answer.

Whether you choose to select the first remaining choice, the second, or the last, the important thing is that you use some preselected standard. Using this approach guarantees that you will not be enticed into selecting an answer choice that looks right, because you are not basing your decision on how the answer choices look.

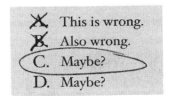

This is not meant to make you question your knowledge. Instead, it is to help you recognize the difference between your knowledge and your impressions. There's a huge difference between thinking an answer is right because of what you know, and thinking an answer is right because it looks or sounds like it should be right.

Summary: To ensure that your selection is appropriately random, make a predetermined selection from among all answer choices you have not eliminated.

Test-Taking Strategies

This section contains a list of test-taking strategies that you may find helpful as you work through the test. By taking what you know and applying logical thought, you can maximize your chances of answering any question correctly!

It is very important to realize that every question is different and every person is different: no single strategy will work on every question, and no single strategy will work for every person. That's why we've included all of them here, so you can try them out and determine which ones work best for different types of questions and which ones work best for you.

Question Strategies

☑ READ CAREFULLY

Read the question and the answer choices carefully. Don't miss the question because you misread the terms. You have plenty of time to read each question thoroughly and make sure you understand what is being asked. Yet a happy medium must be attained, so don't waste too much time. You must read carefully and efficiently.

☑ CONTEXTUAL CLUES

Look for contextual clues. If the question includes a word you are not familiar with, look at the immediate context for some indication of what the word might mean. Contextual clues can often give you all the information you need to decipher the meaning of an unfamiliar word. Even if you can't determine the meaning, you may be able to narrow down the possibilities enough to make a solid guess at the answer to the question.

☑ PREFIXES

If you're having trouble with a word in the question or answer choices, try dissecting it. Take advantage of every clue that the word might include. Prefixes can be a huge help. Usually, they allow you to determine a basic meaning. *Pre-* means before, *post-* means after, *pro-* is positive, *de-* is negative. From prefixes, you can get an idea of the general meaning of the word and try to put it into context.

☑ HEDGE WORDS

Watch out for critical hedge words, such as *likely, may, can, sometimes, often, almost, mostly, usually, generally, rarely,* and *sometimes.* Question writers insert these hedge phrases to cover every possibility. Often an answer choice will be wrong simply because it leaves no room for exception. Be on guard for answer choices that have definitive words such as *exactly* and *always.*

☑ SWITCHBACK WORDS

Stay alert for *switchbacks.* These are the words and phrases frequently used to alert you to shifts in thought. The most common switchback words are *but, although,* and *however.* Others include *nevertheless, on the other hand, even though, while, in spite of, despite,* and *regardless of.* Switchback words are important to catch because they can change the direction of the question or an answer choice.

10

⊘ Face Value

When in doubt, use common sense. Accept the situation in the problem at face value. Don't read too much into it. These problems will not require you to make wild assumptions. If you have to go beyond creativity and warp time or space in order to have an answer choice fit the question, then you should move on and consider the other answer choices. These are normal problems rooted in reality. The applicable relationship or explanation may not be readily apparent, but it is there for you to figure out. Use your common sense to interpret anything that isn't clear.

Answer Choice Strategies

⊘ Answer Selection

The most thorough way to pick an answer choice is to identify and eliminate wrong answers until only one is left, then confirm it is the correct answer. Sometimes an answer choice may immediately seem right, but be careful. The test writers will usually put more than one reasonable answer choice on each question, so take a second to read all of them and make sure that the other choices are not equally obvious. As long as you have time left, it is better to read every answer choice than to pick the first one that looks right without checking the others.

⊘ Answer Choice Families

An answer choice family consists of two (in rare cases, three) answer choices that are very similar in construction and cannot all be true at the same time. If you see two answer choices that are direct opposites or parallels, one of them is usually the correct answer. For instance, if one answer choice says that quantity x increases and another either says that quantity x decreases (opposite) or says that quantity y increases (parallel), then those answer choices would fall into the same family. An answer choice that doesn't match the construction of the answer choice family is more likely to be incorrect. Most questions will not have answer choice families, but when they do appear, you should be prepared to recognize them.

⊘ Eliminate Answers

Eliminate answer choices as soon as you realize they are wrong, but make sure you consider all possibilities. If you are eliminating answer choices and realize that the last one you are left with is also wrong, don't panic. Start over and consider each choice again. There may be something you missed the first time that you will realize on the second pass.

⊘ Avoid Fact Traps

Don't be distracted by an answer choice that is factually true but doesn't answer the question. You are looking for the choice that answers the question. Stay focused on what the question is asking for so you don't accidentally pick an answer that is true but incorrect. Always go back to the question and make sure the answer choice you've selected actually answers the question and is not merely a true statement.

⊘ Extreme Statements

In general, you should avoid answers that put forth extreme actions as standard practice or proclaim controversial ideas as established fact. An answer choice that states the "process should be used in certain situations, if..." is much more likely to be correct than one that states the "process should be discontinued completely." The first is a calm rational statement and doesn't even make a definitive, uncompromising stance, using a hedge word *if* to provide wiggle room, whereas the second choice is far more extreme.

☑ Benchmark

As you read through the answer choices and you come across one that seems to answer the question well, mentally select that answer choice. This is not your final answer, but it's the one that will help you evaluate the other answer choices. The one that you selected is your benchmark or standard for judging each of the other answer choices. Every other answer choice must be compared to your benchmark. That choice is correct until proven otherwise by another answer choice beating it. If you find a better answer, then that one becomes your new benchmark. Once you've decided that no other choice answers the question as well as your benchmark, you have your final answer.

☑ Predict the Answer

Before you even start looking at the answer choices, it is often best to try to predict the answer. When you come up with the answer on your own, it is easier to avoid distractions and traps because you will know exactly what to look for. The right answer choice is unlikely to be word-for-word what you came up with, but it should be a close match. Even if you are confident that you have the right answer, you should still take the time to read each option before moving on.

General Strategies

☑ Tough Questions

If you are stumped on a problem or it appears too hard or too difficult, don't waste time. Move on! Remember though, if you can quickly check for obviously incorrect answer choices, your chances of guessing correctly are greatly improved. Before you completely give up, at least try to knock out a couple of possible answers. Eliminate what you can and then guess at the remaining answer choices before moving on.

☑ Check Your Work

Since you will probably not know every term listed and the answer to every question, it is important that you get credit for the ones that you do know. Don't miss any questions through careless mistakes. If at all possible, try to take a second to look back over your answer selection and make sure you've selected the correct answer choice and haven't made a costly careless mistake (such as marking an answer choice that you didn't mean to mark). This quick double check should more than pay for itself in caught mistakes for the time it costs.

☑ Pace Yourself

It's easy to be overwhelmed when you're looking at a page full of questions; your mind is confused and full of random thoughts, and the clock is ticking down faster than you would like. Calm down and maintain the pace that you have set for yourself. Especially as you get down to the last few minutes of the test, don't let the small numbers on the clock make you panic. As long as you are on track by monitoring your pace, you are guaranteed to have time for each question.

☑ Don't Rush

It is very easy to make errors when you are in a hurry. Maintaining a fast pace in answering questions is pointless if it makes you miss questions that you would have gotten right otherwise. Test writers like to include distracting information and wrong answers that seem right. Taking a little extra time to avoid careless mistakes can make all the difference in your test score. Find a pace that allows you to be confident in the answers that you select.

⊘ KEEP MOVING

Panicking will not help you pass the test, so do your best to stay calm and keep moving. Taking deep breaths and going through the answer elimination steps you practiced can help to break through a stress barrier and keep your pace.

Final Notes

The combination of a solid foundation of content knowledge and the confidence that comes from practicing your plan for applying that knowledge is the key to maximizing your performance on test day. As your foundation of content knowledge is built up and strengthened, you'll find that the strategies included in this chapter become more and more effective in helping you quickly sift through the distractions and traps of the test to isolate the correct answer.

Now that you're preparing to move forward into the test content chapters of this book, be sure to keep your goal in mind. As you read, think about how you will be able to apply this information on the test. If you've already seen sample questions for the test and you have an idea of the question format and style, try to come up with questions of your own that you can answer based on what you're reading. This will give you valuable practice applying your knowledge in the same ways you can expect to on test day.

Good luck and good studying!

Professional Conduct and Regulation

CODE OF ETHICS AND PROFESSIONAL RESPONSIBILITY

PREAMBLE AND APPLICABILITY

The Code of Ethics and Professional Responsibility, composed and published by the Certified Financial Planner Board of Standards, was adopted to outline the principles and rules that apply to all certified financial planners. In other words, all those people who use the CFP certification mark and count themselves as Certified Financial Planners are bound by these principles and rules. In addition, the Code of Ethics applies to those candidates for the CFP certification exam who have been registered as such with the CFP Board. The CFP Board of Standards recommends that every CFP candidate study the Code thoroughly before examination.

COMPOSITION, SCOPE, AND COMPLIANCE

The Code of Ethics and Professional Responsibility is divided into two parts. The first part covers principles and the second part covers rules. Principles are statements that express in general terms the ethical and professional ideals that the CFP Board expects certified financial planners to exhibit in their professional activities. Basically, the principles are designed to provide a source of guidance for CFP Board designees. The rules section, on the other hand, contains descriptions of the standards of ethical and professionally responsible behavior that the Board expects of designees in specific situations. Of course, the varied nature of financial planning means that all of the rules will not be applicable to all designees at all times. The CFP Board does require, however, that all CFP designees adhere to this code at all times.

CLIENT, CFP BOARD DESIGNEE, COMMISSION, COMPENSATION, AND CONFLICTS OF INTEREST

The Code of Ethics and Professional Responsibility defines a number of terms that are essential to the practice of financial planning. A client is a person, persons, or entity who engages a financial planner and for whom professional services are rendered. A CFP Board designee is any person who currently holds a CFP certificate, is a candidate for certification, or has any entitlement to the CFP certification marks. A commission is the compensation an agent or broker receives when this compensation is calculated as a percentage of the amount of his or her sales or purchase transactions. Conflicts of interest are problems that arise when a CFP Board designee's work could be impaired by a personal interest, business relationship, or other circumstances.

FEE-ONLY, FINANCIAL PLANNING ENGAGEMENT, AND PERSONAL FINANCIAL PLANNING

The Code of Ethics and Professional Responsibility defines a number of terms that are essential to the practice of financial planning. The term fee-only refers to a method of compensation in which the financial planner receives compensation only from the client and receives no compensation that depends on the purchase or sale of any financial product. A financial planning engagement is said to exist when a client is relying on the information or services provided by a CFP Board designee using the financial planning process. Personal financial planning, also known just as financial planning, refers to the process of determining the proper means for an individual to achieve his or her financial goals through the financial planning process.

PERSONAL FINANCIAL PLANNING PROCESS

The Code of Ethics and Professional Responsibility defines a number of terms that are essential to the practice of financial planning. The personal financial planning process, sometimes just known as the financial planning process, is the process that includes (but is not necessarily limited to) six basic elements: establishing and defining the client-planner relationship; gathering client data,

15

objectives, and goals; analyzing and evaluating the client's financial status; developing and presenting financial planning recommendations; implementing the financial planning recommendations; and, finally, monitoring the financial planning recommendations.

PERSONAL FINANCIAL PLANNING SUBJECT AREAS AND PERSONAL FINANCIAL PLANNING PROFESSIONAL

The Code of Ethics and Professional Responsibility defines a number of terms that are essential to the practice of financial planning. Personal financial planning subject areas are the main subject fields in financial planning. Specifically, these subject areas are financial statement preparation and analysis; investment planning (including portfolio design); income tax planning; education planning; risk management; retirement planning; and estate planning. A personal financial planning professional is someone who is able and qualified to offer accurate, honest, and comprehensive financial advice to individuals who are trying to reach specific financial goals.

PART ONE, PRINCIPLES

The principles on the Code of Ethics and Professional Responsibility outline the general ethical considerations of a financial planner. These principles apply to all CFP Board designees and are meant to provide guidance to financial planners as they go about their business. The seven principles are qualities that an ethical financial planner will cultivate. They are integrity, objectivity, competence, fairness, confidentiality, professionalism, and diligence. Though these principles in general have the well being of the client in mind, they do not assert that a financial planner should manipulate facts in order to please a potential client. On the contrary, the second principle, objectivity, directly asserts that financial planners should remain objective regarding the achievable goals for each client.

RULES 101, 102, AND 103

The second section of the Code of Ethics and Professional Responsibility contains specific rules for handling common financial planning situations. Rule 101 asserts that a financial planner should not solicit clients through false or misleading communications or advertisements. Rule 102 asserts that a financial planner should not engage in any conduct that involves dishonesty, fraud, deceit, or misrepresentation. Rule 103 is more complex; it lists the specific responsibilities a Board designee has to his or her clients. These are as follows: acting in accordance with the authority set forth in the governing legal instrument; identifying and maintaining records of funds and other property held by a client; delivering any funds or other property to which the client is entitled; not commingling client funds with the designee's own personal property; and showing the care required of a fiduciary.

RULES 201, 202, 301, AND 302

The Code of Ethics and Professional Responsibility outlines some specific rules for situations that are common to a financial planner. Rule 201 states that a financial planner must exercise reasonable and prudent professional judgment. Rule 202 states that a financial planner must act in the interest of the client. Rule 301 states that a financial planner must stay informed of developments in the field of financial planning and participate in continuing education. Rule 302 states that a financial planner must offer advice only in those areas in which that financial planner has competence. In those matters in which the financial planner is not competent, he or she should seek the counsel of qualified individuals.

RULE 401

The Code of Ethics and Professional Responsibility has specific rules for situations that are common in financial planning. Rule 401 requires that a financial planner disclose to the client any important material information, including conflicts of interest and any changes in business affiliation, address, telephone number, credentials, qualifications, licenses, compensation structure, and agency relationships. Also, Rule 401 states that a financial planner must disclose the information required by all laws applicable to the relationship in a manner that is consistent with the relevant laws. Rule 401 is based on the Principle of Fairness, insofar as its objective is to ensure that the client has all of the information needed to make informed decisions about a financial planner.

RULE 402

Rule 402 of the Code of Ethics and Professional Responsibility is designed to support the Principle of Fairness, ensuring that clients have the necessary means to make decisions in their own best interests. Specifically, Rule 402 states that a financial planning practitioner shall make timely written disclosure of all material information relative to the professional relationship. This information always includes conflicts of interest and sources of compensation. A source document is considered in compliance if it includes: a statement of the designee's philosophy; resumes for those individuals who can be expected to contribute to the client's financial plan; a source of compensation and referral fees; a statement describing the designee's compensation system; any material agency or employment relationships with third parties; and a statement identifying any conflicts of interest.

RULES 403, 404, AND 405

In the Code of Ethics and Professional Responsibility, Rule 403 states that before the client relationship is established, a financial planner must disclose in writing any relationships that could reasonably compromise the financial planner's objectivity or independence. Rule 404 states that if a conflict of interest should develop during the course of the financial planning process, the financial planner should immediately disclose the conflict. Rule 405 states that the disclosure of compensation must be made annually to ongoing clients. This means offering clients a current copy of the Securities and Exchange Commission Form ADV, Part II, or all of the disclosure information described in Rule 402.

RULES 406, 407, 408, 409, AND 410

The rules in the 400 series of the Code of Ethics and Professional Responsibility relate to the Principle of Fairness. Rule 406 of the states that the compensation of a financial planner should be fair and reasonable. Rule 407 states that references may be provided that include recommendations from present or former clients. Rule 408 states that the scope of the authority of a financial planner must be clearly defined and properly documented. Rule 409 states that all CFP Board designees are obliged to adhere to the same standards of disclosure and service. Rule 410 states that a financial planner must perform his or her professional services with strict dedication to the lawful objectives of the employer and in accordance with the Code of Ethics and Professional Responsibility.

RULES 411, 412, AND 413

Rule 411 of the Code of Ethics and Professional Responsibility states that a CFP designee must advise his or her employer about any outside affiliations that may reasonably compromise his or her service to an employer. This rule also states that a financial planner must provide timely notice to the employer and clients, unless this is precluded by contractual obligation, in the event of change of employment or change in CFP Board certification status. Rule 412 states that a CFP Board designee must act in good faith with partners. Rule 413 states that a CFP Board designee must disclose to his or her partners all relevant and material information regarding credentials, competence, experience, licensing, legal status, and financial stability.

RULES 414, 415, AND 416

The rules in the 400 series of the second part of the Code of Ethics and Professional Responsibility relate to the Principle of Fairness. Rule 414 states that a CFP Board designee who is a partner or co-owner of a financial services firm must withdraw in compliance with any applicable agreement and in a fair and equitable manner. Rule 415 states that a CFP Board designee must disclose to an employer any compensation or other benefit arrangements in connection with his or her services to clients that are in addition to compensation from the employer. Rule 416 states that if a CFP Board designee enters into a business transaction with a client, the transaction shall be on terms that are fair and reasonable to the client.

RULE 501

The rules in the 500 series of the Code of Ethics and Professional Responsibility relate to the Principle of Confidentiality. Rule 501 states that a financial planner should not reveal any personally identifiable information relating to the client relationship without the client's consent. There are only a few sets of circumstances in which such use is reasonably necessary: to establish an advisory or brokerage account, to effect a transaction for the client, or to carry out any other aspect of the client engagement; to comply with legal requirements or the legal process; to defend the CFP Board designee against charges of wrong-doing; and in connection with a civil dispute between the CFB Board designee and the client.

RULES 502, 503, 601, 602, AND 603

Rule 502 of the Code of Ethics and Professional Responsibility states that a CFP Board designee must maintain the same standards of confidentiality to employers as clients. Rule 503 states that a financial planner must adhere to reasonable expectations of confidentiality while in business and thereafter. Rule 601 states that a financial planner must use the marks in compliance with the rules and regulations of the CFP Board. Rule 602 states that a CFP Board designee must show respect for other financial planning professionals and related occupational groups by engaging in fair and honorable competitive practices. Rule 603 states that a financial planner must inform the CFP Board when another CFP designee has undoubtedly committed a violation of the Code of Ethics.

RULES 604, 605, AND 606

Rule 604 states that a financial planner must inform the appropriate regulatory and/or professional disciplinary body when there is any unprofessional, fraudulent, or illegal conduct by another CFP Board designee or another financial professional. Rule 605 states that a financial planner must disclose illegal conduct to the supervisor and/or partners if illegal conduct is suspected. Rule 606 states that a financial planner must perform his or he services in accordance with all applicable laws, rules, and regulations of governmental agencies and other applicable authorities. Also, it states that a financial planner must act in accordance with all the applicable rules, regulations, and other established policies of the CFP Board.

RULES 607, 608, AND 609

Rule 607 of the Code of Ethics and Professional Responsibility states that a financial planner must not engage in any conduct that reflects adversely on the profession. Rule 608 states that a financial planner must disclose to clients the firm's status as registered investment advisers. It is appropriate to use the term registered investment adviser if the designee is registered individually. If the designee is registered through his or her firm, then the firm is a registered investment adviser. Rule 609 states that a CFP Board designee must not practice any other profession or offer to provide such services unless the CFP Board designee is qualified to practice in those fields and is licensed as required by state law.

Mometrix

RULES 610, 611, AND 612

Rule 610 of the Code of Ethics and Professional Responsibility states that a financial planner must return the client's original records in a timely manner whenever the client should request them. Rule 611 states that a financial planner should not bring or threaten to bring a disciplinary proceeding under the Code of Ethics, or report or threaten to report information to the CFP Board pursuant to Rules 603 and/or 604, for no substantial purpose other than to harass, embarrass, and/or unfairly burden another CFP Board designee. Rule 612 states that a financial planner should comply with all applicable renewal requirements that have been established by the CFP Board.

RULES 701, 702, 703, 704, AND 705

Rule 701 of the Code of Ethics and Professional Responsibility states that a financial planner should provide services diligently. Rule 702 states that a financial planner should enter into an engagement only after securing sufficient information to satisfy him or herself that the relationship is warranted by the client's needs and objectives and that the designee has the ability to provide competent service or to involve professionals who can. Rule 703 states that a financial planner should implement only those recommendations that are suitable for the client. Rule 704 states that a financial planner should make a reasonable investigation regarding the financial products recommended to clients. Rule 705 states hat a financial planner should supervise subordinates with regard to their delivery of financial planning services.

FINANCIAL PLANNING PRACTICE STANDARDS
PURPOSE AND APPLICABILITY

The Practice Standards are designed to set the level of professional practice required of a CFP designee engaged in personal financial planning. The Practice Standards advance professionalism in financial planning and enhance the value of the financial planning process. These standards are set also to help practitioners focus on what clients need. There are ten standards that have been drafted by the Board of Practice Standards, with one or more being assigned to each step in the financial planning process. The Practice Standards do not require that financial planners provide comprehensive planning for clients. Compliance with Practice Standards is discussed in Rule 606 (b) of the Code of Ethics.

100 AND 200 SERIES

The 100 series of the Practice Standards is about establishing and defining a relationship with a client. Standard 100-1 states that the scope of the engagement should be defined before any financial planning service is provided. The 200 series of the Practice Standards is about gathering client data. Standard 200-1 states that a financial planner should determine a client's personal and financial goals, needs, and priorities before making or implementing any recommendations. Standard 200-2 states that a financial planner must obtain quantitative information and documents before making or implementing any recommendations. If such information or documentation is not obtained, the engagement should either be limited or terminated.

300 AND 400 SERIES

The 300 series of the Practice Standards pertains to analyzing and evaluating the financial status of the client. Standard 300-1 states that a financial planner should analyze in order to understand the client's financial situation and to determine how the client's goals can be met. The 400 series is about developing and presenting financial planning recommendations. Standard 400-1 states that a financial planner should identify and evaluate the financial planning alternatives that can achieve the client's goals, needs, and priorities. Standard 400-2 states that a financial planner should

19

develop his or her recommendations from this set of alternatives. Standard 400-3 states that a financial planner should the present his or her recommendations to the client.

500 AND 600 SERIES AND ENFORCEMENT

The 500 series of the Practice Standards is about implementing the financial planning recommendations. Standard 500-1 states that the financial planner and the client should agree on the implementation responsibilities. Standard 500-2 states that they should also select products and services for implementation. The 600 series involves monitoring the implemented strategies. Standard 600-1 states that the financial planner and client must mutually define monitoring responsibilities. CFP designees are required to practice in a manner consistent with these Practice Standards. The enforcement of the Practice Standards is based on the disciplinary rules and procedures established by the CFP Board and administered by the Board of Professional Review and Board of Appeals.

DISCIPLINARY RULES AND PROCEDURES

BOARD OF PROFESSIONAL REVIEW

The Board of Professional Review is charged with investigating, evaluating, and taking whatever action is appropriate when violations of the Code of Ethics are alleged to have occurred. The Board of Professional Review is also called in when there is an allegation that a financial planner has not complied with the Practice Standards. The Board can be divided into two panels: an Inquiry Panel (which investigates and assesses allegations) and a Hearing Panel (which administrates hearings regarding violations). Each panel will have a chair. No member of one panel is allowed to serve on the other panel in regards to the same matter.

STAFF COUNSEL AND GROUNDS FOR DISCIPLINE

The staff counsel maintains a central office for the filing of requests for the investigation of CFP Board designee conduct, for the coordination of investigations, for the enforcement of disciplinary enforcement proceedings carried out pursuant to these procedures, for the prosecution of charges of wrongdoing against CFP designees, and for any other duties designated by the Board. Individuals may be subject to discipline any time they commit an act that violates the Code of Ethics and Professional Responsibility. Individuals may be subject to discipline for acts that do not comply with the Practice Standards, acts that violate the criminal laws of any state or of the United States, acts that are the proper basis for professional suspension, a failure to respond to a Board request, or presenting any false or misleading statement to the CFP Board.

FORMS OF DISCIPLINE AND INVESTIGATION

If the CFP Board determines that there are no grounds for disciplinary action, then they will take no action. The Board has the right to force a designee to complete additional education or remedial work. The Board may privately censure a designee. The Board may also issue a public Letter of Admonition, which is a reproach against misbehavior. The Board may order that a designee be suspended for a certain length of time. The Board may also permanently revoke the license of a designee. When allegations are made and an investigation is begun, the designee has 20 calendar days from the notice of the investigation to file a written response with the Board. If there is no response, the Hearing Panel takes up the matter; otherwise, the Inquiry Panel takes up the matter.

RULES OF CONDUCT

DEFINING THE RELATIONSHIP WITH THE PROSPECTIVE CLIENT OR CLIENT

It is important to set the client's expectations as to what she or he may expect from the client/certified financial planner (CFP) relationship that he or she is entering. The initial meetings with the client should be spent clarifying each party's roles and responsibilities. The CFP professional should explain any services he or she will provide, how he or she bills those services, and how the client will pay the bill. It is also crucial to set expectations with the client about how long the engagement will last. Lastly, as part of the relationship definition, the client should be made aware of the reasoning of decisions and why the CFP professional made those decisions.

CERTIFIED FINANCIAL PLANNERS BOARD DISCLOSURES REQUIREMENTS

The Certified Financial Planners (CFP) Board requires that certain disclosures be made in writing, while others may optionally be made verbally. Before entering into a business relationship with a client, the CFP professional must disclose verbally or in writing the obligations of the planner and the client, pertinent information about how the CFP professional or affiliates will be compensated, if proprietary products will be offered, and any situation by which the CFP professional may use other parties to fulfill the agreement. The disclosures that must be in writing are as follows: the parties to the agreement, the date and length of the client-planner engagement, how either party may terminate the agreement, services provided, how the planner will be paid, any conflicts of interest, contact information for the planner, and information about the planner that may influence the client's decision as to whether or not to enter a planning relationship.

PROSPECTIVE CLIENT AND CLIENT INFORMATION AND PROPERTY

The Certified Financial Planners (CFP) Board establishes that CFP professionals have an expectation of fiduciary conduct regarding clients' information and property. There is an expectation of confidentiality in each relationship. If the confidentiality is breached, it could result in censure of the planner or termination of his right to use the CFP mark. This applies to physical as well as electronic information. The CFP professional should ensure that the client has access to all information necessary to make informed decisions about the recommendations. The CFP professional may generally not borrow money from the client, although there are exceptions, such as when the client is a business in the business of loaning money. If the CFP professional takes possession of the client's property, excellent records should be kept accounting for the property, and it should not be commingled with the CFP professional's property. Planner-retained property should be returned to the client immediately on client request.

OBLIGATIONS TO PROSPECTIVE CLIENTS AND CLIENTS

The Certified Financial Planner (CFP) Board dictates that certificants treat client and prospects fairly and with integrity and objectivity. Certificants are also under onus to only offer advice in areas in which they maintain competence. They must maintain compliance with applicable regulatory authorities (FINRA, the Securities and Exchange Commission, etc.) and exercise reasonable and prudent judgment when providing recommendations. This judgment should also extend to third parties contracted by the certificant. Only suitable recommendations should be made to the client, and certificants should make any client or perspective client aware of their suspension or revocation by the CFP board.

OBLIGATIONS TO EMPLOYERS AS ESTABLISHED BY THE CFP BOARD

The Certified Financial Planner (CFP) Board establishes that CFP professionals' obligations are not only to their clients, but also to their employer, should they have one. CFP professionals are to diligently pursue their employer's goals and objectives, as long as those goals and objectives are legal. If the company's methods are not legal, perhaps they should rethink employment. The CFP Board acknowledges that it only has authority over certificants and none over each individual CPF professional's employer, but offers its support to employers if they should decide to enact CFP Board-approved codes of conduct.

OBLIGATIONS TO THE CFP BOARD

The Certified Financial Planners (CFP) Board requires that certificants abide by all terms and agreements made with the CFP Board. This includes when they may and may not use the CFP marks. They also proscribe meeting all continuing education requirements to be able to use those marks. CFP professionals are obligated to inform the CFP Board of updates to their personal information (i.e., email address, physical address, phone number, etc.) within 45 days of the change. The CFP professional must also inform the board of any conviction of crime (excluding minor traffic offenses) or professional discipline within 30 days of its occurrence. This applies also to changes in the status of a matter that was previously disclosed to the CFP Board. Finally, CFP professionals are not to engage in activities that will affect their reputation or the reputation of the CFP marks negatively.

FUNCTION, PURPOSE, AND REGULATION OF FINANCIAL INSTITUTIONS
BANKS AND CREDIT UNIONS

Banks are the primary depository for checking accounts as well as the primary source of short-term financing for corporations. The Federal Deposit Insurance Corporation (FDIC) insures banks. Credit unions also serve as a depository for checking accounts, and they also provide short-term financing to corporations. However, credit unions are nonprofit, cooperative financial institutions that are owned and run by members. In a credit union, the members make loans by pooling their own funds and elect a volunteer board to oversee the credit union's operations. Credit unions are generally created to serve people in a particular community or a group of employees. The National Credit Union Administration (NCUA), an agency of the federal government, insures credit unions.

BROKERAGE COMPANIES AND INSURANCE COMPANIES

Brokerage companies are the primary depositories of investment accounts for the purpose of trading stocks and bonds. Brokerage firms used to be more distinct from banks than they are now. The Glass-Steagall Act of 1933, which forbids banks from underwriting corporate securities, outlines the main difference at present. The Securities Investor Protection Corporation (SIPC) insures brokerage firms. Insurance companies are the primary vendors of life, health, property, and disability insurance. According to the McCarran-Ferguson Act, the federal government can regulate insurance if the state governments are not doing a good job. The National Association of Insurance Commissioners is composed of the commissioners of insurance from each state; this group has no power over insurance regulation, but is charged with administering the law and recommending new laws.

FDIC

The FDIC will reimburse a depositor for any losses up to the amount of $250,000, even if the depositor is not a U.S. citizen or resident of the United States. The FDIC insures all types of deposits received by a financial institution regularly but not Treasury securities. Deposits made in different institutions are insured separately, as are deposits maintained in different in different categories of legal ownership.

SECURITIES INVESTOR PROTECTION CORPORATION (SIPC)

The Securities Investor Protection Corporation protects the customers of broker-dealers so long as that broker-dealer is a member of the SIPC. If this member's registration with the Securities and Exchange Commission is terminated the membership in the SIPC will also be terminated. The brokerage firms that are members of the SIPC pay the cost of the insurance. If a brokerage firm fails, the customers will get back all of those securities which are registered or in the process of being registered in their names. If the firm does not have enough funds in its customer accounts to satisfy these claims, the SIPC will pay the rest out of its reserve funds, up to $500,000 per customer. Commodity futures contracts, currency, and investment contracts are ineligible for SIPC protection.

FINANCIAL SERVICES REGULATIONS AND REQUIREMENTS
REGISTRATION AND LICENSING (FINRA)

The Financial Industry Regulatory Authority, Inc., or FINRA registers all people who sell stocks, bonds, tax-sheltered investments, options, mutual funds, and other securities. FINRA is an independent group supervised by the SEC. In order to register with FINRA, securities dealers have to fill out a Uniform Application for Securities Industry Regulation, a Form U-4, and pass one or more exams. FINRA has designed a series of exams to test the competence of various financial professionals, from commodities traders to investment advisers. Once the individual passes the appropriate tests, he or she can become a registered representative and is licensed to sell certain securities.

REGISTRATION AND LICENSING (INSURANCE, SEC RELEASE NO. IA-770)

There are 3 ways in which insurers sell insurance, and therefore there are 3 different ways for them to register. Insurance agents are direct representatives of an insurance company; insurance brokers act as liaisons between the insurance companies and the insured, though they actually represent the insured; and insurance service representatives are hired by insurance companies to assist insurance agents, and may not require licensure. According to the SEC, the Investment Advisers Act of 1940 provides the foundation for the regulation of financial planners. SEC Release No. IA-770 states that a financial planner must give investment advice as part of his or her business; must give advice that is specific and action-oriented; and must receive compensation for this advice.

REGISTRATION AND LICENSING (INVESTMENT ADVISERS ACT OF 1940 AND EXEMPTIONS FROM REGISTRATION)

According to the Investment Advisers Act of 1940, financial planners are not subject to the control of the act if they are: a bank or holding company that is not an investment company; a lawyer, accountant, engineer, or teacher who provides investment advice incidentally; a broker, dealer, or registered representative whose advice is incidental; the publisher of a magazine or journal that discusses financial planning; a person whose advice is limited to those securities guaranteed by the federal government; or any other person not within the law as specified by the SEC. Also, financial professionals may be exempt if they provide advice only to people who live within the same state, if they provide advice only to insurance companies, if they have fewer than 15 clients every year, or if they provide advice exclusively to churches.

REGISTRATION AND LICENSING (INVESTMENT ADVISERS SUPERVISION COORDINATION ACT OF 1996 AND REGULATION OF INSURANCE INDUSTRY)

According to the Investment Advisers Supervision Coordination Act of 1996, financial planners must be registered with either the SEC or with the state authorities, but not necessarily with both. There are some specific provisos: advisers with more than $30 million in assets under their control must register with the SEC, and those with less than $30 million must register with the state (these asset thresholds were later modified by the Dodd-Frank Act of 2010). There are a few ways that the government tries to regulate the insurance industry. For one, the legislative bodies in each individual state frequently create laws that restrict the insurance industry. The courts may also rule on the constitutionality of state insurance laws and adjudicate disputes between policyholders and insurance companies. Finally, each state's Commissioner of Insurance enforces the insurance laws and may recommend specific investigations.

MODIFICATIONS TO INVESTMENT ADVISER REGISTRATION BY THE DODD-FRANK ACT OF 2010

When passed by the Obama Administration in 2010, the Dodd-Frank Act modified the Advisers Supervision Coordination Act of 1996 by establishing new asset thresholds for investment advisers. The Act created three distinct thresholds:

- "Small" advisers, which manage less than $25 million in assets
- "Mid-sized" advisers, which manage between $25 million and $100 million in assets
- "Large" advisers, which manage at least $100 million in assets

Small advisers are prohibited from registering with the SEC as long as the principal office and place of business are in a state that regulates advisers (only Wyoming does not). Mid-sized advisers are prohibited from registering with the SEC and must register with their individual state unless their principal office and place of business is not in New York or Wyoming. If the principal office and place of business is in one of those two states, they are required to register with the SEC unless a registration exemption is available. Large advisers must register with the SEC unless a registration exemption is available.

To avoid the burden of frequent changes in registration between the states and the SEC for advisers around the $100 million mark, the Dodd-Frank Act created a buffer or transitional range spanning $90 million to $110 million. Mid-sized advisers whose assets grow to $100 million are required to register with the SEC only after reaching $110 million (but permitted to do so at $100 million), while large advisers who assets decrease below $100 million are required to register with their state only after reaching $90 million (but permitted to do so below $100 million).

REPORTING

When an investment adviser registers with the SEC, he or she will fill out Form ADV, which has two parts. The first part asks for background information about the applicant and his or her expected clients; the second part asks for information about the planned fee structure, services offered, method of business operation, and the adviser's degree of involvement in securities transactions. This form typically restricts advisers from collecting fees based on investment performance, though the adviser may still base fees on a percentage of total holdings. According to the so-called "brochure rule," registered investment advisers (RIAs) are required to submit a written disclosure to potential clients.

COMPLIANCE, STATE SECURITIES, AND INSURANCE LAWS

The SEC requires financial advisers to keep detailed records. Any illegal actions committed by a planner constitute fraud. If an adviser fails to meet any of the requirements set forth by the Investment Advisers Act of 1940 or the process of registration, the SEC is allowed to investigate and confiscate all records. According to the Insider Trading and Securities Fraud Enforcement Act of 1988, investment advisers must keep detailed records in order to prove the absence of insider trading. As for state securities, investment advisers are encouraged to be aware of the "blue sky laws" in the state of their operation. Many states will require a minimum capitalization amount in exchange for registration. The insurance industry is always regulated by the states. Advisers must be registered for each specific product they wish to sell.

CONSUMER PROTECTION LAWS
FTC, TRUTH IN LENDING ACT, FAIR CREDIT BILLING ACT, AND THE EQUAL CREDIT OPPORTUNITY ACT

The Federal Trade Commission is charged with enforcing statutes that relate to competition and consumer protection. The Truth in Lending Act is Title I of the Consumer Credit Protection Act; it

24

requires all creditors to make specified disclosures regarding finance charges and related aspects of credit transactions. This includes stating finance charges in terms of an annual percentage rate. The Fair Credit Billing Act is an amendment to the Truth in Lending Act; it provides protection to borrowers whose credit cards have been lost or stolen, making it impossible for credit companies to adversely adjust their credit rating until an investigation is complete. The Equal Credit Opportunity Act is Title VII of the Consumer Credit Protection Act; it states that creditors cannot discriminate against customers for any reason. Also, it states that creditors must give applicants written reasons when credit is denied.

FAIR DEBT COLLECTION PRACTICES ACT

The Fair Debt Collections Act is Title VIII of the Consumer Credit Protection Act. This act forbids a debt collector from communicating with a consumer regarding the collection of a debt at the consumer's place of employment. The act also defines the appropriate times for contacting a consumer: between eight in the morning and nine at night, at the consumer's residence. According to the Fair Debt Collection Act, a debt collector cannot communicate with any person other than the consumer, his or her attorney, and a consumer-reporting agency. Finally, this act states that if a consumer should notify the debt collector that he or she either does not intend to repay a debt or no longer wishes to hear from the debt collector, the debt collector is required to cease communications except to declare what consequential actions the debt collection agency or creditor will take.

FAIR CREDIT REPORTING ACT

The Fair Credit Reporting Act asserts that consumers have the right to see their own files and request that corrections be made. The act also states that the information contained in a consumer report cannot be provided unless the recipient has a purpose specified in the act. Also, the government is not allowed to see a file unless it is considering hiring the individual, granting some kind of license, considering whether to give the person a security clearance, or if back taxes are owed. Furthermore, the Internal Revenue Service must have a legitimate case in order to receive a report. The act also specifies lengths of time after which information becomes obsolete. Adverse information becomes obsolete after seven years, and bankruptcy information becomes obsolete after ten years.

FIDUCIARY

DUTIES

A fiduciary is any individual or organization that has been given the power to manage the assets of another. Some of the people who are considered fiduciaries are executors, administrators, personal representatives, and custodians. Fiduciaries are required to exercise loyalty in making decisions concerning the estate, meaning that the must be confidential and always act in the best interests of the party they represent. A fiduciary must also exercise care, diligence, and prudence when handling the estate of another. Finally, a fiduciary is charged with preserving and protecting estate assets; this can mean both protecting material assets and making productive investments.

SELECTING

When selecting a fiduciary, one should look for a person who will most likely outlive the testator, has skills in legal and financial affairs, is familiar with the testator, and is an impartial person with strong integrity. Most people will use either a family member/friend or a corporate executor as a fiduciary. The former is likely to know the testator well and to have a personal interest in his or her welfare, while the latter may have more experience in financial matters. Probate attorneys are usually excellent at managing assets during the probate period, and they may have a good working

25

knowledge of financial dealings. On the other hand, the administration costs of an attorney can be very high.

BUSINESS LAW

CONTRACT REQUIREMENTS

In contract law, the person to whom an offer is made is called the offeree; the person who makes the offer is called the offeror. In order for a valid contract to exist, there must be five specific elements. The first is offer and acceptance, in which one part makes a definite, unqualified offer that the other accepts completely. There must then be what is known as genuineness of assent, meaning that there can be no misrepresentation, coercion, undue influence, ambiguities, or willfully incorrect information. There must also be adequate consideration. The offeror and offeree must both be in a situation where they are capable of entering into such a contract. Finally, the terms of the contract must not require that any laws be broken.

TYPES OF CONTRACTS

In a bilateral contract, both parties make legally enforceable promises to one another. In a unilateral contract, one party makes a promise in exchange for another party either doing something or not doing something. Insurance contracts are considered unilateral, since the insured doesn't have any specific obligations. In an enforceable contract, all of the terms are present and clear. In a void contract, one or more of the elements required for a contract to be legal are missing. A voidable contract is one that is legally enforceable, but from which one of the parties could potentially escape because of some lack of genuineness of assent. A quasi-contract is not a legal contract itself, but may function as one if one party has unjustly received a benefit. An unenforceable contract is one that seems to have all the necessary elements for enforceability, but from which one party will be able to escape for some other reason.

The statute of frauds states that a contract need not be in writing to be enforceable, unless it is a promise to answer for the debts of another; a contract to transfer interest in real estate; a contract that cannot be fulfilled within one year; or a contract on goods of more than $500 in value. The parole evidence rule states that when a written contract is the subject of a trial, there is a limit on the additional information that can be introduced to dispute it. Nonperformance of a contract may be excused when: one party has committed a material breach or one party dies and is therefore released from obligations to perform services. If a breach of contract occurs, the party that did not breach the contract may be awarded compensatory damages, punitive damages, or liquidated damages.

TORTS

A person can commit two types of misdeeds: public and private. Public misdeeds are a violation of the individual's compact with society and are called crimes, while private misdeeds are violations of the rights of another person and are known as torts. The person who commits such a wrong is known as a tortfeasor. There are two kinds of torts: intentional and unintentional. Intentional torts are intentional infringements on the rights of others, such as assault, libel, trespass, or invasion of privacy. Unintentional torts are performed through negligence or carelessness. Liability insurance is unlikely to protect the insured from legal penalties resulting from intentional torts or criminal behavior.

AGENCY

When we discuss a two-party relationship in which one party (agent) has permission to act on behalf of the other (principal), we are referring to agency. When an agent acts on behalf of a principal, he or she has the fiduciary duty to act in the principal's best interest, not his or her own.

When an agent is an independent contractor, the principal has no control over his or her actions. When an agent is an employee of the principal, however, the principal may direct the behavior of the agent. There are a few kinds of agent authority that determine the degree to which an agent can bind a principal in a contract: express authority is granted for a specific purpose; implied authority is granted to carry out any acts that are relevant to accomplishing a particular goal; and apparent authority is granted to perform any act which the principal could reasonably want performed. Principals are liable for all torts committed by agents in their employ.

NEGOTIABLE INSTRUMENTS

A negotiable instrument is a written contract that is used as a substitute for money. A negotiable instrument may be either a promissory note (a promise to pay) or a draft (a three-party promise to pay). The holder of a negotiable instrument is entitled to payment unless: the owing party is an infant; the instrument was created under extreme duress; the paying party goes bankrupt; or a fraud has been committed. A valid negotiable instrument is in writing and signed by the maker, includes an unconditional promise to pay, is payable at a definite time, and is payable to a certain party. Banks have a similar obligation to honor checks owed to customers, though banks may also be required to honor a customer's request for them not to pay. Such a stop order is valid for 14 days if given orally and six months if submitted in writing.

PROFESSIONAL LIABILITY

The Practice Standards were designed to protect financial planners from any liabilities created by the practitioner-client relationship. Financial planners are potentially responsible for breach of contract, fraud, tort, or negligence. Financial professionals may take out both malpractice insurance and errors and omission insurance to protect themselves from liabilities. Financial planners may be charged with a fiduciary liability because they have an obligation to their client that is similar to but also more intense than that of a trustee. In the event of a dispute between a client and a financial planner, arbitration and mediation may be a positive alternative to litigation.

General Financial Planning Principles

FINANCIAL PLANNING PROCESS
GOAL, BENEFITS, AND COMPONENTS

A financial planner's goal is simple: to provide sound, organized financial advice to individuals and their families. People can benefit from the services of a financial planner in several ways. Financial planners provide a coordinated strategy for managing the immediate and long-term needs of clients who may be too busy to stay informed on financial issues. Financial planners are able to synthesize the information provided by various financial specialists and determine the best course of action for a particular client. Financial planners can serve as a liaison between clients and other financial professionals. There are five major components of financial planning: insurance, investments, income tax planning, retirement planning, and estate planning.

STEP ONE

The first step in the financial planning process is to establish a client-planner relationship in which both parties state their expectations. The relationship must be based on a firm trust to be successful. The first part of building such a relationship is identifying what services need to be provided. Then, the financial planner should disclose his or her rate of compensation. Next, both the financial planner and the client should work together to outline the responsibilities that each party will bear in the relationship. After that, the two parties may decide on the duration of the agreement. Finally, the client and financial planner should provide any additional information necessary to adequately define or limit the work to come.

STEP TWO

After a solid relationship has been established between the financial planner and his or her client, the financial planner should gather all the data necessary to do the job effectively. This includes determining the client's goals and expectations. Only by collecting thorough and accurate data will the financial planner be able to create a viable financial strategy. This means collecting both quantitative and qualitative data. Quantitative data assesses the client's current financial situation and is found using a fact-finding questionnaire. Qualitative data, on the other hand, gives a more subjective picture of the client. Specifically, it tells the financial planner why the client has set his or her goals. Qualitative data is obtained during a goals (broad-based projections) and objectives (specific steps for reaching goals) interview.

STEP THREE

After the financial planner has established a solid working relationship and acquired the data necessary to construct a good financial plan, he or she should seek to painstakingly assess the client's current financial status. This can only be done by rigorously analyzing and evaluating the client's insurance and risk management, special needs, investments, taxation, employee benefits, retirement, and estate planning. Of course, not all of these subjects will be applicable for each client. The purpose of this assessment should be to identify the strengths and weaknesses of the client's financial situation. Once this is done, it may be necessary to revise the goals set forth by the client during step two of the financial planning process.

STEPS FOUR, FIVE, AND SIX

Once the financial planner and client have set out achievable, realistic goals based on an accurate assessment of the client's financial status, the financial planner can begin to develop a suitable financial plan. This means creating a set of financial strategies that are suited to the client's objectives and goals. Once the client has agreed to a plan, the financial planner will move to implement that plan. This may involve motivating the client as well as incorporating the advice and aid of outside experts as required. Once the plan has been fully implemented, the financial planner must constantly monitor it. This includes evaluating performance, reviewing changes in the client's circumstances (as well as any relevant changes in tax law), and adjusting the plan as necessary.

RESPONSIBILITIES OF FINANCIAL PLANNER, CLIENT, AND OTHER ADVISERS

All of the parties involved in the financial planning process have certain responsibilities. The financial planner must evaluate the needs of the client, explain complicated financial concepts, analyze the financial circumstances of the client, prepare financial plans, clarify client goals, and, finally, implement and monitor the financial plan. The client is responsible for making known his or her goals and objectives, for being receptive to creative financial plans, and for working to advance the agreed-upon plan. The other advisers that are brought in to assist in the financial planning process are responsible for fulfilling whatever their particular task may be as designated by the financial planner with the approval of the client.

BALANCE SHEET (STATEMENT OF FINANCIAL POSITION)

A balance sheet is basically a freeze-frame of an individual's wealth at a particular time. There are three categories on a balance sheet: assets, liabilities, and net worth. Net worth is total assets minus total liabilities. Net worth increases due to an appreciation in the value of assets, an increase in assets from retaining income, an increase in assets from gifts or inheritances, or a decrease in liabilities from forgiveness. Net worth is unchanged by the paying off of debt or the purchase of an item with cash. Assets and liabilities are given at fair market value. Assets may be either categorized as cash and cash equivalents (checking or savings account), invested assets (stocks, bonds, mutual funds), or use assets (homes, furniture, cars). Liabilities are either current liabilities (credit card balances, for instance) or long-term liabilities (auto loans, life insurance loans, or real estate mortgages).

CASH FLOW STATEMENT

A cash flow statement shows where an individual's financial resources are going. To be accurate, it must indicate the period of coverage, which is usually a calendar year. The first step in constructing a cash flow statement is to estimate the family's annual income. Then, estimate both fixed and discretionary expenses. Next, determine the excess or shortfall of income during the budget period. The net cash flow is the total income minus the total expenses. Once this is determined, consider ways of increasing income or decreasing expenses. Finally, calculate income and expenses as a percentage of the total to determine a better flow of resources.

QUANTITATIVE ANALYSIS

Financial planners use modeling and simulation as tools to analyze the possible effects of planned financial decisions. Probability analysis is used to determine the likelihood that a certain event will occur. This is often used to forecast the development of insurance rates and insurance risk. Probability analysis is often combined with modeling and simulation to give financial planners a window into the possible performance of planned investments. Sensitivity analysis is a form of modeling in which financial planners consider how small changes in the market or in investment will affect the client's portfolio. An independent variable is adjusted to see how much change it will cause in the dependent variable.

PRO FORMA STATEMENT

A pro forma statement forecasts future balance sheets and cash flow statements. Sometimes, the best way to create a pro forma statement is to consider three scenarios: the worst-case budget, in which income is lowest and expenditures are highest possible; an average-case budget, in which both income and expenditures are at a reasonable level; and a best-case budget, in which income is highest and expenditures are at lowest possible. These three measures typically are enough to create pro forma statements that can serve as a rough guide to the potential cash flow over the coming year.

PERSONAL INCOME STATEMENT

The personal income statement, also known as the statement of cash flows, is a physical representation of a client's cash flows during a certain period of time. The most common time period for this statement is January 1 through December 31 of a given year. Contained on the income statement are the client's various forms of income, fixed and variable outflows, and payments of taxes. Fixed outflows include such items as monthly auto loans, home mortgages, and property taxes. Variable outflows cover expenses such as monthly food spending, entertainment spending, and other unpredictable expenses. The most common taxes shown on the income statement are the client's property taxes, income taxes, self-employment taxes (if any), and FICA taxes. The income statement is useful in helping illustrate to clients whether or not their lifestyle is within their means.

BUDGETING

DISCRETIONARY VERSUS NONDISCRETIONARY

Budget expenses can be either discretionary or nondiscretionary: discretionary expenses can be changed or timed depending on convenience. Nondiscretionary (fixed) expenses can be changed somewhat, but must be paid at some time. A variety of strategies are used to maximize income and minimize expenses. Debt restructuring is the process of consolidating a number of different debts into one low personal line of credit. Asset reallocation is the process of changing underperforming assets to more productive investment assets. Expenditure control is the process of reducing consumption. Incorporating children's assets is the process of saving for a child in a custodial account in order to avail oneself of the lower tax rate for children.

FINANCING STRATEGIES

People can use a number of financing strategies in personal budgeting. One common strategy is to consolidate credit card or student loan debt, so as to lock in a low interest rate. A person may also take a cash-out refinance, in which a first mortgage is renewed and additional cash is disbursed to the mortgager. People also often take out a home equity loan or home equity line of credit. Sometimes, an individual will use the cash value of a life insurance policy for a loan. Another common financing strategy is tapping into a company savings plan. Finally, individuals often use the after-tax money from a Roth IRA; this money can be taken out without any penalty or tax consequences.

SAVINGS STRATEGIES

Individuals can use a few common savings strategies when budgeting. One basic strategy is setting goals. The goals that are set should be realistic, and known to all the involved parties. Another common savings strategy is to decide ahead of time to take all of the money that is saved and devote it to some special purchase. Some people use a savings-first approach, in which they save first and pay cash in order to avoid the high interest charges on loans. They may also earn interest by investing their savings. Many people force themselves to save by having money automatically deducted from their paycheck and placed into a savings account. This may include money that is placed directly into mutual funds or money that is contributed to a company retirement plan.

EMERGENCY FUND PLANNING

Most people feel comfortable if they have set aside three to six months of monthly expenses in case of an emergency. If a family has only one income, they may want to set aside enough money to cover expenses for a longer period. The marketability of an asset is the ease with which an asset may be bought or sold, while the liquidity of an asset is the ease with which it can be converted into cash with little loss of principal. Both of these factors should be considered when planning emergency funds. Real estate is considered illiquid because it can often take a long time to sell, but it is considered marketable because it is easy to sell in a moment of desperation. Some liquidity substitutes are checking and savings accounts, money market accounts, CDs, life insurance policies, US Treasury bills, and home equity loans.

CALCULATION
BUYING AN AUTOMOBILE

There are certain considerations that a consumer can make when deciding to buy rather than lease an automobile. First, if a taxpayer is purchasing a car for business use, he or she may use the standard mileage rate at first and then switch to the actual expense method later on should it become more favorable. It may also be a good idea to buy rather than lease if the consumer intends to keep the car for more than four years, or if the consumer has cash available to make a down payment. Finally, it will make more sense to buy an automobile if it will be driven more than 15,000 miles a year, since most lease agreements will charge the consumer extra for miles driven over this limit.

LEASING AN AUTOMOBILE

In some situations, it may make more sense for a consumer to lease rather than buy an automobile. For instance, some leases will offer lower monthly payments with a very small down payment. A lease may also be preferable for those individuals who plan on acquiring a new car every three or four years, or for those who would have to borrow money in order to pay for a new car. For such individuals, the trade-in value will be less than the loan value, which would result in a loss. The advantages offered by a lease are service, convenience, and flexibility. The tax advantages of leasing increase as the quality of the car rises, so individuals in need of a nice car for business may be better off leasing. When a vehicle is bought for business, interest is not deductible; if a vehicle is leased, the cost of interest is included in the payment, which is entirely deductible.

BUYING OR LEASING A HOUSE

There are a few factors consumers should consider before deciding whether to buy or lease a home. Most of the time, people will lease (or rent) when they do not have the requisite funds to make a down payment. Purchasing a home creates a number of tax advantages for the buyer. In addition, creditors tend to give better treatment to homeowners. A purchased home may become an appreciating asset for the owner. Also, in most cases a monthly payment made on a purchased home is more stable than the cost of renting, which is more commonly affected by changes in the market. Still, it often makes more sense to rent a home if the consumer knows that his or her stay in that home will be brief.

ADJUSTABLE AND FIXED RATE LOANS

Fixed rate loans may be preferable for clients that are less able to take financial risks because they have a set interest rate that remains constant for the duration of the loan. On the other hand, some clients may prefer an adjustable rate loan in which there are provisions for changing the interest rate periodically. An adjustable rate mortgage (ARM) on a home is preferable if the home is only going to be owned for a brief time, as the initial interest rates will tend to be lower. When an ARM is

31

said to have a 2/6 cap, this means that there is a 2 percent maximum interest rate increase every year, and 6 percent over the life of the loan. A fixed rate loan is best in a low or increasing interest rate environment, and a variable rate loan is better in a high or decreasing interest rate environment.

PURCHASED, LEASED, OR RENTED ASSETS
EFFECTS ON BALANCE SHEET AND CASH FLOW STATEMENT

Leased and rented assets are not entered on the balance sheet unless a sum of money was taken from one of the listed assets in order to pay for the leased asset. This initial payment will create a decrease in cash and a decrease in net worth. Assets purchased entirely with cash will not cause any change in net worth, since the reduction in cash will be balanced by an increase in the form of the asset itself. Assets purchased with a loan will cause a reduction in cash or whatever other liquid asset was used for the purchase or down payment. If a loan was secured in order to purchase the asset, the loan will be entered as a liability and there will be no change in net worth. As for the cash flow statement, any purchase of an asset or lease payment will be shown as an outflow of cash.

DIVORCE
SETTLEMENT, CAREER ASSETS, FAMILY BUSINESS, AND HOUSE

A divorce settlement is supposed to be equitable, which means not that it will be equal but that it will be fair. Many times, one spouse will have a significant amount of assets invested in his or her career. These assets may include life, health, disability, and long-term care insurance; vacation and sick pay; Social Security payment; stock options; pensions; and retirement plans. In divorce settlements, it is assumed that both spouses jointly own career assets. There are three available options when dividing a business and/or house: one spouse may keep the house or business by buying out the other's interest; both spouses may continue to own the business/home; or the business/home may be sold and the proceeds divided.

RETIREMENT PLANS, ALIMONY, AND CHILD SUPPORT

There are two ways to divide a retirement plan during a divorce settlement. In the buy-out (or cash-out) method, the nonemployee spouse receives a lump-sum settlement in return for the employee's right to keep the retirement plan. In the deferred division (or future value) method, each spouse will receive an equal share of the benefits when they are paid. Alimony may be arranged as a series of payments from one spouse to another, or to a third party on behalf of the receiving spouse. The taxable income goes to the recipient, and usually the tax-deductible expense goes to the payer. Child support payments will be set by the court and based on the ratio of each parent's income. Child support cannot be deductible by the payer and cannot be included in the income by the recipient.

SPECIAL SITUATIONS
DISABILITY, TERMINAL ILLNESS, AND NONTRADITIONAL FAMILIES

Many people do not know that they are more likely to become disabled before retirement than to die. For this reason, it is always a good idea to purchase a disability income policy that carries full protection. Work-related injuries should be covered by a worker's compensation plan. In the case of terminal illness, long-term care insurance will fund nursing and hospice treatment not covered by Medicare, while viatical agreements are arrangements in which a terminally ill person sells his or her life insurance policy to a company in order to help finance present care. Nontraditional families should be sure to carefully plan estates through wills and trust, as there is no unlimited marital deduction if a couple is not married. Single parents also need to plan carefully and should probably carry more insurance.

JOB CHANGE, JOB LOSS, AND DEPENDENTS WITH SPECIAL NEEDS

Most people should maintain an emergency fund with enough to cover between three and six months of expenses in case of job loss. Although there are state unemployment insurance programs that will help individuals who want to work but cannot, these funds are limited and subject to many restrictions. State unemployment income is taxable. When a client has a dependent with special needs, he or she will need to set aside extra emergency funds to cover unforeseen expenses. An individual with special needs is one who has serious physical, emotional, and/or cognitive problems. Some people elect to create special-needs trusts, which will help preserve state-provided benefits that may otherwise be unreasonably expensive.

SUPPLY AND DEMAND

DEMAND CURVE

According to the law of demand, higher prices will reduce the demand for an item and lower prices will increase demand. As the price of a product increases, consumers will find more substitutes, products that fill a similar role, and consumers will be more responsive to price when more viable substitutions are available. A demand curve, then, will slope down and to the right. Price elasticity exists when a small change in price results in a large change in sales. When perfect elasticity exists, the demand curve is exactly horizontal. Price inelasticity, on the other hand, exists when a large price change produces only a small change in sales. A vertical demand curve indicates perfect price inelasticity.

SUPPLY CURVE AND INCOME ELASTICITY

The law of supply states that a higher price will increase the supply of a good. A supply curve is elastic when a price change leads to a great change in the quantity supplied; the curve is inelastic when a price change produces only a small change in supply. The change in quantity supplied is simply movement along the supply curve. Factors that can cause movement along the supply curve include changes in resource prices, changes in technology, natural disasters, or other disruptive events. Income elasticity is the sensitivity of demand to changes in consumer income. An inferior good will have negative income elasticity, meaning that as income increases, the quantity demanded will decrease. The relation will be opposite for a normal good, which is said to have positive income elasticity.

FISCAL POLICY

Fiscal policy is the action taken by the government to influence the economy by raising or lowering government spending and taxes. For instance, if the government wants to stimulate economic activity, it can do so by implementing expansionary fiscal policy. Specifically, it does so by increasing spending or reducing taxes. Usually, expansionary policy creates an increased gross domestic product and higher price levels. Conversely, the government may want to use restrictive fiscal policy in an effort to slow the economy. Restrictive fiscal policy generally consists of decreasing spending or increasing taxes, which usually causes the gross domestic product to decrease and price levels to drop.

MONETARY POLICY

The Federal Reserve System, or Fed, uses monetary policy to influence the money supply. The Fed has three tools at its disposal when creating monetary policy. The first is to adjust the required reserve ratio, which is the minimum amount that a bank is allowed to have in its reserves. When this ratio is lowered, the money supply tends to increase. The Fed's most powerful tool is its open market operations, in which it buys and sells government securities, depending on whether it wants to remove or add money to circulation. The Fed can also manipulate the money supply by adjusting the discount rate, the rate charged to member banks when they borrow money from the Fed. A favorable discount rate will encourage banks to borrow more money and put it into circulation.

SUPPLY OF MONEY

In the short-run, an unanticipated increase in the money supply tends to increase aggregate demand. If the increase is anticipated, however, there will be negligible impact on aggregate demand or interest rates. There are a few definitions for the money supply. M-1 is the simplest definition, and includes currency in circulation, checkable deposits, and traveler's checks. M-2 is a bit broader; it includes everything in M-1 along with savings deposits, time deposits less than $100,000, and money market mutual fund shares. When money leaves the system, interest rates will rise, which will tend to drive down the value of stock (since the required rate of return will increase and the firm's earnings will likely decrease).

ECONOMIC INDICATORS

Investors whose livelihoods depend on knowing the relationship between security prices and economic activity will want to be able to guess the direction of economic activity. The ten leading economic indicators (as compiled by the National Bureau of Economic Research) are: stock prices; average weekly work hours; average unemployment claims; manufacturer's new consumer goods orders; manufacturers' new orders for nondefense capital goods; vendor performance; new building permits; the difference in interest rates for ten-year Treasury bonds and the federal funds rate); inflation-adjusted M-2; and consumer expectations as measured by the University of Michigan Research Center.

METHODS OF MEASURING INFLATION

The behavior of investors is determined in large part by their perception of inflation, which is the general rise in prices. There are two common indices for evaluating inflation. The Consumer Price Index is calculated using statistics from the Bureau of Labor. This index, commonly known as the CPI, measures the cost of a basket of goods and services over a set time period. The Producer Price Index, known as the PPI, is calculated by the United States Department of Labor. It takes a slightly different look at the price of goods by measuring the wholesale cost of a certain set of goods over a determined period of time.

BUSINESS CYCLES

A business cycle is a pattern of changing economic output and growth. The peak of a business cycle is generally accompanied by an increased rate of inflation; when this occurs, unemployment rises and national output declines, creating a recession. A recession is defined as a period in which real GDP declines for two or more consecutive quarters; a depression is simply a severe recession. The most common means of measuring economic activity is gross domestic product, which is the total value of all final goods and services newly produced within a country by domestic factors of production. Most of the time, economists will use real GDP (GDP adjusted to exclude the impact of inflation) and the unemployment rate to determine the phase of the business cycle.

INFLATION AND DEFLATION

When inflation occurs, investors will try to avoid interest-sensitive securities and long-term debt instruments that pay fixed amounts of interest. Often, investors will seek to acquire short-term instruments whose yields will increase with the rate of inflation. In an inflationary environment, investors should expect to benefit from stocks whose asset bases will be enhanced by increased asset values. In a period of deflation, however, investors should try to secure assets whose values will not fall. The safest strategy in a deflationary period is to acquire short-term liquid assets, like bank deposits, since deflation will increase the purchasing power of money. Long-term debt is not

34

so bad in a deflationary period, as the value of the payments will decrease. Only bonds of excellent quality should be purchased in a deflationary period, as many firms may go out of business.

RECESSION AND ECONOMIC STAGNATION

Typically, the Fed will try to jolt the economy out of a recession by putting more money in circulation and expanding the supply of credit. Meanwhile, the federal government will implement expansionary fiscal policy, lowering taxes and increasing government expenditures. Investors will then attempt to move out of short-term money market instruments and into the stocks of firms that will benefit from expansionary monetary and fiscal policy. An individual investor may want to pursue a conservative strategy, purchasing a number of convertible securities and common stocks of firms with low beta coefficients. On the other hand, a more aggressive investor may want to increase the potential for capital gains by purchasing common stocks from firms that have low payout ratios if these firms are using the earnings to finance expansion.

YIELD CURVE

A yield curve is a graph that shows the relationship between term to maturity and yield to maturity. A yield curve will show the relationship between interest rates and time, typically as relating to government Treasury securities. This graph is helpful for investors because rates do not usually change by the same amount as basis points across maturities. Yield curve risk is the risk that yields for different maturities may not change by the same amount of basis points across maturities. This risk can be measured with the help of duration, which is a measure of bond price sensitivity to interest rates. In general, short- and intermediate-term rates are lower in an upward-sloping yield curve.

PRESENT VALUE AND FUTURE VALUE

Present value is determined by taking the future value of an amount of money and then calculating, using a discount rate, what it will be worth today. The formula for present value is:

$$PV = \frac{FV}{(1+i)^N}$$

The higher the discount rate, the smaller the present value will be as compared to the future value. Future value, on the other hand, is the future amount of a sum invested today if it grows over time through compounding interest. For a single cash flow, the formula for finding future value is:

$$FV = PV(1+i)^N$$

ORDINARY ANNUITY, ANNUITY DUE, AND NET PRESENT VALUE

An annuity is a succession of equal cash flows that occur at regular intervals over a period of time. For instance, if an individual were to receive $5,000 at the end of every year for ten years, that would be considered an annuity. Ordinary annuities are those in which the cash flows begin at the end of the year, and annuities due are those in which the cash flow begins on the same date as the initial investment. Net present value, meanwhile, is the amount of cash flow, expressed in terms of present value, that a project will generate after repaying invested capital and the required rate of return on that capital. When NPV is positive, shareholder wealth increases. NPV is considered to be a better measure than IRR because it measures profitability in dollars added to shareholder value. NPV assumes that the reinvestment rate of cash flows is the cost of capital.

INTERNAL RATE OF RETURN (IRR) AND IRREGULAR CASH FLOW

The internal rate of return (IRR) is the rate of return at which the present value of a series of cash inflows will equal the present value of the cost of a project. It can also be described as the rate of return at which the net present value for a project is zero, assuming that all cash flows are reinvested in the internal rate of return. IRR will be equal to the yield to maturity, the geometric average return, and the compounded average rate of return. If the IRR is less than the cost of the capital, a project should be rejected. The stream of cash flows may change from year to year from certain investments. In order to determine the future and present values of an irregular cash flow, you will need to find the future and present values for each cash flow and then add them up.

INFLATION-ADJUSTED EARNINGS RATE AND SERIAL PAYMENTS

Investors will require the following nominal rate of return: nominal risk-free rate = (1+ real risk-free rate) x (1+ inflation rate) – 1. The real risk-free rate can be calculated: real risk-free rate = [(1+ nominal risk-free rate) / (1 + inflation rate)] – 1. Serial payments are those that increase at a constant rate on an annual basis. The constant rate for a serial payment scheme is often the rate of inflation. Typically, then, the last serial payment will have the same purchasing power as the first. Unlike annuities, serial payments are not fixed payments. The first of the serial payments will be less than the annuity payment, but the last serial payment will be more than the annuity payment.

CLIENT ATTITUDES AND BEHAVIORAL CHARACTERISTICS
CULTURAL

When we refer to the cultural characteristics of a client, we mean the values and beliefs that are common to the group of which the client is a member. The aspects of a client's culture that are relevant to financial planning may be obvious, as in the cases of language or race, or less obvious, as in the cases of obscure customs or beliefs. Acquiring a more complete understanding of a client's culture will make it easier to provide that client with superior service. One way that many financial planners seek to do this is by establishing relationships with many different people in a particular community so that a variety of perspectives from the same group can be considered.

FAMILY

A financial planner's clients will no doubt have many goals and objectives that relate to their family. For instance, many clients will want to save money to put their children through college or in case of some emergency relating to their children. Also, clients with families are likely to want to set aside funds to protect against financial disaster. Moreover, a client's willingness to assume a financial risk will often depend on his or her family situation. Clients who have small children are generally less likely to pursue risky financial ventures, as they realize that there may be some unexpected and large financial costs in the future.

EMOTIONAL

The emotional characteristics of a client will often influence their financial plan. In many cases, individuals will let their emotions drive their financial decisions; one of the important roles of a financial planner is to guide clients towards reasonable and prudent financial decisions. Also, investors are too often influenced by sensational stories in the media, and so a financial adviser must encourage calm here as well. Investors may be averse to admitting their mistakes, and a financial planner should help them to acknowledge unsuccessful strategies and make positive changes. One way to keep emotions from guiding investment decisions is to diversify investments so that no one investment carries too much emotional emphasis.

36

LIFE CYCLE AND AGE (ACCUMULATION AND CONSOLIDATION PHASES)

A financial planner should acknowledge four main phases in the life cycle. The accumulation phase is typically the client's first forty years, during which he or she wants to earn funds to help his or her family avert financial disaster; save money for homes, automobiles, and college; and develop some assets for long-term security. Individuals in the accumulation phase usually are willing to accept some high-risk investments if there is the promise of above-average return. In the consolidation phase, individuals are usually less willing to accept high-risk ventures, but will attempt some moderate-risk investment. In the consolidation phase, individuals will have paid off all of their loans and funded the education of their children, but will need to keep saving for retirement. Individuals are usually in the consolidation phase between the ages of 40 and 60.

LIFE CYCLE AND AGE (SPENDING AND GIFTING PHASES)

When an individual reaches the spending phase of his or her life cycle, he or she will begin to seek investments that offer security and the preservation of capital. Although individuals in this phase will want to stick with low-risk investments, it is a good idea for them to maintain some more adventurous investments as a partial protection against inflation. The spending phase typically begins at retirement. The gifting phase can occur at the same time as the spending phase. In this phase of the life cycle, the individual seeks to disburse his or her capital to loved ones and preferred institutions. In this phase, a financial planner will mostly be helping with estate planning. The gifting phase is basically an individual's preparations for death.

LEVEL OF KNOWLEDGE, EXPERIENCE, EXPERTISE, AND RISK TOLERANCE

As a client develops his or her knowledge and experience in investment, he or she is likely to be more tolerant of risk. However, clients who are approaching retirement will probably be less willing to make risky investments. It is essential for a financial planner to identify his or her client's level of knowledge so that he or she can be careful not to encourage too much investment in instruments that the client does not understand. As for measuring the general risk tolerance of an investor, this has less to do with assessing knowledge than with assessing the emotional and financial ability of the investor to withstand a loss. Most financial planners try to classify clients by the level of risk they're willing to take on: high, medium, or low.

COMMUNICATIONS WITH THE PUBLIC

Communications with the public (FINRA Rule 2210) - a qualified registered principal must approve all retail communication before its use or filing with FINRA, unless another member has already filed it and it has been approved and the member has not altered it. For institutional communications, members are to establish written procedures for review by a qualified registered principal of institutional communications. The procedures are to be designed to ensure that institutional communications company with the standards. All communications, retail and institutional, are to be retained according to requirements, and must include:

- A copy of the communication
- The name of any registered principal approving of the communication
- If not approved by a registered principal prior to first use, the name of the person who prepared it
- Information about the source of information used in graphic illustrations
- If approval is not required for retail communication, the name of the member that filed it with FINRA, as well as the letter from FINRA

WRITTEN COMMUNICATION

Written communication - written communication that is a road show is not required to be filed. A road show written communication does have to be filed if the offering is for common equity or convertible equities under an issuer that is not at the time required to file reports with the SEC, unless there is a bona fide electronic version of the road show made available.

Bona fide electronic road show - a written communication regarding the offering of a security transmitted graphically and that involves a presentation of members of management.

TELEMARKETING

The types of communications covered under FINRA Rule 3230 include:

- Outbound calls from a member or associated person of a member to a non-broker dealer, including to wireless telephone numbers.
- Outbound calls that have been outsourced to a third party.
- Abandoned calls, which are those not answered by someone at the member within two seconds of the person's completed greeting.
- Prerecorded messages.

For purposes of this rule, the term telemarketing is defined as consisting of or relating to a plan, program, or campaign involving at least one outbound telephone call, for example cold-calling. The term does not include the solicitation of sales through the mailing of written marketing materials, when the person making the solicitation does not solicit customers by telephone but only receives calls initiated by customers in response to the marketing materials and during those calls takes orders only without further solicitation.

ELECTRONIC COMMUNICATION NETWORK

An electronic communication network, or ECN, is a system by which securities orders are matched to bypass the need for a third party. The matching is performed electronically and allows buyers and sellers of securities to communicate directly without the need for a third party to facilitate their trading. ECNs must register with the Securities and Exchange Commission (SEC) as a broker/dealer, and collect a fee for their services. ECNs facilitate trading by displaying the optimal bid/ask prices for the same securities, and then automatically execute the transaction on behalf of the buyers and sellers. ECNs greatly reduce the time it takes to match orders for buyers and sellers. In addition to serving retail investors, ECNs also facilitate trading for institutional investors.

OPTIONS COMMUNICATIONS

The standards that must be followed in communications regarding options include:

- Options communications must only provide general descriptions, including the registered clearing agency, the way in which the exchange on which the options trade operates, and a basic description of how options are priced
- Options communications must provide the ways in which a copy of the options disclosure document may be obtained
- Options communications may not provide statements regarding performance (past or future), rates of return, or the names of any specific options
- Options communications must include any statements so dictated by state laws
- Options communications may include marketing designs (logos, pictures, graphics, etc.) so long as they are not misleading

CREDIT AND DEBT MANAGEMENT
RATIOS

A client should always have enough liquid assets for an emergency fund. Consumer debt should never be greater than 20% of income. The monthly payments on a home should be no more than 28% of the owner's gross income. The total monthly payment on all debts should never be more than 38% of gross monthly income. A renter's expenses should always be less than or equal to 30% of his or her gross monthly income. It is always preferable to have more than one source of income. When an individual only has one source of income, he or she needs to do more planning. It is a good rule of thumb to have at least 5-10% of gross income going into savings and investments, not including reinvested dividends and income.

CONSUMER DEBT

Consumer debt is the most widely known form of debt that a financial planner will need to address. There are three main varieties of consumer debt: thirty-day or regular charge accounts; revolving and optional charge accounts; and installment purchases or time-payment plans. These last can occur either when an individual buys on time from the seller or borrows money from a credit institution, generally in the form of a credit card. The most common sources of consumer credit are commercial banks, consumer finance companies, credit unions, savings and loan associations, life insurance companies, brokerage companies, and auto dealers.

HOME EQUITY LOANS, HOME EQUITY LINE OF CREDIT, AND SECURED AND UNSECURED DEBT

A home equity loan is any cash that is given up front at a fixed rate. A home equity credit line, on the other hand, gives the individual the chance to use the money only when it is needed, but at a variable rate that is usually tied to the prime rate. Oftentimes, individuals will keep the current first mortgage and get a second loan for the necessary cash amount. If the current mortgage rates are more than the rates for the existing first mortgage, a home equity loan gives the borrower the opportunity to maintain the lower first mortgage rate. According to the 2017 Tax Cuts and Jobs Act, the interest on a home equity loan is tax-deductible within certain limits (so long as it's used to buy, build, or substantially improve a home). A secured loan is one in which collateral is used to keep the debtor from defaulting; an unsecured loan will have higher interest rates to the borrower because no collateral is used.

BANKRUPTCY CODE
CHAPTER 7 BANKRUPTCY

Congress established the Bankruptcy Code in 1978 in accordance with Article I, Section 8 of the Constitution. Title 11 of the United States Code governs bankruptcy proceedings. There is a bankruptcy court for each judicial district in the country. Chapter 7 bankruptcy has to do with liquidation; in order to qualify for this form of bankruptcy, the debtor must be an individual, partnership, or corporation. The debtor is allowed to retain certain property, but a trustee liquidates all other assets. The discharge of Chapter 7 bankruptcy will extinguish the debtor's responsibility for dischargeable debts. Such a discharge is available to individual debtors only and not to partnerships or corporations.

CHAPTER 11 AND CHAPTER 13 BANKRUPTCY

In Chapter 11 bankruptcy, the person, firm, or corporation is allowed to reorganize in order to meet the obligations of debt. After this is done, the court will either confirm or reject the plan of reorganization. Typically, the debtor will remain in possession of his or her assets and will continue to operate the business, though these operations may be subject to the oversight of the court. In Chapter 13 bankruptcy, an individual is allowed to set up a repayment plan. The debtor is allowed to hold on to his or her property as long as he or she makes regular payments. Debtors will often file for Chapter 13 bankruptcy if they are threatened with foreclosure. Many of the debts that cannot be discharged through Chapter 7 can be discharged through Chapter 13.

ESTATE, QUALIFIED RETIREMENT PLANS, TAX-ADVANTAGED SAVINGS PLAN, AND EXEMPTIONS

In a bankruptcy settlement, the property of the estate is all the property that is not exempt from being divided. Typically, the trustee sells the property of the estate and creditors are paid from the proceeds. The Supreme Court has ruled that creditors cannot seek to take funds from the retirement plans of a debtor. This includes almost all pensions and 401(k) plans. If retirement savings are a part of the estate, they may be exempted under the available exemption statutes. Exemptions are the forms of property that, according to state law, are beyond the reach of creditors. In sixteen states, debtors have the ability to choose whether they would like to honor the state or federal set of exemptions; in all other states, the state exemptions must be selected.

DISCHARGEABLE AND NONDISCHARGEABLE, AND ALTERNATIVES

If a debt is discharged, the debtor is freed from any personal liability and the creditor may not take any actions to collect the debt. Most unsecured debt is dischargeable. Secured debt, on the other hand, will survive bankruptcy as a charge on the property to which it attaches unless a court order modifies the lien. There are a few types of debt that cannot be discharged in either Chapter 7 or 13 bankruptcy. These include debts that were not listed in the bankruptcy papers, child support, alimony, debts for personal injury or death caused by driving while intoxicated, student loans, fines incurred by breaking the law, recent income tax debts, and some long-term obligations like home mortgages. Instead of declaring bankruptcy, a debtor may elect to consolidate debt, negotiate debt, take out a home equity loan, or start a line of credit.

Education Planning

CREDITS AND TAX PLANNING
NEEDS ANALYSIS

When a client wants to establish an appropriate saving schedule to fund his or her child's college education, a financial planner needs to learn the child's age, the age at which the child will enter college, the after-tax earnings rate of the parents, the inflation-adjusted interest rate, and the current cost of tuition, as well as the rate of increase.

AMERICAN OPPORTUNITY TAX CREDIT

The American Opportunity Tax Credit (AOTC) is a tax credit available for the first four years of undergraduate study. The credit is worth up to $2,500 per student per year, calculated as 100% of the first $2,000 in "qualifying educational expenses" plus 25% of the next $2,000, with $1,000 of the credit being refundable. Qualifying educational expenses include not only tuition but also books, supplies, equipment, and student fees. Further, the student must be enrolled on at least a half-time basis for his educational expenses to qualify. This credit phases out for MFJ taxpayers over the AGI range of $160,000 through $180,000, and for single taxpayers over the AGI range of $80,000 through $90,000.

LIFETIME LEARNING CREDIT AND STUDENT LOAN INTEREST

The Lifetime Learning Credit is a tax credit that, unlike the American Opportunity Tax Credit, is available for all the years of undergraduate and graduate study. Tuition is a qualified expense, though books and supplies are not if they are not bought from the school directly. The credit is good for 20% of the first $10,000 paid for all eligible students; the maximum amount per family, then, is $2,000. None of this credit is refundable. Taxpayers are also allowed to deduct up to $2,500 of interest on qualified education loans as an adjustment to income. This deduction phases out as the modified adjusted gross income reaches a certain level. Any voluntary payments of interest are also deductible. Any nontaxable education benefits, such as distributions from an ESA, will reduce the amount of the deduction.

QUALIFIED TUITION PROGRAMS

Qualified tuition programs, also known as QTP or 529 plans, are state-sponsored, tax-advantaged plans that can be used to pay for education, especially undergraduate and graduate education. The Tax Cuts and Jobs Act expanded 529 plans to permissibly fund K-12 education, not merely college expenses. The owner of the account selects the beneficiary, though the contributor will stay in control and will have the freedom to withdraw funds at any time. If the designated beneficiary does not attend college, the owner may select a new beneficiary from the same family. There is a tax-free growth of earnings if funds are withdrawn for qualified educational expenses, which include tuition, room and board, and books and supplies. The SECURE Act of 2019 also permits 529 funds to be used on up to $10,000 of student loan debt. The funds are treated as a gift of present interest, qualifying for the $16,000/$32,000 gift-tax exclusion (as of 2022). Contribution limits vary by state. These plans will have some effect on the amount of financial aid the student is likely to receive. These plans are only successful when they are begun while the child is very young.

EDUCATION IRAS
PART ONE

An education IRA, also known as a Coverdell ESA, is an education savings plan used for undergraduate and graduate-level expenses. The owner of the account will select the beneficiary.

Typically, a parent or guardian will establish the account and can elect to maintain control of the account for educational purposes. Withdrawals are paid to the beneficiary and are not refunded to the person who started the account. If the beneficiary does not attend college, the beneficiary may be changed to a member of the beneficiary's family under the age of 30. Any withdrawals are tax-free as long as they are not greater than the beneficiary's qualified education expenses for the year.

PART TWO

Contributions to an education IRA can be made after the beneficiary reaches the age of 18 only if the beneficiary is a special needs beneficiary. Contributions are not deductible from taxes and can be made to more than one IRA as long as total contributions do not exceed the contribution limit. Withdrawals may be made for tuition, room and board, books, and supplies without penalty. Any earnings are taxed as ordinary income and are subject to a 10% penalty for nonqualified use. The parent or guardian will have a broad choice of investment vehicles for the IRA. An individual may claim the American Opportunity, Hope and Lifetime Learning Credit in the same year that he or she receives a tax-free distribution, so long as the distribution is not used to cover the same expenses for which the credit is claimed.

SAVINGS BONDS

Savings bonds are sold at a discount and pay no annual interest. The interest earned on savings bonds is not taxable at the state and local levels, but it is subject to federal tax. Interest will be excluded from federal income tax if it is used for higher education expenses in the same year that bonds are redeemed. For this to happen, though, the person must be at least 24 years old at the time of issuance and the bond must be registered in the name of the purchaser or the child (if it is intended for the child's education). The qualified educational expenses for a savings bond include and fees; the cost of books and lodging, however, is not considered a qualified expense. Exclusion is phased out with a high AGI and is not available for married taxpayers filing separately.

COLLEGESURE CD

A CollegeSure CD can be purchased from the College Savings Bank and is sold in both whole and fractional units. The annual interest for a CD of this kind is calculated on the basis of the Independent College 500 Index. There is no ceiling on how much a CollegeSure CD can earn, and it is guaranteed to keep up with the cost of college. Even if the cost of college does not go up in a given year, the CD will earn a minimum of 4%. The FDIC insures CollegeSure CDs for up to $250,000, and investors who hold them will pay no fees or commissions. If the student should earn a scholarship or choose not to go to college, the parents will get back all of the money invested plus the accumulated interest.

OTHER EDUCATIONAL FUNDING
GOVERNMENT GRANTS AND SCHOLARSHIPS, PERKINS LOAN

Pell Grants are distributed on the basis of financial need; the greatest amount that can be distributed in a given year is $8,370 for the 2022-23 school year. These grants are available only to undergraduates. Federal Supplemental Educational Opportunity Grants (FSEOGs) are distributed on the basis of financial need, with the maximum amount that a student can receive in a year being $4,000 as of 2022. These grants are available to both full- and part-time students, though the grants are reduced for part-time students. Perkins Loans are funded by the federal government but administered by the schools. They are distributed on the basis of financial need, with the limit being $5,500 for undergraduates and $8,000 for graduate students. The loans have a 5% rate of interest, and there is a 9-month grace period after graduation before payment is due.

STAFFORD LOANS, PLUS, AND SLS

Stafford Loans are available to part- and full-time undergraduates and graduate students. These loans are based on financial need, though there are limits on how much an individual may receive both in a single year and cumulatively. Loans can be either subsidized, meaning the student will not be charged interest until repayment begins, or unsubsidized, where repayment begins at the inception of the loan. The interest rate on any unsubsidized Stafford Loan and a subsidized graduate school Stafford Loan is currently fixed at 6.8%; subsidized undergraduate Stafford Loans have a fixed interest rate of 7.9%. The Parent Loan to Undergraduate Students (PLUS) allows parents to borrow money for college; like the Supplemental Loans to Students (SLS), they are not tax-based and are not available to part-time students.

COLLEGE WORK STUDY, UGMA, AND UTMA

College work-study programs are funded by the federal government and administered by individual schools. Eligibility for these programs is based on financial need, and they are available to both graduates and undergraduates. Students in work-study programs are provided with employment at which they can earn a maximum amount of money while attending school. The Uniform Gifts to Minors Act (UGMA) and Uniform Transfers to Minors Act (UTMA) were both established to allow parents to set up custodial accounts in a child's name to help pay for the child's education. Parents may want to transfer assets to their children in order to reduce the income taxes on the earnings. The money transferred to such an account is an irrevocable gift, and the child may choose to use it for something other than education.

SECTION 2503(C) MINOR'S TRUST AND ZERO-COUPON BONDS

A Section 2503(c) Minor's Trust allows the transferred trust property to be treated as if it were a gift of a present interest to a child. For this reason, it qualifies for annual gift tax exclusion. A trust like this is used either when the grantor's income tax bracket is high and the recipient's tax bracket is low, or when the grantor doesn't want an appreciating asset included in the gross estate. If income from the trust is distributed every year, it is taxable to the recipient; if income accumulates, it is taxed to the trust. Another way of funding education is through zero-coupon bonds, which offer no interest during the life of the bond, but the payment of the principal at maturity. These bonds are sold at a discount. Zero coupon bonds are made somewhat less attractive by the fact that the IRS taxes the accrued interest even before the investor receives the funds.

OWNERSHIP OF ASSETS

The ownership of assets will affect the amount of financial aid a student is offered. The firm that evaluates a student's financial aid will use a methodology formula known as the expected family contribution. Parents can use as much as 47% of after-tax income to pay for college, but no more than 5.6% of assets; capital gains are treated as income. The family will be expected to contribute less to the cost of education if the family saves money in the parents' rather than the child's name, as the formula asks students to contribute 35% of their assets to the cost of college. Also, parents can minimize their expected contribution by investing in a 401(k) or other tax-sheltered retirement plan; investments in these plans are excluded when calculating the total value of the assets owned by the parents.

Risk Management and Insurance Planning

RISK

Risk is the potential for loss. A financial risk is the type of risk with which insurance is concerned. A dynamic risk is one that is associated with changes in the economy, whether in price level or consumer tastes. Static risks are those that are more easily covered by insurance, since they pertain to common economic risks. Fundamental risks are those that are not particular to any one individual, and as such are the responsibility of society. Particular risks are felt by individuals and so are more commonly treated by insurance. A pure risk has only two possible results: loss or no loss. A speculative risk, on the other hand, has the potential for both gain and loss. An insurable risk must be definable, measurable, somewhat predictable, and must create losses that are random and not catastrophic.

PERIL, HAZARD, THE LAW OF LARGE NUMBERS, AND ADVERSE SELECTION

A peril is a reason for loss. Perils include fire, windstorm, and theft. A hazard is some condition that is likely to increase the chance of loss in the event of peril. There are three types of hazards: physical hazards are physical properties (like volatility) that increase hazard; moral hazards are qualities in individuals (like dishonesty) that increase the risk of loss; and morale hazards are the dangers that one faces by being indifferent to risk. The law of large numbers states that as the number of independent trials increases, the instances of a certain event will approach the number predicted by probability. In other words, when something occurs many times, it is easier to predict aspects of it. The concept of adverse selection states that the people who are aware of their vulnerability to a certain peril are more likely to acquire insurance against it.

RESPONSE TO RISK AND MORTALITY VS. MORBIDITY

Risk retention is the voluntary or involuntary submission to risk and is especially common in situations where potential loss seems to be small. Risk transfer is the shifting of a risk from one individual to another who is more equipped to handle it. Risk control is the process of minimizing losses, while risk financing is the process of developing the means to pay for losses. Risk reduction involves taking active steps to minimize the damage caused by risks with high frequency but low loss. Risk avoidance is the total refusal to perform a risky behavior. Mortality is the rate at which a population dies, while morbidity is the likelihood of disability. Insurance companies use the mortality and morbidity rates of certain populations to set insurance rates.

RISK EXPOSURE

PERSONAL

Life insurance is intended to allow a person's dependents to carry on when he or she dies. There are two main ways to design it. The human life value approach determines the present value of the portion of a person's income that will be necessary to support his or her dependents. A needs analysis, on the other hand, compares the needs that will arise after the person's death with the means already in place to fulfill these needs. Individuals are also at risk of becoming disabled, in which case they may need insurance to cover their own cost of living. Many individuals have insurance to protect themselves against a general decline in health, unemployment, or, conversely, the problem of superannuation, in which a person lives so long that they run out of money.

PROPERTY AND LIABILITY

All the real estate owned by a person is at risk of many different perils, and therefore there are many insurance policies to protect real property. Other tangible and intangible assets that a person owns are also in danger of damage, and insurance policies may be taken out on them as well. Damage to automobiles is so common that the government requires drivers to take out auto insurance. As for liabilities, individuals may become subject to claims on their assets because they have been convicted of a tort. This tort may be intentional, as in the case of libel or assault, or it may be unintentional, as in the case of negligence. In either case, very few nonspecific insurance policies will cover the liabilities arising from a tort.

NEGLIGENCE

Negligence is defined as any conduct that is below the standard of care established by the law for the protection of others against unreasonable risk of harm within the scope of reasonable expectation. In order to prove tort liability for negligence, it must be proven that the defendant owed a duty to the plaintiff, that the defendant failed to do this duty, that the plaintiff was damaged in some way, and that the breach of duty was the cause of this damage. A person accused of negligence may use one of several defenses: that the plaintiff assumed a risk by participating in some activity; that the plaintiff contributed to the damage by risky behavior of his or her own; that their negligence was only responsible for part of the damages; or that the plaintiff had a "last clear chance" to avoid damage.

COLLATERAL SOURCE RULE, VICARIOUS LIABILITY, LIBEL, SLANDER, AND MALPRACTICE

The collateral source rule states that a person injured through the negligence of another may receive a compensation awarded in a lawsuit in addition to personal insurance compensation. A person may be guilty of vicarious liability if he or she is a principal and his or her agent commits a negligent act. Parents, for instance, are generally considered to be liable for the acts of their children. Libel is the printing of false and defamatory information about another person and is considered an intentional tort. Slander is stating out loud false and defamatory facts about another person. It is also an intentional tort. Malpractice is professional misconduct or incompetence in the performance of a professional act. The practitioner will be liable for the damages or injuries caused by malpractice.

BUSINESS-RELATED RISK, PROPERTY AND CASUALTY INSURANCE CALCULATION

Worker's compensation laws make employers absolutely liable for injuries to employees. The death or disability of the operator or partner in a business may make it difficult for the business to continue. Homeowners insurance covers the dwelling and other structures on a replacement cost basis. This means that if the amount of insurance coverage is at least 80%, the loss will be paid without deduction for depreciation, and not on an actual cash basis, in which the payment is the replacement cost minus depreciation. If the amount of insurance is less than 80% of the replacement cost, the company will pay either the actual cash value or the proportion of the replacement cost of the loss that the amount of insurance bears to 80% of the replacement cost value of the building, whichever is larger.

HEALTH INSURANCE CALCULATION AND LIFE INSURANCE CALCULATION

In the calculation of health insurance, the deductible is the retained risk. If covered expenses are incurred, the first part of the expenses is applied to the deductible, which must be paid by the insured. After the deductible, the coinsurance must be paid. This is split between the insured and the insurance company. The stop-loss limit is the maximum amount that the individual can be required to pay out of pocket. There are three factors that influence the premiums of a life insurance policy. Mortality is the probability of dying or living at a certain age. An insurance company will also calculate rates of interest, so that they do not need to collect the full amount of future losses from policyholders. Finally, insurance companies will calculate what is known as loading. Loading is the portion of the premium that will cover expenses, profit, and margin for contingencies. Mortality and interest are used to calculate the net premium, which is combined with operating expenses to figure gross expenses.

INDEMNITY, INSURABLE INTEREST, AND CONTRACT REQUIREMENTS

Insurance contracts are said to be contracts of indemnity, because the insurer will reimburse the insured either up to the extent of the insured's covered financial loss or the amount of coverage, whichever is less. Typically, the insured party will be given the actual cash value of the damaged property rather than a replacement piece of property. According to the common law doctrine of subrogation, the insurer will assume whatever rights the injured party has against a responsible third party, meaning that the insurance company can sue the third party if they so choose. Insurance can only be issued if the applicant has an insurable interest in whatever is to be insured. In order for a valid contract to exist, there must be five elements: offer and acceptance, genuine assent, adequate consideration, capacity, and legality.

INSURANCE CONTRACT CHARACTERISTICS

Insurance contracts are specific to the person who is being insured. They are unilateral, meaning that only one party may be forced into compliance. They are also considered contracts of adhesion, meaning that the insured can only accept or reject the contract as it is written. They are also called aleatory contracts, because it is possible for one party to receive much larger benefits than the other. Insurance contracts are contracts of utmost good faith, meaning that they can be voided if one party commits fraud or misrepresentation. In an insurance contract, a warranty is a statement made by one party to another that, if false, would have the effect of voiding the contract. Concealment is the failure to disclose known information. Estoppel states that one cannot deny a fact that has already been proven. Rescission means that insurance contracts may be rescinded if one party misrepresents itself.

CATEGORIES FOR THE ANALYSIS OF INSURANCE CONTRACTS

In an insurance contract, declarations are the factual statements identifying the people, properties, and activities involved. The definitions section of the contract contains an explanation of the key policy terms. The insuring agreement is the basic premise of the insurance contract. Exclusions are those exceptions to the coverage offered by the insurer. Conditions are the things the policy owner must do in order for the contract to obtain. The policy continuation provision of the contract indicates the right of the owner to continue coverage. The valuation of losses indicates any sharing of losses that will have to be absorbed by the insured party. The endorsements and riders section contains any add-ons that the insured may obtain for an extra charge.

PROPERTY INSURANCE

Real and personal property consists of a person's land, anything attached or affixed to his or her land, and the rights that are inherent in ownership. Insurance can help protect real and personal property against both named perils (in which coverage is only provided for those perils listed on the policy) and all-risk perils (in which coverage from is included for all perils unless specifically excluded). There are eight standard homeowner forms: HO-1, which is the basic form, for owner occupants of one- to four-family dwelling units; HO-2, the broad form, for the same; HO-3, the special form, for the same; HO-4, the contents broad form, for renters; HO-5, the comprehensive form, for owner-occupants of one to four-family dwellings; HO-6, the unit-owners form, for condo owners; HO-8, the modified coverage form, for owner-occupants of one- to four-family dwellings; and HO-15, the Homeowners Special Personal Property Coverage Form, for basic personal property.

HOMEOWNER FORMS

Homeowner forms have two major sections: the first covers property, and the second provides liability and medical payment coverage. In the first section, Coverage A insures the house and anything attached to it; Coverage B insures any other structures on the property; Coverage C insures the personal property of the owner at actual cash value; Coverage D pays for any loss of use; Coverage E insures against personal liability; and Coverage F insures for any medical payments that need to be paid to other people. This coverage is provided under the conditions that the insured must give notice to the insurance company, must protect property from further damage, must prepare an inventory of damages, and must submit a signed statement within sixty days of the loss.

AUTOMOBILE INSURANCE

A personal auto policy (PAP) is a package insurance policy that provides both property and liability insurance for the members of a family. A PAP offers four kinds of insurance: liability coverage, which covers the people named in the policy when they are liable for damages caused by their own auto; medical coverage, in the event that the insured or anyone in the insured's car needs medical treatment; uninsured motorist coverage, which protects drivers when they are in an accident with another driver who is not insured; and coverage for damage to the insured's automobile. This last section contains both collision coverage, which insures against accidents with other cars, and comprehensive physical damage, which insures against every other kind of damage.

BUSINESS AND BUSINESS ACTIVITY INSURANCE

Commercial property insurance protects real and personal property used during the course of business. Business income insurance protects individuals against a loss of income incurred after business property is damaged. Crime insurance protects businesses against losses suffered because of burglary, extortion, or employee dishonesty. Commercial general liability insurance protects the owners of a business from any claims made by customers. Worker's compensation and employer's liability insurance covers employers when employees are hurt on the job, even when the injury is due to employee negligence. Commercial auto insurance covers employers for cars that are used in the everyday operations of the business.

UMBRELLA INSURANCE POLICY

An umbrella insurance policy is designed to provide coverage in addition to that provided by a basic liability policy. Umbrella policies can usually only be taken out when the insured has an underlying basic liability policy. In cases where an insured party fails to maintain basic liability coverage, umbrella policies will often only pay the amount that they would have had to if a basic policy had been in place. There are a few general exclusions to umbrella liability coverage. These include owned or leased aircraft or watercraft, failure to render professional services, claims covered by worker's compensation, intentional injury, and damage to property owned by the insured.

GENERAL BUSINESS LIABILITY

Professional liability insurance provides coverage for the legal liability that arises when a person demonstrates incompetence in his or her profession. Professionals may take either errors or omissions insurance, which covers liability for financial and property damage, or malpractice insurance, which covers liability for bodily injury. Directors and officers liability insurance is purchased by a corporation on behalf of the officers and directors; it protects these people from lawsuits that may be brought by stockholders, creditors, competitors, and governments. Product liability insurance protects individuals against claims brought against a product that is manufactured by their business.

47

HEALTH INSURANCE
HOSPITAL-SURGICAL AND MAJOR MEDICAL

Hospital-surgical insurance policies provide benefits only when the insured needs surgery or needs to be hospitalized; in other words, they do not cover trips to the doctor's office. These policies may not be adequate to cover long-term illness. Hospital-surgical plans often have the lowest premiums because they offer the fewest benefits. Major medical plans cover just about every kind of health condition and may provide $1 million or more in coverage. In these plans, the insured party may choose who provides their insurance, though they may receive reduced benefits if their doctor is outside a care network. One major variable in major medical plans is their coverage of prescription drugs: some plans cover all medication, while others only carry medication up to a certain point.

TRADITIONAL INDEMNITY AND PREFERRED PROVIDER ORGANIZATION

Traditional indemnity plans provide a comprehensive medical expense plan. This includes medical, hospital, surgical, and diagnostic service. There may be a limit on the amount of reimbursement that can be received, but patients are allowed to choose their own doctor. Managed care plans are similar, though they specify which doctors may be used. Managed care plans also take more of an effort to encourage preventive care, so that customers may avoid illness. A preferred provider organization (PPO) is a benefit plan that an insurance company has established with a network of health professionals to provide health care at a reduced rate. The insured party will have incentives to use services within the network of the PPO.

HEALTH MAINTENANCE ORGANIZATION AND POINT-OF-SERVICE PLAN

A health maintenance organization (HMO) is an organized health care system that provides a range of medical services on a prepaid basis to individual subscribers, all of whom live in a particular geographic region. HMOs emphasize preventative care, though they do offer comprehensive packages of health care services. The subscribers to an HMO pay an annual premium with no deductible or co-payment. A point-of-service plan is a hybrid of the HMO and the PPO: these resemble HMOs for network services and PPOs for non-network services. Point-of-service plans may be either open-ended HMOs, in which is the insured has the option to visit doctors outside the network, or gatekeeper PPOs, in which the customer selects a primary care physician who is responsible for determining whether the customer needs to go outside the network for care.

MEDICARE SUPPLEMENT INSURANCE AND BLUE CROSS AND BLUE SHIELD

Medicare supplement insurance provides benefits for some of the specific expenses that are not covered by Medicare, including deductibles, coinsurance, copayments, and other expenses that are beyond Medicare coverage, like prescription drugs and treatment outside the United States. When individuals receive coverage of this kind, it is usually called Medigap coverage. The National Association of Insurance Commissioners has developed ten insurance plans for the federal government. These plans typically cover hospitalization, medical expenses, and blood. Blue Cross and Blue Shield provide for medical care for prepaying subscribers. Blue Cross plans mainly give coverage for hospital expenses, while Blue Shield plans are mainly used to cover physician's expenses.

DISABILITY INCOME INSURANCE
OCCUPATIONAL DEFINITIONS AND APPLICATIONS

If an injury or illness is not debilitating, no benefit need be paid. There are four types of disability in current policies: the inability to engage in one's own occupation; the inability to engage in an occupation for which one has been trained or educated; the inability to engage in any occupation; and a reduction in income due to disability. Many companies use what is called a split definition of disability, meaning that they give "own occupation" coverage for a while and then modify the coverage. Many disabilities that occur on the job are covered by worker's compensation rather than disability. Total disability benefits provide for the full policy benefit, partial benefits pay a reduced benefit if the insured can still fulfill some functions, and residual benefits help the disabled person receive a bit of extra income even after returning to work.

BENEFIT PERIOD, ELIMINATION PERIOD, AND BENEFIT AMOUNT

Short-term disability coverage provides benefits for only a period of about six months and almost never more than a year. There may be a waiting period before the customer can receive benefits during a sickness, although there will be no waiting period after an accident. Long-term disability coverage offers extended benefits, often lasting up to two year. These policies may be subject to an even longer waiting period. The elimination period for a disability policy is just the deductible; these are used o prevent fraud by the insured. Disability benefits are structured to provide a percentage of regular earnings. Short-term disability plans typically provide benefits ranging from 50-100%, while long-term plans may range from 50-70%. Plans may have a maximum dollar amount.

RIDERS

A cost-of-living allowance allows the disability income benefit to be increased after the insured becomes disabled. A presumptive disability provision states that the loss of two limbs, or of either sight or hearing, will be treated as a total disability. A guaranteed insurability provision allows the insured party to buy additional coverage if his or her income should increase. An automatic benefit increase means the benefit will rise if the cost of the policy rises. A waiver of premium provision exists should the insured become totally disabled for a long period of time. A Social Security substitute rider allows disability insurance to be coordinated with the Social Security insurance program.

A probation period is the period of time after a disability policy is issued during which certain injuries are not covered. A preexisting conditions clause acknowledges any physical condition which the insured had before coverage began. Preexisting conditions are generally not covered by disability plans. A change of occupation provision allows the insurer to reduce benefits if the insured moves to a more dangerous line of work. A relation of earnings to insurance clause states that disability benefits cannot exceed the insured's earned income. A noncancelable policy is one that the insurer cannot cancel and in which the premiums may not be raised. A guaranteed renewable policy is one that the insurer may not cancel, but on which premiums may be raised for a whole class of policy owners. The insurer has the right to cancel a conditionally renewable policy and has total control over a policy with no provision.

TAXATION OF BENEFITS

Disability benefits received from an employer-provided disability policy are fully included in taxable income. Disability benefits received from an employee-paid disability policy are excluded from taxable income. Disability benefits received from a policy paid by both employer and employee are included in income to the extent of the employer pro rata share of premiums. For example, if an employee pays 60% of the cost of his or her disability premium, then 40% of any disability income payments are tax-free to the employee, and 60% are taxable as income. The contributions made by the employer are deductible, but the contributions made by the employee are not tax-deductible.

LONG-TERM CARE INSURANCE
POLICY PROVISIONS

There are special terms, like "adult day care," that may only be used in a long-term care insurance policy if they are defined. The renewal provisions are considered guaranteed if the premiums can be adjusted and are considered noncancelable if they cannot be adjusted. Exclusions are generally prohibited, unless in the case of: alcoholism or drug addiction; mental and nervous disorder; suicide and war; and services available under Medicare or other social insurance programs. Policies must contain the right to purchase more coverage or nonforfeiture options. Inflation protection benefits must also be offered. Policies must contain a provision that waives premiums if the insured has been receiving benefits for a given amount of time. Policies cannot be contested on the grounds of misrepresentation after two years.

MARKETING PROVISIONS

An applicant for a long-term care insurance policy must receive an outline of coverage, a shopper's guide, and a free 30-day period to examine the policy. The insurer must provide accurate comparisons with competing policies. The insurer must also ask clear questions when evaluating the applicant's health. Policies cannot be issued until the applicant is given the option to identify a third party to be notified of any pending lapses because of the failure to pay premiums. Insurers must report lapse rates, replacement sales, and denied claims for each year. All of the advertisements used by the insurance company must be filed with the state regulatory authority. Contracts will have a defined period of incontestability.

ELIGIBILITY

The Health Insurance Portability and Accountability Act (HIPAA) created a definition for long-term care plans. HIPAA grants favorable tax treatment to qualified long-term care insurance contracts. For a contract to qualify, only long-term care insurance can be provided; the policy cannot pay for expenses reimbursed under Medicare, the policy cannot have a cash surrender value or loan provision, and any premium refunds and policy dividends must be used to reduce future premiums or increase future benefits. Qualified long-term care services, on the other hand, are defined as the necessary diagnostic, preventive, therapeutic, curing, treating, and rehabilitative services and maintenance or personal care services required by a chronically ill person and provided by a plan of care developed by a licensed health care practitioner.

To be classified as chronically ill, a person must be unable to perform at least two activities of daily living (ADLs) or must require substantial help to keep healthy and safe. Activities of daily living include eating, bathing, dressing, transferring from bed to chair, using the toilet, and maintaining continence. Benefits are typically paid out a certain dollar amount per day. They may be provided on an indemnity basis that covers 80-100% of charges up to a given maximum. The duration of a long-term care policy is influenced by the elimination period and the maximum benefit period. The premium will increase proportionally to the maximum benefit period and inversely proportional to the elimination period.

ELIMINATION PROTECTION, INFLATION PROTECTION, AND NURSING HOME AND IN-HOME CARE

The benefits of a long-term care insurance plan do not begin until after a specified period of time during which the insured has been receiving long-term care. The cost of inflation protection is added into the initial premium, so the premiums will not increase during the annual increase. There are a few varieties of care provided for in long-term care plans: skilled-nursing care, in which a registered nurse is available at all times; intermediate care, in which less attention from nurses is required; custodial care, in which medical services are not needed; home health care, in which a person requires daily or weekly nurse visits; assisted living care, for elderly people who don't need the care provided by nursing homes; and respite care, which is occasional full-time care provided for a person in his or her own home.

COMPARING POLICIES

Consumers should make a few considerations before settling on a long-term care insurance policy. First, a policy should always be guaranteed renewable for life. Also, a three-month waiting period will usually offer the best value relative to the premium. A policy should provide coverage for skilled, intermediate, and custodial care. It may be prudent to select a policy that does not require hospitalization before entering a nursing home. It should be noted that not every policy provides coverage for Alzheimer's disease. One should always select a policy that provides for unanticipated rises in the cost of long-term care. Finally, one should select a policy that provides for a waiver of premiums in the event of disability and that provides level premiums for life.

TAX IMPLICATIONS AND QUALIFICATION AND APPROPRIATENESS OF COVERAGE

There are some excellent tax benefits of qualified long-term care contracts. For one thing, individuals are allowed to deduct a premium paid for long-term care in excess of 10% (or sometimes 7.5%) of adjusted gross income. The individual's age determines limits on the amount that can be deducted. Contributions made by an employer are deductible to the employer and will not create taxable income for the employee. Benefits are received tax-free, unless the contracts are written on a per diem basis, in which case the proceeds may be excluded from income at a rate of up to $390 a day (as of 2022). It should be noted that the young as well as the elderly sometimes require long-term care.

AUTOMOBILE INSURANCE
GENERAL PROVISIONS

Although automobile insurance contracts can vary widely, most contracts currently in effect include a few standard provisions. Most auto insurance contracts will specify that the term of the policy can only be changed or waived by an endorsement signed by the company. Also, the contract will state that the insurer will not cover any accidents or losses reported by an insured party that has made fraudulent statements. In addition, the policyholder is allowed to cancel the policy by notifying the company in writing. Finally, most contracts include a subrogation clause that applies to all coverage.

DISCOUNTS AND AREAS OF NO COVERAGE

Many insurance companies will give discounts for: higher deductibles, elimination of collision coverage for older cars, no accidents over a certain period of time, no smoking, good grades in school, completion of a defensive driving course, airbag, automatic seat belts, individuals over age 25, women, and married people. There are three main circumstances in which automobile insurance may not provide coverage. One is when a person is living in the same house as the insured but is not listed on the policy. Another common event that may not be covered is when the accident occurs during business use. Finally, auto insurance may not cover accidents that occur after the driver has rejected insurance coverage through a rental company.

LIFE INSURANCE
FUNDAMENTALS

All insurance policies insure not against death in general, but against untimely death. Life insurance contracts are not contracts of indemnity, as they make no attempt to restore the individual to his previous position. There are two types of life insurance. Term (or pure) insurance has no cash value; it pays a death benefit if a person dies within the term of the policy. Permanent insurance, on the other hand, never expires, has a cash value, and contains the advantage of a tax-deferred investment income. The cash value of a permanent insurance policy is a kind of savings fund for the policyholder. The level premium concept states that the cash value reserve will accumulate over time, allowing the premium to remain the same.

TERM INSURANCE

There are a few different types of term life insurance policies. A yearly renewable term policy is established annually and is renewable for periods of one year. These policies typically have a fixed face amount and a premium that increases every year. Level-term insurance offers the guarantee of a fixed premium and face value for up to ten years or, sometimes, for twenty years. Decreasing-term insurance policies offer less protection every year they are maintained. This kind of insurance is often used to provide funds to pay for a mortgage. These policies usually have a fixed, level premium. Term policies offer both renewability and convertibility. Convertibility is the right to exchange a term policy for a permanent policy without demonstrating insurability.

WHOLE LIFE INSURANCE

Because the annual insurance costs in a whole life policy are spread out over the life of the insured, these policies offer a level premium. Whole life policies provide a guaranteed but fixed death benefit and a balance between cash accumulation and protection. There are four basic types of whole life insurance. Ordinary whole life has the lowest premium rate and a low cash value; it assumes that the premium rate will be payable throughout the life of the insured. Limited-pay whole life provides protection for life without forcing the insured to pay after he or she retires. Single-premium whole life is a good tax-deferred investment; it is set up with a single lump sum payment. Graded premium whole life insurance has a relatively low initial premium that increases for several years. This allows individuals who anticipate an increased income to gradually increase their payments.

UNIVERSAL LIFE INSURANCE

Individuals who hold a universal life insurance policy may increase or decrease their benefit as long as they maintain insurability. The interest charged to the policy's cash value is adjusted for current interest rates. Universal life insurance is referred to as unbundled insurance, because operating expenses, mortality charges, and cash buildup can all be viewed in the annual statement. Universal life insurance policies are somewhat similar to whole life policies, except that the premium payment is flexible, the death benefit is adjustable, and both the investment and the mortality risks are transferred to the policyholder from the insurance company. The cash value of a universal life policy will increase more than that of a whole life policy when the interest rates increase. Death benefits in such a policy may be paid as either the face amount of the policy or at the stated face amount plus the cash value at the time of the insured's death.

VARIABLE LIFE INSURANCE

In a variable life insurance policy, the policy owner is allowed to choose the investments to which the savings element will be directed. There is no guaranteed cash value or crediting rate in a policy of this kind. Investments will be held in separate accounts that resemble mutual funds but are classified as different. These policies generally have between five and fifteen separate accounts from which an individual may choose; one of these is always a conservative, interest-bearing account. The holder of a variable life insurance policy runs the risk of being charged a substantial amount just to keep the policy active in a down market. A variable life insurance policy puts the investment risk on the insured party and lets him or her direct the policy's cash value into the securities market. Only licensed insurance and securities agents can sell these policies.

Mometrix

VARIABLE WHOLE LIFE INSURANCE AND VARIABLE UNIVERSAL LIFE INSURANCE

In variable whole life insurance policy, the policyholder pays the fixed premiums as in a whole life policy. There is a guaranteed death benefit, also, just as in a whole life policy. However, a variable whole life insurance policy also has the investment flexibility of a variable life insurance policy and has no guaranteed cash values. A variable universal life insurance policy has premium flexibility, just like a universal life insurance policy. Also, there is death benefit design flexibility in such a policy, just as there is in a universal life insurance policy. The differences between a variable universal life insurance policy and a universal life insurance policy are that the variable policy offers investment flexibility and has no guaranteed cash values.

ENDOWMENT POLICIES

A less-common kind of life insurance policy is known as an endowment policy. In an endowment policy, the death benefit will be equal to the cash value at maturity. The purchaser of an endowment policy can specify the maturity date of the policy (these are usually terms of ten, fifteen, twenty, or more years). At age 100, the life insurance will be identical in design to an endowment, as cash value equals the death benefit. A change in federal income tax law made in 1984 eliminated the tax-advantaged buildup of an endowment's cash value. The current sale of endowment contracts is very limited in the United States.

JOINT-LIFE INSURANCE

FIRST-TO-DIE POLICY AND SECOND-TO-DIE POLICY

There are a few different kinds of joint-life policies. A first-to-die policy is usually made for the continuation of a business. The policy will insure all of the owners of the business, and when the first owner dies, the insurance company will make a payment that the other owners use to purchase the deceased's share of the business. Second-to-die policies are more common in estate tax payment. These policies are usually purchased by married couples. When the first spouse dies, the estate transfers to the living spouse, and when he or she dies the estate is subject to a tax that the insurance policy pays. These policies tend to eliminate liquidity problems. If a deceased person owned the policy, it is included in the estate, even if the deceased is not the beneficiary.

FAMILY INCOME POLICY AND FAMILY LIFE INSURANCE POLICY

There are a few different types of joint-life insurance policies. A family income policy is a combination of decreasing term insurance and some form of whole life insurance. The whole life insurance will pay a lump sum, and the term rider will provide an income designed to end at a certain date in the future. A family life insurance policy, on the other hand, has a base policy (usually whole-life) on one adult in the family. Such a policy also covers other members of the family. Policies of this kind are often sold in units; a given unit will include a certain amount of money on the primary insured, a lesser amount on the spouse, and an even lesser amount on each child.

LIFE INSURANCE

CONTRACTUAL PROVISIONS

There are a few contractual provisions that distinguish life insurance policies. In a participating policy, for instance, dividends may be paid to the policy owner. However, there will be a small extra margin in the premium of such policies, which will not be found in nonparticipating policies (which do not pay dividends). Also, a participating policy will be capable of responding to changes in the economy. For instance, when interest rates rise rapidly, a participating policy can adjust to give the policy owners a better chance to earn interest. An insurance contract is also declared to be a whole contract; that is, no other contract can be said to control it. An insurance contract must state that

53

someone with an insurable interest in the insured holds the policy, and that, though the policy may be transferred, the insurance company must approve the transfer.

A life insurance contract will have to state a beneficiary. The owner of the policy will have the ability to change the beneficiary unless that designation was made irrevocably. Changes must be made in writing to the insurance company in order to be effective. A primary beneficiary is the individual first designated to receive the proceeds of the policy; contingent beneficiaries are those who are entitled to receive proceeds if the primary beneficiary has died. If a life insurance contract has what is known as collateral assignment, the owner may use the policy as collateral. This arrangement is often made when life insurance is taken in a business situation.

Some life insurance contracts will contain what is known as an incontestable clause. This clause gives the insurance company two years in which to discover any information about the insured that would affect the decision to issue the policy. If adverse information is discovered, the company will have the right to void the contract. Insurance contracts also contain language regarding misstatement of age: if an individual turns out to be a different age than he or she asserted at the time the policy was made, then death benefits will be adjusted to what the premium would have purchased. Life insurance contracts will also contain a statement of the grace period, an automatic extension of the period in which the premium may be paid. This period is usually 31days.

Life insurance contracts contain language that indicates that if the premium is paid after the end of the grace period, the policy will lapse. A reinstatement provision allows the policyholder to reinstate a policy if insurable interest still exists and if the insured is still insurable. Reinstatement is usually automatic if it is requested within 30 days of the end of the grace period. Many life insurance contracts will contain provisions for an automatic premium loan, where the insurance company loans the individual the money for an unpaid premium automatically. This is only done in cash value policies. Some insurance contracts will contain a suicide clause stating that the insurance company must pay only cumulative premiums plus interest if the insured commits suicide within two years of the policy being issued.

Life insurance contracts may contain some rather obscure provisions. An aviation and war clause denies coverage for any death that occurs during flight or war. Such policies are now very rare. A policy loan provision allows the owner to borrow money from the insurance company at a specified interest rate, using the policy as collateral. A simultaneous death clause states that if both the insured and the beneficiary die at the same time, the insurance company will assume that the beneficiary died first, and therefore will distribute the proceeds as if the insured had survived the beneficiary. In other words, proceeds will be paid to the secondary beneficiary or to the estate of the insured.

Some life insurance contracts contain what is called a common disaster clause, in which the settlement of the policy proceeds is withheld for a predetermined number of days after the death of the insured and any beneficiary that dies during this period is considered to have predeceased the insured. Therefore, proceeds are distributed as if the insured had survived the beneficiary. A contract that contains a guaranteed purchase option gives the owner some protection against becoming insured by giving him or her the option to purchase more insurance at a specified later date without having to prove insurability. A waiver of premium states that if the insured should become disabled, the insurance company will waive the premiums on the life insurance policy during the continuance of the insured's disability.

The accelerated benefits provision of a life insurance contract, also known as an accelerated death benefit, allows an insured individual who is terminally ill to withdraw a portion of the policy's death benefit before death. The portion of the death benefit that is taken out prematurely is income tax-free. There are also some provisions that are prohibited in a life insurance contract. For one thing, nonpayment of a loan is not grounds for forfeiture of the policy. Also, insurance companies cannot promise something in the declarations made about the policy and then take it away in the fine print.

DIVIDEND OPTIONS

Participating life insurance policies will offer several dividend options. Dividends may be paid to the owner in cash in what is considered a return of the premium (these dividends are income tax-free). Dividends may also be paid as a reduction of premiums or treated as an accumulation of interest. This interest will then be taxed as ordinary income. Sometimes, dividends are used to purchase small amounts of permanent paid-up insurance (on which no future premiums will be due). Other times, dividends will be used to buy insurance for shorter periods of time. Finally, many insurance companies will allow the policy owner to apply the dividend to any interest or principal of a policy loan.

NONFORFEITURE OPTION

The nonforfeiture option of a life insurance policy gives the owner a few choices concerning how to use the policy's cash value. The owner may want to surrender for cash; that is, withdraw the cash value of the policy. Or, the owner may want to purchase an annuity to provide income for life or over a specified period. Additionally, the owner may want to buy a reduced amount of paid-up permanent insurance. This gives the owner a zero-premium policy of a reduced amount. Finally, the owner may want to buy the same amount of extended term insurance. This makes the amount of the term insurance the same as the face amount of the original policy, but the period of coverage will only be for the time frame identified in the policy.

SETTLEMENT OPTIONS

A life insurance policy will have several different settlement options. An interest-only option can be used to delay before choosing a final settlement. While this arrangement is in effect, the insurance company will send a quarterly check for interest. If a lump sum payment is chosen, no income tax is charged. A cash settlement like this allows the beneficiary to pay funeral costs, pay outstanding debts, create a fund for emergencies, and invest in the market. One common fixed annuity option (those which provide partial taxability) is the fixed income option, in which the recipient tells the insurance company how much income is needed each month, and the insurance company tells the recipient how long payments can continue at that rate.

There are a few different kinds of fixed annuity options, all of which provide partial taxability. A fixed-period option is the arrangement in which the recipient tells the insurance company how long the money needs to last, and the insurance company then determines the amount for each payment. There are also four life income options. In a straight life income arrangement, the beneficiary will receive a specified amount for as long as he or she lives, but will receive nothing after his or her death. In a life income with period certain arrangement, the beneficiary is paid an income for as long as he or she lives, with a guaranteed minimum number of payments in case the beneficiary dies early.

In a life income with refund settlement, the beneficiary will be paid a life income for the rest of his or her days, and if the amount of the original lump sum has not been paid out by the time he or she dies, the rest of the proceeds will be paid out to the secondary beneficiary. In a joint-and-survivor income settlement, benefits continue after the death of one beneficiary until the death of a second beneficiary. Variable annuity options can also be used in settlements. These settlements offer a return consistent with the market by investing proceeds in mutual funds. This is in contrast to a fixed annuity option, which is basically a savings account earning a fixed rate of interest.

POLICY REPLACEMENT

A policy owner may wish to terminate or change a policy for a number of reasons. This is often done if the insurance company that issued the policy is in financial trouble, or if the policy is performing poorly. One may want to replace a policy if one has quit smoking and is now eligible for a better premium. Sometimes, people replace a short-term policy with a long-term policy if they feel they can reduce cost. An owner may want to reconsider replacement if he or she will have to pay policy acquisition costs again; if the new policy will have a new contestable period and/or suicide clause; if some of the new provisions or riders are less favorable; if the new premium will be based on the policyholder's age at the time of the switch; or, if the savings generated by eliminating the fee from an old policy don't offset the cost of replacement.

TAX ISSUES AND STRATEGIES (INCOME TAXATION OF DEATH PROCEEDS)

Life insurance is defined in IRC section 101(a). If a given policy doesn't qualify as life insurance, then earnings are considered ordinary income for tax purposes. If the policy does qualify as life insurance, earnings are tax-deferred and the death benefit is income tax-free. To determine whether a policy is life insurance, the IRS usually administers either the cash value accumulation test (determining that the most that can be paid into a policy is the same as the net single premium to pay up the policy), or the guideline premium and corridor test (determining whether the ratio-to-death benefit is within a certain range). According to the transfer for value rule, income tax exclusion is lost when a life insurance policy is transferred unless it is transferred to the insured, to the insured's corporation, or to a partner of the insured.

TAX ISSUES AND STRATEGIES (INCOME TAXATION OF LIVING PROCEEDS)

Cash buildup in a life insurance policy is not subject to taxation as long as it remains in the policy. If the cash is taken out or loaned, it is not taxable unless the policy is a modified endowment contract (MEC). A policy is a MEC if the total premium paid into the policy at any time during the seven-year testing period is more than the sum of the net level premiums that would be needed to result in a paid-up policy after seven years. If this is the case, the death benefit remains income tax-free, but the amount of the loan that is the part of the gain in the policy is taxed as ordinary income if the policy cash value exceeds the premiums paid and the policy owner borrows against the policy. MECs are subject to LIFO tax treatment with respect to loans and distributions from the company. If the policy qualifies as life insurance, it receives FIFO tax treatment.

According to the IRS, dividends paid on life insurance policies are a return of the excess premium. So, if a policy owner receives dividends from an insurance company, they are not subject to income tax. The only exception to this policy occurs when the dividends exceed the cumulative premiums, in which case excess dividends must be reported as ordinary income. The taxable amount of the cash surrender is the total amount surrendered minus the policy owner's current basis in the policy. According to IRC Section 1035 Exchange, life insurance policies or annuities can be exchanged for similar contracts without incurring any adverse income tax consequences. The basis in the old policy will simply become the basis in the new policy.

TAX ISSUES AND STRATEGIES (GIFT TAXATION, ESTATE TAXATION)

When life insurance policies are transferred from one individual to another, or to a trust, there is the potential for a gift tax to be levied. The value of the policy is called the interpolated terminal reserve, which is usually very close to the cash value of the policy. The gift tax may apply in cases where a policy owned by one individual on another's life matures because of the other person's death, and a person other than the policy owner is named as the beneficiary. As for estate taxation, if a person owns a policy on his or her life, then the death benefit will be included in the estate for the purposes of determining whether estate taxes must be paid. Furthermore, any individuals who had an incident of ownership within the three years prior to their death will have the proceeds included in their estate.

POLICY OWNERSHIP ISSUES AND STRATEGIES

There are three common ownership strategies designed to include the proceeds from a life insurance policy in the estate of the deceased. Often, if the owner of the policy is an irrevocable trust, the insured will make payments to the trust to cover premiums, so that the trust will be the beneficiary and can determine how benefits will be distributed. Another common strategy is to choose a charity to be the owner and beneficiary of the insurance policy; an annual, tax-deductible gift to the charity will cover the cost of the premium. People also often make their children the beneficiaries and owners of their life insurance policies so that they may pay the premiums without being subject to a gift tax. In split-dollar life insurance, either the employer will own the policy and have the responsibility for paying premiums (the endorsement method), or the employee will own the policy and pay the premiums (the collateral assignment method).

VIATICAL AGREEMENTS

LEGAL PRINCIPLES, REQUIREMENTS, AND TAX IMPLICATIONS

In a viatical agreement, a terminally ill policy owner the viator) sells his or her life insurance to a third party (the viatical settlement provider) in exchange for a lump sum of cash. Typically, this lump sum is 40-80% of the death benefit. In order for this process to take place, the insured must be terminally ill or chronically ill. Also, the viatical settlement provider must be licensed with the state and must meet the requirements of the NAIC Model Act. Viatical agreements are not subject to income tax so long as the above requirements are met. If they are transferred for value, there may be some capital gains resulting from the difference between the settlement received and the total premium paid.

PLANNING, ETHICAL CONCEPTS AND PLANNING

Alternatives to setting up a viatical agreement include establishing an accelerated death benefit provision, accessing the cash value through a loan, or using the cash value as collateral to secure a loan from a bank or from someone else. The proceeds from a viatical agreement may make the viator ineligible to receive help from Medicaid or Supplemental Security Income. The proceeds may also be subject to the claims of creditors. When setting up a viatical agreement, clients should make sure to include provisions protecting their privacy. Also, it is quite common for viators to receive less than they expect from a viatical agreement. The new owner will have no insurable interest in the life of the insured, a scenario that makes many insurance companies uneasy.

BASICS OF KEY EMPLOYEE INSURANCE

Key employee insurance is insurance taken out on a certain valuable employee. This insurance is owned by the business, which is also considered the beneficiary. The premiums in a policy of this type are not deductible to the business. Death benefits acquired through a policy of this type are tax-free. Generally, key employee insurance is taken out in order to protect the business against the loss of business income and also to ensure that funds will be available to find and train a replacement for the key employee.

INSURANCE NEEDS ANALYSIS
LIFE INSURANCE AMOUNT REQUIRED

Financial planners may conduct a financial needs analysis to determine how much life insurance a family needs if the principal sum is liquidated in the process of meeting the client's financial objectives for surviving members of the family. The liquidation approach (using investment earnings and capital) creates the risk of running out of funds prematurely, while the nonliquidation approach (using investment earnings only) may provide too small of a monthly income. A capital needs analysis (analysis of capital retention) doesn't liquidate the lump sum principal received after death; it uses a high capitalization rate to derive income benefits solely from investment income. The human life value analysis method tries to determine what will be lost if a certain person should die; this is calculated as the present value of that person's estimated future earnings that will be used to support future dependents.

DISABILITY, LONG-TERM CARE, HEALTH, PROPERTY, AND LIABILITY INSURANCE

If a disabling injury should occur, the financial risk taken by the client is calculated as the difference between income needs and income sources. Individuals with no dependents will need disability insurance more than they need life insurance. Individuals probably need to achieve a minimum of wealth before they consider purchasing long-term care insurance, and most will wait until around age 60 to purchase it at all. When purchasing basic health insurance, individuals should be mainly conscious of protecting against the chance of catastrophic loss. Most purchasers of property insurance will accept the financial burden of small losses in order to avoid paying outrageous premiums. As for liability insurance, it is crucial that the limits be coordinated with homeowner and auto insurance in an umbrella policy.

INSURANCE POLICY SELECTION
PURPOSE OF COVERAGE, LENGTH OF TIME REQUIRED, RISK TOLERANCE, AND CASH FLOW CONSTRAINTS

The purpose of insurance is threefold: to protect existing assets; to protect income, so that it will not be interrupted by loss; and to protect both income and assets in the case of liabilities or emergency needs. Life insurance policies may be taken out for short-term needs, as when it is used to hedge a mortgage or a loan, or it may be taken out permanently, in order to augment or increase retirement income in the future. There are some basic assessments of risk tolerance that will determine the coverage appropriate for a given client: clients who are primarily seeking to invest may want a variable form of insurance; clients seeking to protect themselves should consider term insurance; clients who want flexible premiums should take universal and variable universal life; and clients mainly concerned about surviving dependents should take a joint or survivorship life policy. Families should always have enough disability and health insurance, even at the expense of life insurance.

INSURANCE COMPANY SELECTION
FINANCIALS AND RATIOS

The most important factor used in evaluating an insurance company is financial strength, but customers should also consider the willingness and ability to pay claims, the number of lines of coverage offered, the service provided before and after a claim, the cost of the coverage, and the age of the company. Typically, companies that sell only life insurance will have more financial stability than those that offer a number of different types of insurance. Also, companies that mainly sell term insurance are likely to be less stable. The NAIC Watch List is a compilation of 12 financial ratios that measure the financial strength of insurers. The risk-based capital ratio measures the minimum amount of capital that an insurance company needs to maintain to support operations. The lapse ratio measures the number of policies that are cancelled. Policy persistency measures the relative longevity of policies.

Ratings and Mutual vs. Stock

These five companies provide the best ratings of financial strength: A.M. Best; Fitch; Moody's; Standard and Poor's; and Weiss. These ratings are typically based on underwriting results, economy of management, adequacy of reserves for undischarged liabilities, adequacy of policyholder's surplus to absorb shocks, and the soundness of investments. In stock insurance companies, stockholders assume the risks of the insured, the premiums charged are nonnegotiable, earnings are distributed to shareholders as dividends, and the capital invested by shareholders creates a surplus to protect against emergency. In a mutual insurance company, policyholders own the company, premiums are not fixed, there are no dividends or capital stock, and the company must be sure to accumulate a surplus in case of emergency.

Reinsurance and Investments

Reinsurance is the insurance purchased by insurance companies. Reinsurance exists so that, in the event of catastrophic events, losses can be diversified. Also, reinsurers aid small insurance companies by removing part of the burden of accumulating reserves in case of emergency. When insurance companies receive premiums, they usually invest them, though state law strictly governs this process. Insurance companies that specialize in life insurance tend to make most of their investments in long-term securities, since they do not need to have highly liquid investments. Other companies are likely to invest more in government securities, since the insurance contracts they offer are of shorter duration.

Underwriting, Federal Law, and State Law

Underwriting is the process whereby insurance applications are selected and classified. This process obviously involves rejecting some applicants. Underwriting is performed at the time of the original application and at every subsequent renewal. Information for underwriting is obtained from the applicant, the agent, claims department, and other outside agencies. The government regulates insurance through legislation, judicial action, and administrative action. The NAIC drafted the McCarran-Ferguson Act of 1945, which gives the power to regulate insurance companies to states. The NAIC also can recommend legislation. Two common areas are solvency regulation (concerning the licensing of companies, regulation of reserves, etc.) and marketing regulation (concerning unfair practices, consumer complaints, etc.).

Investment Planning

INVESTMENT VEHICLES

CERTIFICATES OF DEPOSIT

Certificates of deposit, also known as CDs, are time deposits with specified dates of maturity. A certificate of deposit may be either negotiable or nonnegotiable. Negotiable CDs are those that can be sold by the depositor in the open market at any time before the CD reaches maturity. A nonnegotiable CD is one in which the maturity date must be reached before the initial depositor may receive the funds. There is an early withdrawal penalty when the funds in a nonnegotiable CD are withdrawn before they reach maturity. If an investor has more than $100,000 to invest, a depository institution may sell him or her a negotiable or jumbo CD. The maturities on these tend to be up to one year; for the most part, certificates of deposit of less than $100,000 are nonnegotiable.

MONEY MARKET MUTUAL FUNDS AND US TREASURY BILLS

Money market mutual funds are primarily short-term securities and are offered as an alternative to other money market instruments. These mutual funds are typically made up of a group of the short-term instruments available in the open market, such as Treasury bills, commercial paper, banker's acceptances, certificates of deposit, and repurchase agreements. US Treasury bills are issued by the federal government and are sold in denominations of $1,000 to $1,000,000 and have maturity periods of three to twelve months. These treasury bills are usually sold at a discount. The interest acquired through them is subject to federal income tax, but not state or local tax.

COMMERCIAL PAPER, BANKER'S ACCEPTANCES, AND REPURCHASE AGREEMENTS

Commercial paper is the unsecured short-term promissory notes that are issued by corporations. There is a small risk of default on these, because only firms with excellent credit ratings are allowed to issue them. Commercial paper is usually sold at a discount, and has a maturity period of less than 270 days. Banker's acceptances, on the other hand, are the short-term promissory notes that a bank guarantees. The bank takes responsibility for repaying these loans, which are generally sold on a discounted basis and used during international trade. Repurchase agreements, or repos, are sales of short-term security in which the seller pledges to buy it back at a specified price and date. The price at which the seller pledges to buy it back is higher than the original sale price.

TREASURY NOTES AND BONDS

Treasury notes are sold in denominations ranging from $1,000 to $1,000,000 and have maturity periods of between 2 and ten years. Treasury bonds are the government's long-term debt; they have maturity periods longer than ten years. Treasury notes and bonds are both offered as coupon securities and are considered to be the safest medium- and long-term investments because the government backs them up. Because they offer such safety, they generally have yields lower than high-quality corporate bonds. The interest earned on treasury notes and bonds is subject to federal income tax but is exempt from state and local taxes.

US GOVERNMENT SAVINGS BONDS

There are a few kinds of US government savings bonds. The Series E bond was established to encourage more saving; it was offered in small denominations, at a discount, and paid no interest. The Series EE bond replaced the Series E, adding a variable rate of interest that allowed investors to benefit from rising interest rates. The interest on E and EE bonds is not taxable until they either reach maturity or are cashed in.

TREASURY INFLATION PROTECTED SECURITIES (TIPS) AND TREASURY STRIPS

Treasury inflation-protected securities are issued by the federal government and have coupon payments that periodically adjust to changes in the inflation rate. These changes in inflation are represented in the principal rather than the coupon. The appropriate coupon payment is calculated by multiplying the inflation-adjusted principal by the real rate (which represents the fixed coupon rate net of inflation). Treasury STRIPS (separate trading of registered interest and principal securities) are zero coupon bonds that constitute direct obligations of the federal government. STRIPS do not pay a coupon, but the interest will be taxed as it accrues. These are considered more risky than other government bonds during periods in which interest rates fluctuate widely.

MUNICIPAL BONDS

GENERAL OBLIGATION BONDS AND REVENUE BONDS

General revenue bonds are not considered to be very risky because they are backed by the taxing power of the issuing government. Revenue bonds, on the other hand, are only supported by the revenue of a project, and so are considered a bit more risky. Often, municipal bonds suffer from poor marketability and liquidity. There may be a very small market for them. Most of the time, state and local governments issue debt that is long-term serial issue because these give the buyer the comfort of knowing when they will mature. The federal government does not tax the interest earned on municipal bonds. Also, many states exempt the bond interest on municipal bonds.

INVESTMENT GRADE CORPORATE BONDS

Investment grade bonds are those that offer debt of high quality. There are a few different types. Secured bonds have a claim to the assets of a corporation in the event of insolvency, liquidation, or default. Unsecured bonds, on the other hand, are not backed by collateral. Debentures are promissory notes not backed by collateral but by the reputation of the firm. During bankruptcy, debentures can only be redeemed after all other secured debt has been paid off. Zero coupon bonds are sold at a discount with no coupon and are redeemed for face value at maturity. Interest is accrued over the life of a zero coupon bond. Individuals cannot avoid tax by buying zero coupon bonds, though the taxes earned on accrued interest can be avoided in retirement accounts because the tax is deferred until the money is withdrawn.

HIGH-YIELD AND CONVERTIBLE CORPORATE BONDS

High-yield corporate bonds, often referred to as junk bonds, are low-quality bonds that have many of the same features as investment grade debt but offer higher yields. These bonds are usually rated below triple B. High yield securities may have a call feature and a sinking fund; they are often debentures but some do have collateral. Convertible bonds are those that give the holder the right to convert a bond into shares of common stock. Investors will have to pay for this privilege. Investors like these bonds because they offer the safety of debt along with the potential for capital gains. Both the underlying stock and interest rates will cause changes in the price of convertible bonds. The conversion ratio is the number of shares a bond may be converted into; it is calculated by dividing the face value of the bond and by the conversion price.

CORPORATE BONDS

CALLABLE BONDS

Firms will usually place a call provision on their bonds that allows them to buy the bonds back at a specified price before maturity. Call provisions are often used after a period of high interest rates, when it makes sense for firms to refinance new debt at a lower interest rate. The call price is typically less than the market price; otherwise it doesn't make sense for the issuer to call the bonds. Purchasing a callable bond carries with it an increased interest rate risk and an increased reinvestment risk along with a reduced potential for capital appreciation. Basically, in a time of falling interest rates the call price will act as a ceiling. The price of bonds without call provisions will continue to rise as interest rates fall.

WAYS TO RETIRE DEBT

Serial bonds are issues in which specified bonds will mature every year. Interest is paid off at different intervals. These nonamortizing securities are popular among local governments seeking to finance capital improvements. When a corporate bond is said to have bullet maturity, this means that the entire principal is paid off in one payment at the maturity date. Amortizing securities make both interest and principal payments. Sinking funds are a series of staggered payments that retire a portion of the bond issue prior to maturity. When new debt is issued in order to generate proceeds for paying off old debt, it is known as refunding. Some bonds are nonrefundable, though they may still be callable.

EMBEDDED OPTIONS

Corporate bonds may include a number of different embedded options, which are rights given to the issuer or to the bondholder. A call provision, whereby the issuer may call the bond at any point before maturity, is one common option. Many bonds will contain a prepayment provision, allowing the borrower to pay off the loan balance before maturity. These are often used with home mortgages and car loans. An accelerated sinking fund provision allows the issuer to retire more bonds than required under a sinking fund. A put provision gives the bondholder the option to sell the bonds back to the issuer at a predetermined price. This option is common when bonds are trading below average because of high interest rates.

PROMISSORY NOTES AND INSURANCE-BASED INVESTMENTS

Promissory notes are documents that have been signed by a borrower pledging to repay a loan under certain stated terms. Promissory notes are unsecured and may be made for the short term or the long term. Insurance-based investments may be either guaranteed investment contracts or annuities. Guaranteed investment contracts, commonly known as stable value funds, are securities sold to pension plans by insurance companies. The rate of return for these is guaranteed over a certain amount of time. Annuities are contracts issued by insurance companies. The holder of an annuity receives a regular payment from the insurance company. Annuities may be either fixed or variable.

COMMON STOCK

TYPES OF COMMON STOCK

There are six basic categories of common stock. Blue chip stocks are those that are highly regarded for investment. Blue chip stocks will consistently pay dividends. Income stocks pay regular and steady dividends and typically appreciate enough to keep up with inflation. Growth stocks are those for firms whose sales, earnings, and market shares tend to grow at an above-average pace. Cyclical stocks are those that perform in a manner consistent with the market. Interest-sensitive stocks are affected greatly by changes in interest rates. Insurance companies, utilities, and banks all have interest-sensitive stock. Defensive stocks are generally unaffected by changes in the market.

CONTROL AND STOCK PRICE ADJUSTMENT

When common stock is said to be noncumulative, then each share gives the holder one vote for each member of the board of directors. If the stock is cumulative, then the shareholder has a number of votes that is equal to the number of positions on the board multiplied by the number of shares owned. These votes can be allocated however the shareholder likes. Cash dividends, the payments made to the shareholders of a corporation, will be paid as the stock price is adjusted. The price of the stock will decrease by the amount of the dividend per share on the ex-dividend date. The balance sheet of the firm will also be affected by dividend payments, as the levels of cash and retained earnings will decline by the amount of the dividends paid.

PROCESS OF PAYING DIVIDENDS

There are a few important dates in the process by which dividends are paid to shareholders. The declaration date is the date on which the board of directors passes a resolution to pay a dividend. The ex-dividend date is set two business days before the date of record; if the stock was purchased before the ex-dividend date, then the holder of the stock is entitled to a dividend. The date of record is the day on which the holders of record are supposed to receive the dividend. The corporation will draw up a list of all the individuals believed to be stockholders in order to determine who is to receive the dividend. Finally, the date of payment is the day when dividends are mailed to the stockholders.

STOCK SPLIT, STOCK DIVIDEND, AND EFFECTS ON BALANCE SHEET

Sometimes dividends on common stock will not be paid out in cash. When a stock split is made, for instance, the firm has increased the number of shares it has outstanding, so every shareholder now owns more individual shares. A stock dividend, on the other hand, is a payment made by the firm in the form of additional stock. There is no value gained by a shareholder through a stock split or stock dividend, since the price of the stock will decline by the same percentage as the stock split or dividend. Stock dividends, then, do not alter the stockholder's total equity. Stock splits reduce the par value of the stock but do not affect the common equity part of the balance sheet. There is no overall change in equity after a stock split.

PREFERRED STOCK

Preferred stock typically pays a fixed dividend that is not guaranteed. This dividend is expressed as a percentage to par or dollar amount. Dividends are paid from earnings and are given priority over common stock dividends. In cumulative preferred stock, dividends are not paid but accumulate. In noncumulative preferred stock, dividends do not accumulate and are paid. Investors who are seeking a fixed stream of income usually purchase preferred stock. Unlike bonds, preferred stock is perpetual, and so a firm does not have to generate a certain amount of funds in order to retire it. Preferred stock is considered to be less risky than common stock; it also has a greater market fluctuation than do bonds.

WARRANTS

Warrants are equity call options issued directly by a corporation that give the purchaser the right to purchase stock at a specified price over a specified period. Unlike with ordinary call options, the exercise of a warrant increases the number of outstanding shares of stock, and this dilutes the firm's earnings. Typically, an individual warrant will give the right to buy one share of stock, though this is not always the case. The actual price paid for a warrant is usually higher than the theoretical price, as investors will often flock around warrants if they anticipate that the underlying stock price is going to rise above the exercise price. Warrants tend to have more percentage change in price relative to the underlying stock because of the leverage effect.

RIGHTS

There are a few different kinds of rights that may be purchased with respect to corporate stock. Preemptive rights are the rights held by current stockholders to maintain their proportion of ownership in the firm. If a firm decides to issue new stock, it will hold what is known as a rights offering, in which existing shareholders are allowed to buy new shares before those shares are made available to the general public. Rights, then, are simply the options held by stockholders to buy additional shares of stock at a specified price during a specified time period.

DERIVATIVES

OPTIONS

Derivatives are securities that have a value tied to the value of some underlying securities. Options are contracts that give the owner the right to trade in an asset for a predetermined price at a later date. The price paid for an option is referred to as a premium. Options may be classified as either a call or a put. A call gives the holder of the option the right to buy an asset at a predetermined price; a put gives the holder the right to sell the asset at a predetermined price. The person who sells an option contract is called an option writer: that person is obliged to buy or sell the asset at the predetermined price. The strike price of an option is the predetermined price. The expiration date is the date at which the option can no longer be exercised.

An option with value is said to be in-the-money; an option with negligible value is said to be out-of-the-money; and an option with minimal value is said to be at-the-money. All listed stock options expire on the Saturday after the third Friday of the expiration month. American stock options may be exercised at any point, though European options can only be exercised at the date of expiration. The intrinsic value of an option is defined as the minimum price for which it can be bought. The intrinsic value of a call option is calculated as stock price less strike price; the intrinsic value of put options is calculated as strike price less stock price. The time value of an option is the premium less the intrinsic value.

FUTURES

Futures contracts are formal agreements between a buyer, a seller, and a commodity exchange. When purchasing a futures contract, the buyer agrees to accept a specific commodity at a predetermined date. When a futures contract is sold, the seller agrees to deliver a specified commodity at a specified date. The buying position, also known as the long position, will increase in value if the underlying commodity increases in value. Future price is the price in the contract for the future delivery of a commodity; spot price is the current price of the commodity. The daily limit is the maximum daily change allowed in a commodity future's price. In order to purchase a futures account, one must have a margin account with an initial deposit and a minimum balance.

EXCHANGE TRADED FUNDS AND INDEX SECURITIES

With exchange traded funds (ETFs), investors can invest in a bundle of stocks that all closely reflect an underlying benchmark index. These stocks trade daily on stock exchanges and are continuously being priced. ETFs can be bought and sold on margin and charge lower annual expenses than index mutual funds, though investors must pay a commission to buy or sell these shares. ETFs offer flexibility, low cost, and are not subject to taxation other than changes to capital gains. Index securities, on the other hand, are a portfolio of underlying equities or bonds that attempt to reflect the performance of a particular index. Index securities offer low costs, lower taxes, and manage to keep pace with the index, but they cannot hold cash, so there is no ability to mitigate losses in a down market, and owners may be forced to sell shares when investors become nervous.

INVESTMENT COMPANIES

Investment companies come in a variety of forms. Unit investment trusts are sold in $1,000 packages and contain a fixed portfolio of assets. The assets of such an investment trust are frozen, and so no new securities can be purchased. Unit investment trusts are self-liquidating; after a while, such a trust is sold and funds are distributed to stockholders. These funds are set up to perform particular functions, like earning interest. Open-end mutual funds do not trade on the secondary markets; these shares are purchased straight from the fund at net asset value plus any applicable sales charge. Closed-end investment companies, on the other hand, issue a specified number of shares of stock or a combination of stock and debt. Shares issued by a closed-end investment company cannot be redeemed, and new shares will not be offered after the initial offering.

REAL ESTATE INVESTMENT TRUST

A real estate investment trust (REIT) is a closed-end investment company that is publicly traded. These trusts invest in managed, diversified portfolios of real estate or real estate mortgages and construction loans. REITs can be sold for premiums or discounts to the net asset value. They are traded on exchanges. There are three basic types of REITs: equity REITs, which acquire ownership interests in commercial, industrial, and residential properties; mortgage REITs, which lend the funds for construction and mortgages; and hybrid REITs, which are a combination of the other two types. REITs offer limited liability, no corporate-level tax, the ability to leverage, and liquidity, but they also give investors little control, lower potential returns, and no flow-through of tax benefits.

REAL ESTATE (INVESTOR-MANAGED)

Real estate properties may be either income properties (residential or commercial) or speculative properties (raw land and investment). To determine value in a real estate investment analysis, a financial planner must consider the objectives of the investor, the features of the property (including geographic area, time horizon, and property rights), the determinants of value (supply and demand, the local property transfer process), and the local valuation of property. The cost approach to estimating market value works best for evaluating newer properties; it evaluates the value of property by considering the cost of rebuilding it. The comparative sales approach evaluates a piece of property by comparing it to similar and nearby properties that have recently sold. The income approach evaluates a property at the present value of all future cash flows.

PRIVATE PLACEMENT

Private placements operate by selling securities directly to high-level investors. They may only operate for a predetermined length of time, in which case they do not require a SEC license. Rule 505 of Section D exempts the issuance of securities of up to $1 million in a year to an unlimited number and type of investors; Rule 505 of Regulation D exempts issuance of up to $5 million in a year; Rule 506 of Regulation D exempts the issuance of an unlimited amount of securities in a private placement. Investors who are not accredited and seek to make purchases through a private placement must be sophisticated, meaning that they have special knowledge and experience in financial matters.

LIMITED PARTNERSHIPS AND ASSET-BACKED SECURITIES

A limited partnership is a business owned by both limited and general partners. In such an arrangement, the general partners manage the business and can be held accountable and liable for the actions of the business. Limited partners are considered to be investors and are only liable for the amount of their investment. Limited partners may lose their liability protection if they take an active management role. Asset-backed securities stand for pools of asset-linked debts. In these arrangements, investors receive payments on a monthly basis that consist of a scheduled principal and interest; they may also receive any prepayments. Prepayments for asset-backed securities are mainly unaffected by changes in the market interest rates, which result in predictable cash flows.

MORTGAGE PASS-THROUGH SECURITIES

Mortgage pass-through securities represent a self-amortizing pool of mortgages. The payments for these are made on a monthly basis and are composed of a scheduled principal and interest. If no prepayments are made, then monthly cash flows will be consistent. There are several benefits of mortgage pass-through securities, especially for fixed-income investors: they may have yields up to 200 basis points higher than comparable government and corporate fixed-income debt; they are considered to have a higher quality of credit than AAA corporate bonds because they are issued by federal agencies; they tend to be very liquid in the marketplace; and they are a good source for investors interested in receiving a monthly income. There is a bit of reinvestment rate and interest rate risk associated with these policies.

COLLATERALIZED MORTGAGE OBLIGATIONS AND NATURAL RESOURCES

Collateralized mortgage obligations (CMOs) are derivatives of pass-through securities that are held by a trust and in which prepayment and reinvestment risk are reduced. CMOs are divided into different classes (called tranches) that receive different cash flow payments. Principal repayments are directed to the first tranche until it is retired and then paid into the next tranche. Investors in the longer tranches accept a higher rate of interest when they accept a later repayment of capital. Another investment vehicle is natural resources; individuals may invest in resources like timber and oil. Natural resources have an elastic demand and are therefore price sensitive to demand. Increases in demand will cause the value to rise, and decreases in demand will cause their value to drop.

TANGIBLE ASSETS AND AMERICAN DEPOSITARY RECEIPTS

Tangible assets are things, like collectibles, that have a strong secondary marketplace with little or no government regulation. The risk of liquidity and fraud can be very high in the tangible assets marketplace. American depositary receipts (ADRs) are a means for foreign firms to get their shares traded on American exchanges. There are two ways to do this: firms can make their shares directly available for trading by listing them on the exchanges, or firms may issue American depositary receipts. ADRs stand for indirect ownership in the shares of a foreign company. US banks have possession of the physical shares, which are held on deposit in foreign banks. The US bank will then issue receipts for these shares to investors. ADRs provide a means of investing in foreign countries without having to worry about currency problems.

INFLATION RISK AND INTEREST RATE RISK

Inflation risk, also known as purchasing power risk, occurs when the cash flows from a security vary because of inflation. Another kind of risk associated with investment is interest rate risk. When market interest rates go up, the prices of stocks and bonds tend to go down, and vice versa. This inverse relation between market yields and bond prices also applies to the bond's coupon. If the market yields should fall beneath the value of the bond's coupon, the price of the bond will always exceed par value. At this point, the bond is said to trade at a premium. When the market yield is above the coupon, the price of the bond will always be less than par value. In this scenario, the bond is said to be trading at a discount.

When investors believe that interest rates are going to rise, they are also anticipating that bond prices will fall. If they predict that interest rates are going to fall, they also predict that bond prices will rise. The maturity and coupon of a bond will affect the magnitude of change in the price of a bond; those bonds that have long maturities and low coupons are subject to more price volatility than others. As the yield for a bond increases, the price curve will become flatter, and so changes in the yields will have a smaller effect on the bond's price when the yields increase. If the yields should drop, the price curve will get steeper and any changes in yields will have a smaller effect on the price of the bond. In other words, yields are proportional to the volatility of price.

SYSTEMATIC RISK, BUSINESS RISK, AND LIQUIDITY RISK

Systematic risks affect the entire market and therefore cannot be avoided through diversification. Systematic risk can be determined by beta when calculating risk for a diversified portfolio. Unsystematic risks, then, are those that only affect a particular business or industry, and therefore can be avoided through diversification. It has been demonstrated that unsystematic risk can be avoided by having a portfolio with as few as 10 or 15 stocks. Marketability risk is the relative ease with which a security may be bought or sold. Liquidity risk, on the other hand, refers to the relative ease with which a security can be sold at a fair price without the risk of loss. The best measure for liquidity is the size of the spread between bid and ask. A larger spread is indicative of an illiquid market.

REINVESTMENT RISK, POLITICAL RISK, AND EXCHANGE RISK

Reinvestment risk results when amortizing securities repay their principal, exposing investors to the hazards of investing these funds at a lower interest rate. Political risk, which is also known as regulatory or country risk, is the chance that changes in government, restrictions imposed on foreign exchange flows, and/or environmental and other regulations may expose a firm to unforeseen costs. Exchange (currency) risks occur when the interest and dividend payments of a particular security are set up in a foreign currency and the value of that currency changes in relation to the home currency. If the value of the foreign currency increases in relation to the home currency, then each unit will be worth more, and if the value of the foreign currency decreases in relation to the home currency, each unit will be worth less.

COEFFICIENT OF DETERMINATION, COVARIANCE, AND THE CORRELATION COEFFICIENT

The coefficient of determination, often referred to as R-squared, is often used in investing. Typically, R-squared is systematic risk, and one minus R-squared is unsystematic risk. The volatility of a given return relative to the market is given by the beta coefficient, and the strength of this relationship is given by R-squared. Covariance, meanwhile, is the degree to which any two variables move together over time. If the two variables move together, they have a positive covariance; if they move apart, they have a negative covariance. Large numbers indicate a strong relationship, and small numbers a weak relationship. The correlation coefficient measures the relationship of returns between two stocks. A correlation coefficient of +1 indicates that returns move in the same direction and are perfectly positively correlated; a correlation coefficient of -1 means the returns move oppositely, and are perfectly negatively correlated; a correlation coefficient of zero indicates two uncorrelated returns.

VARIANCE, SEMIVARIANCE, AND STANDARD DEVIATION

The standard measure of total risk is variance; this is the measure of the dispersion of returns around the expected return. Semivariance, on the other hand, is a measure of downside risk, the dispersion of returns that occur below a certain target return like zero or the T-bill rate. Standard deviation is the measure of the variability of returns of an asset compared with the mean or expected value of that asset. It is a measure of total risk: the larger the dispersion around some mean value, the greater the risk and the larger the standard deviation. There is usually a bell-shaped curve for standard deviation, meaning that readings will tend to cluster around the expected mean.

CALCULATION OF HISTORICAL STANDARD DEVIATION

In order to calculate the historical standard deviation for a given security, take the difference between the individual observation and the average return, square the difference, and then sum the squared differences. For a sample with a certain number of observations, then, divide the sum by one less than the total number of observations and then take the square root. It should be noted that the average of the standard deviations for the individual stocks in a portfolio is not the same as the standard deviation of the portfolio. In fact, the standard deviation of a portfolio is usually less than the average standard deviation of the stocks that make up the portfolio.

COEFFICIENT OF VARIATION AND BETA

The coefficient of variation is a measure of relative dispersions (unlike standard deviation, which is the measure of absolute dispersions). The coefficient of variation can be calculated by dividing the standard deviation by the mean. A larger value for the coefficient of variation will indicate a greater dispersion relative to the arithmetic mean of the return. The beta coefficient is the most common measure of systematic risk. It is generally used for analyzing a diversified portfolio. A well-diversified portfolio will only contain systematic risk, and so the beta coefficient can be described as the measure of volatility for a diversified portfolio. A beta of 1.0 indicates that the stock is moving exactly with the market; anything higher indicates that the stick is more risky than the market, and anything less indicates that the stock is less risky than the market. The beta coefficient for individual securities may be risky over time, but it will be fairly stable for a portfolio.

ANNUALIZED RETURN, REAL (INFLATION-ADJUSTED) RETURN, AND RISK-ADJUSTED RETURN

One common method of comparing companies is to use the annual rate of return, or annual percentage rate (APR). APR is calculated by multiplying a given rate by the number of compounding periods needed to annualize it. Real (inflation-adjusted) return is the earnings from an investment that are above inflation. The real rate of return is calculated as

$$\frac{1 + nominal\ rate}{1 + inflation\ rate} - 1$$

An approximation of the real rate of return is to simply subtract the inflation rate from the nominal rate, but such an answer is not precisely correct. It should be noted that when evaluating the returns of a portfolio, a particular high return may not be good and a particular low return may not be bad. The major composite performance measures are the Treynor index, the Sharpe index, and the Jensen index. These indices are used to see whether a given stock actually beat the market.

REQUIRED RATE OF RETURN

The required rate of return for a risky asset can be calculated using the capital asset pricing model. This states that the return an individual receives on an investment will depend on the return the individual earns on a risk-free asset and a risk premium. Risk-adjusted return can be expressed:

$$r = r_f + \beta(r_m - r_f)$$

In which r_f is the risk-free asset and r_m is the return of the market. Risk premium, which is the additional return of the market over the risk-free rate of return (the part in parentheses), will be adjusted by the systematic risk associated with that asset (the beta coefficient).

EXPECTED RATE OF RETURN, AFTER-TAX RETURN, AND HOLDING-PERIOD RETURN

Expected rate of return is the anticipated growth from an investment. It is calculated:

$$E_r = \frac{E_D}{P} + E_g$$

68

In which E_r is the expected return expressed as a percentage, E_D is the expected dividend, P is the price of the asset, and E_g is the expected growth. After-tax return is calculated by multiplying the pretax rate by the quantity one minus the marginal tax bracket of the investor. Holding-period return is the total return and is calculated:

$$HPR = \frac{P_1 - P_0 + D}{P_0}$$

Where P_1 is the sale price, P_0 is the purchase price, and D is the dividend paid.

INTERNAL RATE OF RETURN, YIELD TO MATURITY, AND YIELD TO CALL

The internal rate of return is the discounted rate that allows the present value of the cash outflows to equal the initial cash outflows, such that the net present value equals zero. The yield to maturity is the internal rate of return of a bond if the bond is held until maturity. This measure will consider the current interest return and all price appreciation or depreciation. This is also a measure of risk and is the discount rate that equals the present value of all cash flows. The yield to call can be used to determine the internal rate of return earned by a bond until it is called or retired by the firm. Yield to call is calculated in a manner consistent with the calculation of yield to maturity, except that the expected call date is used instead of the known maturity date, and principal plus call penalty is used instead of principal only.

CURRENT YIELD AND AFTER-TAX YIELD

The measure of current yield only considers the coupon component of a bond. In other words, it does not include any reinvestment income, price appreciation, or price depreciation. The current yield is calculated as annual coupon payment divided by the price of the bond. The after-tax yield on a bond issue after paying taxes is calculated as pretax yield on an equivalent but fully taxable bond multiplied by one minus the marginal tax rate. Taxable equivalent yield is calculated to determine the yield that must be earned on a taxable bond in order to equal the same yield for a tax-exempt municipal bond. It is computed as the tax-exempt yield divided by one minus the marginal tax rate.

REALIZED COMPOUND RATE AND GEOMETRIC RETURN

The realized compound rate of an asset is its actual return based on the present value of future cash flows. The realized compound rate is commonly known as the time value of money, and it is calculated:

$$P_0(1 + r)^n = P_n$$

Where P_n is the purchase price of the security, r is the rate of return for the period, n is the number of periods, and P_n is the price at which the security is sold. Another common way to determine the rate of return over a period of years is to find the geometric average return. The equation for finding the geometric average return is:

$$G = [(1 + x_1)(1 + x_2) \dots (1 + x_n)]^{\frac{1}{n}}$$

BOND DURATION

The duration of a bond is the average amount of time that it takes to capture interest and principal repayments. Bond durations are compared between bonds with different coupons and maturities by assessing the sensitivity of these bonds to changes in the interest rate. Bonds will tend to exhibit more price volatility the longer it takes them to reach maturity. Bonds with a low coupon will tend to be more volatile than those with high coupons. When two bonds have the same maturity, it is typical for the bond with the lower coupon to have a longer duration. Bonds with a longer duration will tend to decline more in price when interest rates go up and will increase more with a decrease in interest rates. The duration of a bond is calculated as the sum of the present value of cash flows weighted by a time period in which payment is received.

BOND CONVEXITY

Bond duration and approximate change in price bear an interesting relation to one another. Actual price change will be greater than estimated price change when yields decrease, and actual price change will be less than estimated price change when yields increase. The greater the change in yields, the less exact will be the measure of duration. This is because actual price as charted on a price-yield graph is a curved line, and the closer it gets to any extreme, the more it departs from the straight line of estimated price. When financial planners are able to measure the degree of bond convexity, they can better predict the price of a bond. Typically, duration is used to calculate the first percentage change in price, and convexity is used to calculate the second, and is added to duration.

CAPITALIZED EARNINGS

Capitalization treats both earnings and dividends as perpetuities. Preferred stock is an instrument of perpetual debt, and its dividends will continue indefinitely because it has no maturity date. The value of a preferred stock is the present value of its dividends counted at the appropriate interest rate over an infinite period of time. The value of a preferred stock can be calculated:

$$V_p = \frac{D}{k}$$

The value of a bond can also be found through capitalization as the present value of future cash flows discounted at the appropriate interest rate.

DIVIDEND GROWTH MODELS

When valuing stock with no dividend growth, one can use the same equation as when valuing preferred stock. The only real difference will be the required rate of return on common stock, which will usually be riskier than that of a preferred stock. When valuing stock with a one-year holding period, one can calculate it as the present value of any dividend received during the year plus the present value of the price of the stock at the end of the year. The model used for considering stocks with a constant dividend growth suggests that dividends will increase at a fixed rate on an annual basis in the future. In order to calculate the value of a common stock with a constant rate of growth, one can use this equation:

$$V = \frac{D_0(1 + g)}{k - g}$$

Where D_0 is the current annual dividend, g is the constant growth rate, and k is the required rate of return.

PRICE/EARNINGS RATIO

The price/earnings (P/E) ratio is used to determine the value of stock. The dividend of the firm is compared to the earnings and to the proportion distributed. Unlike the dividend discount model, the P/E ratio can be applied to stocks that are not paying cash dividends. On the other hand, the P/E ratio cannot tell an investor whether a stock is overvalued or undervalued in relation to its market price, a calculation that is relatively easy to perform with the dividend discount model. Instead, investors will have to take a look at the historical P/E ratios in order to make this determination. To determine the estimated value of a stock, take the P/E ratio and apply it to estimated earnings for the next year.

PRICE/FREE CASH FLOWS RATIO, PRICE/SALES RATIO, AND PRICE/EARNINGS/GROWTH RATIO

The price/cash flow ratio can be defined as the market value divided by the per-share cash flow. The price/free cash flow ratio is frequently used in tandem with the P/E ratio, because it places emphasis on growth in cash flow rather than earnings. The price/sales ratio is the firm's stock price divided by its per-share sales. This ratio is good for assessing distressed firms, which will have a hard time hiding poor sales figures. The price/sales ratio may distort valuation in situations where earnings drop, however. The price/earnings/growth (PEG) ratio is found by dividing the P/E ratio by the estimated earnings growth rate. When the dividends are significant, the dividend yield should be added to the growth rate when calculating PEG ratio. This ratio indicates the price that the market placed on earning expectations.

INTRINSIC VALUE AND BOOK VALUE

The intrinsic value of a stock is the underlying value that a careful evaluation would produce. Efficient markets tend to value stocks at their intrinsic value. According to the dividend discount model, the intrinsic value of a stock is the present value of the stock's expected future dividends discounted at the stock's required rate of return. When a stock trades above its intrinsic value, it should be sold. Book value is the equity of a stockholder divided by his or her outstanding shares. Value investors try to select stocks that are trading below book value. The price/book value is the firm's stock price divided by its per-share book value. A low ratio indicates that a stock is undervalued, though what is considered high or low is basically left up to the discretion of the analyst.

PORTFOLIO THEORY

Portfolio theory strives to understand the relationship between portfolio risk and correlation. Markowitz portfolio theory assumes that a portfolio is efficient if no other portfolio offers a higher expected return with the same or lower risk. The standard deviation of a portfolio will be less than the weighted average standard deviation of the individual stocks in the portfolio. In order to determine the standard deviation of a portfolio, we must find the covariance of returns among stocks. Correlation only affects the risk of a portfolio. Modern portfolio theory has taught us that the correlation coefficient drives the theory of portfolio diversification. The lower the correlation coefficient, the greater will be the diversification. Markowitz' efficient frontier is the set of portfolios that will give the investor the highest return at each level of risk.

CAPITAL MARKET THEORY

Capital market theory builds on the work done by Markowitz portfolio theory. This theory assumes that investors are efficient and have the same expectations and freedom in the market. In graphical form, the combination of a risk-free asset and a risky asset will produce a linear risk/return line. A linear efficient frontier line is called the capital market line. Any two assets that fall on this line will be perfectly correlated with one another. In capital market theory, there is a set of all stocks, bonds, and risky assets in existence that is known as the market portfolio. Any securities that are below the capital market line are considered inefficient and will not be bought. The proper relationship between risk and return is systematic risk and return; beta is the measure of systematic risk.

PERFORMANCE MEASURES
SHARPE RATIO AND TREYNOR RATIO

The Sharpe ratio is the measure of the risk-adjusted performance of a portfolio based on total risk. The measure for total risk is the standard deviation. This measure implies that a portfolio is not widely diversified. It is calculated as:

$$S_i = \frac{r_p - r_f}{\sigma}$$

Where r_p is the portfolio rate of return, r_f is the risk-free rate of return, and σ is the standard deviation of the portfolio. The Treynor ratio, meanwhile, is the relative measure of the risk-adjusted performance of a portfolio based on market risk, and is more appropriate for using on diversified portfolios. It is calculated as:

$$T_i = \frac{r_p - r_f}{\beta}$$

Where beta is the risk of the portfolio.

JENSEN RATIO AND INVESTMENT POLICY STATEMENT

In the Jensen ratio, alpha (α) is used as an absolute measure of performance; specifically, it compares the performance of a managed portfolio with that of an unmanaged portfolio of equal risk. The Jensen ratio measures how much the realized return differs from the required return, and more generally it measures the performance of portfolio managers. An investment policy statement does four things in order to create a structure for making sound investment decisions: it establishes risk and return objectives; it determines constraints; it establishes a set of agreed-upon goals and other criteria for measuring performance; and it reduces professional liability by illustrating how appropriate steps were taken at all points of the portfolio management.

PORTFOLIO MANAGEMENT
APPROPRIATE BENCHMARKS AND DOLLAR-WEIGHTED VS. TIME-WEIGHTED RATE OF RETURN

The evaluation of a portfolio should be done from the perspective of the entire portfolio's composition or from the perspective of certain classes of assets in the portfolio; it is not appropriate to compare unlike securities. The dollar-weighted rate of return applies the concept of internal rate of return to investment portfolios, taking into account all of the cash inflows and outflows. The time-weighted rate of return, on the other hand, doesn't weigh all of the dollar flows in each time period. Instead, it computes the return for each period and averages the results; then, it averages the holding periods. When the investment is for more than one year, it takes the geometric mean of the annual returns to find the time-weighted rate of return for the measurement period. The time-weighted approach is more commonly used in the investment management profession, since it is not affected by the timing of cash flows.

PROBABILITY ANALYSIS

Portfolio managers use a number of simulations to try to predict the behavior of securities. One of the most common methods for solving differential equations is the Monte Carlo simulation, which is usually performed on a computer. If we were to assume that the value of an option depends on two underlying factors, the stock index and the exchange rate for instance, we could use a Monte Carlo simulation to price the option. The computer would create a large number of scenarios for the value, allow all of them to be affected by the two variables, and then create a probability distribution to indicate what the likely prices for the option are. The sum probability of all the probabilities in the probability distribution will have to equal one.

DOLLAR COST AVERAGING, DIVIDEND REINVESTMENT PLANS, BOND LADDERS, AND BOND BARBELLS

Dollar cost averaging is the process wherein securities are purchased over a period of time through periodic investments at a predetermined amount. This is done to reduce risks caused by changes in the market. Dividend reinvestment plans (DRIP) are those in which, for little or no cost, dividends are used to purchase more shares of a firm's common stock. For tax purposes, these reinvested dividends are treated the same as cash. A bond ladder is a series of bonds that have their maturity dates spread out over a period of time. This reduces interest rate risk and makes cash available more often. Bond barbells are portfolios consisting of some long-term bonds and some short-term bonds. If an investor can correctly predict rate change, barbells can offset fluctuating interest rates.

MARKET TIMING AND PASSIVE INVESTING

In the investment strategy known as market timing (or active investing), investors adjust their portfolios based on the changes they predict in the market. This strategy directly conflicts with the efficient market hypothesis, and so is used more often by investors who feel the market is inefficient. Passive investing, on the other hand, is when investors seek to protect their portfolios from market change. They try to stick with a good rate of return and thereby keep transaction costs down. In the strategy known as fundamental analysis, investments are based on an evaluation of the financial strength of the firm in question. Investors making use of fundamental analysis will try to pick the best firms in the most promising industries.

PORTFOLIO IMMUNIZATION AND BUY AND HOLD

In the investment strategy known as buy and hold, investors buy stocks and keep them because they believe that active management only drives up transaction costs without really contributing to a portfolio. Unlike a passive investing strategy, in which asset allocation percentages are maintained by rebalancing the portfolio, the buy and hold strategy does not include periodically rebalancing the portfolio. Another common strategy is portfolio immunization, in which an investor seeks to balance his or her portfolio so as to avoid suffering from any changes in the direction of interest rates. This can be done either by purchasing a series of zero-coupon bonds that have maturities corresponding with the planning horizon or by assembling a bond portfolio in which the duration is equal to the planning horizon.

SWAPS

A swap is an investment technique in which bonds are sold and different bonds are purchased with the proceeds. A swap is conducted for the purposes of deriving advantageous tax treatment, yields, maturity structure, or trading profits. In a substitution swap, bonds with virtually identical characteristics but different yields are swapped. When the difference in yields between the bonds is huge, it is called an intermarket spread swap. When a low-yield bond is sold and a high-yield bond is purchased (typically because it has a longer maturity), it is known as a pure-yield pickup swap. A swap that is designed to handle an expected interest rate change is called a rate anticipation swap. When an investor seeks to lock into a loss, he or she may execute a tax swap, selling a bond only to then buy a similar bond.

TECHNICAL ANALYSIS

When investors perform a technical analysis, they are assuming that prices are determined by supply and demand, which are driven by rational and irrational behavior. They believe that shifts in supply and demand can be observed in the behavior of market price. The major challenge to this belief is the efficient frontier hypothesis, which states that new information in the market will cause instantaneous adjustments in price that cannot be predicted. Whereas technicians believe that new information affects price slowly, fundamentalists assert that it does so quickly, and efficient market theorists assert that it does so almost instantly. Efficient market theorists believe that technical analysis takes too much time for it to be effective.

There are a couple of different views that bear on the technical analysis of investment. Contrarians are those that assert that investors should do the opposite of the general investor, as the general investor is wrong most of the time. Smart money traders are those who simply follow the money movement of individuals who they consider to be sophisticated investors. Contrarians will make use of mutual fund cash positions, the investor credit balances in brokerage accounts, investment advisory opinion, and OTC vs. NYSE volume, whereas smart money traders will make use of the Confidence Index, T-bill yields, Eurodollar rates, short sales by specialists, and the margin debit balances in brokerage accounts.

The Confidence Index, which is used by smart money traders, is the ratio of Barron's average yield on 10 top-grade corporate bonds to the yield on a Dow-Jones average of 40 bonds. Basically, the Confidence Index measures the difference between high-quality bonds and a large cross-section of bonds. Another market indicator used in technical analysis is the Dow Theory, which tries to identify trends in the security markets. Analysts will also consider volume, as a price change on high volume is much more telling than a price change on low volume. They may also examine the breadth of the market, which is the ratio of advancing stocks to decreasing stocks. Other indicators include the short interest ratio (the cumulative number of shares sold short divided by the daily volume of trading), support and resistance levels, relative strength ratio, and moving average lines.

STRATEGIC ASSET ALLOCATION

Strategic asset allocation is when an investor selects a suitable mix of assets based on his or her own portfolio. A client's risk tolerance, for instance, can be deduced from his or her age, and an investment portfolio should match the client's risk tolerance while meeting his or her return objectives. Asset allocation programs are usually marketed in one of five ways: aggressive growth, growth, growth and income, balanced, and fixed income; these are listed above in descending order of return and risk level. Investments will be divided up among stocks, bonds, and cash and money market instruments. Typically, the driving force of strategic asset allocation is the correlation coefficient.

TACTICAL ASSET ALLOCATION, PASSIVE AND ACTIVE PORTFOLIO MANAGEMENT, AND DEALING WITH CONCENTRATED POSITIONS

When an investor engages in tactical asset allocation, he or she is using security selection as the main determinant in developing a portfolio. Regular asset allocation tends to use an investment policy. A passive portfolio management strategy begins by establishing specific percentages for each asset class and then rebalancing occasionally to maintain these percentages. In an active strategy, on the other hand, the most important factor is market timing. When dealing with a tax-deferred retirement account, it is most appropriate to rebalance a portfolio to maintain asset allocation percentages, since the gains on these securities will not be taxed. This is also appropriate for regular accounts, although constant rebalancing can make tax reporting overly complicated.

EFFICIENT MARKET HYPOTHESIS
STRONG FORM AND SEMI-STRONG FORM

The efficient market hypothesis (EMH) asserts that individuals cannot outperform the market on a risk-adjusted basis over an extended period of time because security prices will be very consistent

74

with the amount of risk involved with a certain security. A strong form of the EMH asserts that security process will fully reflect all information. This includes public, private, and nonmarket public information. This form of the theory indicates that an investor should not expect success. The semi-strong form of EMH states that stock prices fully reflect all of the information, and so an investor should not expect to achieve success using a fundamental analysis. In this form of the theory, security prices only include market and nonmarket public information, so insider trading is possible.

WEAK FORM EMH AND TESTS

The weak form of the efficient market hypothesis asserts that stock prices fully reflect all of the available information. The weak form also states that security prices are not correlated to another and that returns are likewise independent. The random walk theory is often used to explain the weak form of the EMH: historical indicators, price behavior, and any other indicators are incapable of providing useful information for investment. There are a few different tests of the EMH. To test the weak form, analysts will frequently conduct statistical tests of the independence of security returns. To test the semi-strong form, they will try to predict future rates of return based on public information. In order to test the strong form, they will use academic tests to isolate the legal use of public information and its effects.

ANOMALIES FROM CROSS-SECTIONAL TESTS

Many studies have shown that the dividend yield, default spread, and term structure spread can all be used to determine the rate of return on stocks and bonds. Moreover, quarterly earnings reports show that the market may not have adjusted stock prices as quickly as expected in order to reflect earning surprises. One should also keep in mind the January effect, which shows that stocks tend to perform well in January. There also is a similar day of the week effect: the days of the weekend tend to generate a lower rate of return. This suggests that investors should try to buy a stock on Monday rather than Friday, as the stock will be more likely to generate returns during the week.

CONCLUSIONS AND ANOMALIES FROM STRONG-FORM ACADEMIC TESTS

Strong-form academic tests indicate that stock exchange analysts have access to information that is essentially monopolistic; for this reason, they derive better-than-average returns. Also, corporate insiders have exclusive information, and they therefore tend to have greater returns than others. In conclusion, market results seem to support the weak-form efficient market hypothesis, while results are spottier for the semi-strong form EMH. Specifically, time-series and cross-sectional tests indicate that markets are not always semi-strong form efficient. For the most part, results support the strong form EMH; the exceptions to this are corporate insiders and specialists.

CAPITAL ASSET PRICING MODEL (CAPM)

The capital asset pricing model (CAPM) calculates the required rate of return for risky investments. This figure is derived from the risk-free rate an investor can earn by investing in risk-free security (like a Treasury bill) and the risk premium. The risk premium is both the additional return an investor will earn and the volatility of the security to the market. If the difference between the market rate and the risk-free rate grows, so does the risk premium. The CAPM is often used to identify overvalued and undervalued assets: if the expected return is greater than the required return, the asset is undervalued; if the expected return is lower than the required return, the asset is overvalued. Similarly, if a stock's expected return falls below the security market line, the stock is overpriced (i.e., the expected return is too low).

MOMETRIX

MULTIFACTOR ASSET PRICING MODEL

The multifactor asset pricing model (also known as the arbitrage pricing theory) was developed because of the variety of factors that influence stock performance. This model assumes that capital markets are competitive, investors will prefer more wealth to less, and that the K-factor model represents the process that generates asset returns. This model, unlike CAPM, does not assume that security returns are normally distributed, that investors have quadratic utility functions, or that the market portfolio contains all securities and is mean variance efficient. This model assumes an unspecified number of risk factors and represents an attempt to calculate the rate of return by evaluating the responsiveness of the stock to all of these risk factors.

DESCRIBE THE OPTION PRICING MODEL

The goal of the asset pricing model known as the option pricing model is to determine the value of a call option. This model assumes that the call option is in the European rather than the American style, meaning it can be exercised only on its expiration date. In the option pricing model, there are four variables: time to maturity, interest rates, the price of the underlying stock, and volatility. The value of a call will typically decrease with an increase in strike price. Put-call parity determines the value of a put option. This indicates that there is a close relation between the prices of puts and calls and the value of stock. Put-call parity ensures that the prices of a call and a put will change with one another and the underlying stock.

MARGINS

If an investor purchases a stock on the margin, then he or she must make an initial payment (much like the down payment on a house) and pay for the rest with borrowed money. The Federal Reserve has at present set the initial margin requirement at 50%. Stock exchanges and brokerage houses will set a maintenance margin requirement, with maintenance margin being the minimum equity an investor must have for a margin position. A maintenance margin protects the brokerage house from having to shoulder too much risk. Margins provide a great deal of leverage to an investor: when the price of stock rises, for instance, the customer's profits will rise much faster. Of course, losses can be much greater as well.

MARGIN CALLS

When a stock or portfolio declines a great deal in price, the result will be a margin call. Margin calls indicate that the equity in the account has dropped beneath the margin requirement. Investors will have to increase their equity by either selling assets or depositing cash or securities. In order to find the price that will trigger a margin call for a certain stock, analysts use the following formula:

$$P_{MC} = P_O \frac{1 - M_I}{1 - M_M}$$

Where P_O is the original price of the stock, M_I is the initial margin required, and M_M is the maintenance margin required.

The rate of return on a margin transaction can be figured by finding the net profit and total investment in the transaction, and then dividing net profit by investment to find the percentage gained or lost.

STRATEGY OF BUYING CALLS AND PUTS

Investors will seek to buy calls when they anticipate that the underlying stock or index is going to rise. Long call positions may be used either speculatively through the use of leverage or conservatively as insurance policies. The absolute gain or loss on a transaction will tend to be

76

smaller than it would be if the stock were owned, since options are less expensive. An investor may seek to buy puts in a situation where he or she anticipates a decline in price in the underlying stock. The maximum gain will increase as stock price decreases, with the maximum loss being the premium paid for the options. Time decay will accelerate as options approach expiration. Often, puts are used as an alternative to selling short.

STRATEGY OF SELLING NAKED CALLS AND NAKED PUTS

The strategy of selling options is frequently referred to as naked call writing. Typically, naked call writing will expose an investor to a substantial amount of risk, because if the call is exercised after a rise in the price of stick, the option writer will be forced to buy the stock back and then sell it to the buyer. The maximum gain in this strategy is the price of the premium, while the maximum loss is unlimited. This strategy is usually used to take advantage of volatility and time decay. Investors may also write naked puts. In this scenario, the option trader assumes the risk of the underlying security in exchange for the premium. Maximum gain is the premium that is received, and maximum loss is the cost of buying the stock at the strike price.

STRATEGY OF COVERED CALL WRITING AND COVERED PUT WRITING

When investors write a covered call (also called covered call writing), they are taking short calls with a long stock position in the underlying stock. When the option is exercised, the seller will supply the stock at the strike price. The call seller will limit the gain on the stock by the premium received plus the strike price, less the price paid for the underlying stock. Maximum gain is made when the stock trades above the strike price at expiration. In the strategy of covered put writing, the investor sells the stock short and sells the put in order to create the covered put. When the put is exercised, the investor buys the shares and uses them to cover the short position. This strategy is only effective when the investor expects a stable stock price.

SHORT SALES

A short sell is when an investor sells borrowed securities because he or she anticipates a drop in price. The investor will profit by selling the securities and then buying them back at the reduced price. The maximum loss of a poor short sell can be unlimited if the value of the stock continues to rise. Typically, the investor does not own the securities that are being sold short; they are sold with a promise of future delivery. There are two technical points that bear on short selling: short sellers have to pay all dividends owed to the lender of the security; and short sellers must deposit margin money to cover the repurchase of the security.

TAX-EFFICIENT INVESTING

MUTUAL FUNDS

In mutual funds, those with a greater portfolio turnover ratio will create more tax consequences for investors. A mutual fund turnover ratio assesses the amount of buying and selling in a certain mutual fund. Even though the returns of a mutual fund are stated before tax, the investor only gets to keep the after-tax returns. A mutual fund is said to be tax-efficient when it can generate returns without creating large amounts of tax obligations. There will be no tax obligations if the fund doesn't generate income or realize any capital gains. Investors should always be aware of the date on which capital gains and income are distributed (either mid-year or year-end). Hidden capital gains can result in unexpected taxes, while hidden capital losses can indicate tax-free gains.

STOCKS, BONDS

With stocks, the returns of a portfolio will be measured by after-tax returns. According to the wash-sale rule, the practice of selling shares at a loss and then buying them back within 30 days makes it impossible to deduct such losses on one's tax return. The disallowed loss amount can then be added to the cost basis of any additional shares purchased, and any taxable gain or loss on the sale of these shares will include the loss incurred on the original shares. This rule also applies to mutual funds and bonds. For bonds, the taxable equivalent yield is calculated as the tax-exempt municipal yield divided by one minus the marginal tax rate. If bonds were purchased at a premium, the investor may want to amortize a part of the premium and reduce the basis by the amount deductible. The SEC yield is a good measure of performance for various bond funds.

INVESTMENT STRATEGIES IN TAX-ADVANTAGED ACCOUNTS

For investors, every gain or loss can be classified as either ordinary or capital. A capital gain or loss will be the result of the sale of a stock or bond; every other gain or loss (for example dividends) will be classified as ordinary. Individuals do not have to pay interest on capital gains and income on tax-deferred accounts as long as the proceeds and payments are left in the account. The net unrealized appreciation is also nontaxable. It is a good idea to fill tax-advantaged accounts with high-income-producing assets, zero coupon bonds, stocks that are held for short-term appreciation, and TIPS. It is a good idea to fill taxable accounts with municipal bonds, treasury bills, notes, bonds, and growth stocks with a long term of appreciation.

TAXATION
MUTUAL FUNDS

In order to determine the basis of a mutual fund, add the cash investments, reinvested dividends, and capital gains, and then subtract returns of capital received. Front-end and other sales charges will adjust the share purchase price and increase the basis, while back-end loads and redemption charges will reduce the proceeds acquired through the sale of securities. When the cost basis of a mutual fund is assessed, an investor must identify the specific shares that have been sold, receive written confirmation from the broker, and then calculate the shares on a first-in, first-out arrangement. In order to figure the average basis, investors calculate the total cost of the shares owned divided by the total number of shares owned.

STOCKS

Stock dividends are reported on Form 1099-DIV, while interest is reported on Form 1099-INT. Any dividend reinvestments are considered constructive receipt and are taxed as ordinary income. In order to calculate the basis, capital gains are recognized not on the settlement date, but on the trade date. Those securities that are purchased have a basis that is calculated by adding the price and any commission charges. Selling expenses are figured against the gross sales price in the calculation of the amount realized on sale. The realized capital gain from the sale of a security is the amount that is realized over the cost basis in the security; realized capital loss is the excess of the basis over the amount realized. When investors choose to have their dividends reinvested, these become the cost basis of new shares.

Capital gains on stocks are reported on Form 1099-B. Taxes will be due the year that a sale occurred in a taxable account. Taxes on tax-deferred accounts will not occur until the liquidation of the account, and they will be subject to ordinary income only. The receipts for stock splits, stock dividends, and rights are considered nontaxable events, since these are just rearrangements of already-owned stocks. Taxable distributions are reported as income, with the taxable dividend being equal to the fair market value of the stock on the date of distribution. Nontaxable distributions will affect the basis of the old shares: the cost basis of old stock is divided by the total number of shares held after distribution. The exercise of a warrant is not a taxable event.

FEDERAL GOVERNMENT BONDS, AGENCY BONDS, AND MUNICIPAL BONDS

The interest on instruments of federal debt is subject to federal income tax but is exempt from state and local taxes. For treasury bills, interest earned is equal to purchase price less the amount paid at maturity. For Treasury notes and bonds, interest is to be paid semiannually and is reported in the year that it is earned. Agency bonds can be taxed at both the federal and the state/local level; interest will be taxed as ordinary income, while treatment of capital gains and losses will be applicable only if the bonds have appreciated or depreciated in value. As for municipal bonds, the interest income they create is excluded from federal taxes. Any state and local bond interest may be taxed by the state or locality in which the investor lives. The treatment of capital gains or losses will apply when the bonds are sold.

ZERO COUPON BONDS AND TIPS

Interest on zero coupon bonds is taxed as if it were received. Original issue discount occurs when a long-term debt instrument is issued at a price lower than par value. Investors are not allowed to defer recognition of the interest income created by original issue discount. In the case of Treasury inflation protected securities (TIPS), the principal will have to be adjusted up or down for inflation or deflation, and the fixed interest rate must also be considered. Interest on TIPS is paid semi-annually, though inflation-adjusted principal is not paid until the bond matures. Investors will have to pay federal income tax on the increasing principal amount as well as on any coupon interest.

CONVERTIBLE BONDS, ACCRUED INTEREST, AND US SAVINGS BONDS

Changing convertible bonds into common stock is not a taxable event. The cost basis for the new common stock is the same as the original cost of the convertible bond. The holding period for shares will begin at the time the convertible was originally purchased. As for accrued interest on investments, the seller is required to report accrued interest in his or her gross income. The purchaser, on the other hand, will deduct the accrued interest from the next interest payment as if it were a return of capital. The interest on US savings bonds is only subject to federal taxation; it is exempt from state and local taxes. The taxpayer has the option of either reporting interest annually or upon redemption of the bond.

ANNUITIES

Although investors are not taxed on the annual buildup in the value of an investment, they are taxed on the gain in an annuity when it is distributed. This gain is treated as ordinary income. Any interest earning will be assumed to be withdrawn first, and then principal; only a portion of the annuity payable will be taxable as ordinary income. Annuities may be subject to full taxation if the taxpayer has not contributed to the cost, or if the taxpayer's entire cost has been recovered. For partially taxable distributions, the percentage of each annuity payment excluded from gross income is the total after-tax contribution of the employee divided by the annual payment multiplied by life expectancy.

GOALS OF FUNDAMENTAL INVESTMENT ANALYSIS

The term fundamental analysis describes the process of analyzing data and applying the data to ratios to determine the relative financial health of what is being analyzed. The three areas of fundamental investment analysis occur at the economic, industry, and individual company levels. Empirical data for each level is analyzed to determine whether the time for investment may be right. If a fundamental investor determines that an entire country at the economic level may not be suitable for investment, he may eschew drilling down further and avoid all investment in the country. Fundamental analysts use ratios to determine the soundness of investing in economies and industries, and if they determine that the time is right for both, they'll move to individual

79

companies where they'll use fundamental analysis to estimate a reasonable fair market value for the stock of the company to determine if there is an opportunity for investment.

TOP-DOWN AND BOTTOM-UP FUNDAMENTAL INVESTMENT ANALYSIS

There are two basic types of fundamental analysis: top down and bottom up. Top-down fundamental analysis describes the analysts beginning with the overall economy of the country in which they choose to invest. After they determine the health of the economy, they'll determine the fundamental financial health of individual industries, and once they've selected an industry, they'll begin evaluating individual companies. Bottom-up analysts, colloquially known as stock pickers, begin at the company level, then move to the industry level, and finally to the economy level. There are proponents for both types of analysis. Top-down analysts may save themselves time and effort by eliminating economies and industries that are not suitable for investment before they drill down to the company level. Alternatively, bottom-up analysts may save themselves time and effort by choosing relatively stable economies and industries and skipping their analysis altogether.

FUNDAMENTAL EVALUATION

Fundamental investment analysis occurs at three levels: the economic level, the industry level, and the individual company level. At the economic level, analysts are studying the health of a given country's finances. Data considered at the economic level includes (but is not limited to) interest rates, fiscal and monetary policy, and legislative environments. At the industry level, the fundamental analyst is endeavoring to determine the health of individual sectors of the economy. Such things as supply, demand, and business cycles are considered at the industry level. Finally, at the individual company level, fundamental analysts are trying to determine the fair market value, or FMV, of individual companies. Ratios such as liquidity and activity ratios using raw data from the companies' financial statements are used to assist in determining their FMV.

Tax Planning

INCOME TAX LAW
STATUTORY LAW AND ADMINISTRATIVE PRONOUNCEMENTS

The Internal Revenue Code of 1986 is the main source of tax law, though the Taxpayer Relief Act of 1997 includes more than 300 modifications and over 300 new provisions. Tax legislation begins in the House Ways and Means Committee. If approved, it moves on to the House of Representatives, Senate Finance Committee, and Senate. If the legislation makes it through all of these steps, the President must approve it before it goes into effect. Treasury regulations, published by the US Treasury, are the official interpretations of statutory tax rules. Revenue rulings stand for the official position of the Internal Revenue Service but have less authority than Code and regulations. Revenue procedures are the official positions of the IRS on matters of tax tables, inflation-indexed amounts, and asset class lives. Letter rulings are more specific interpretations offered by the IRS.

JUDICIAL DECISIONS AND STEPS TO RESEARCHING A TAX QUESTION

Taxpayers who are involved in a tax-related dispute may always bring their claim to the level of the regional appeals office of the IRS. When cases are unresolved, the taxpayer may take it to one of three federal courts: in the US Tax Court, the taxpayer refuses to pay the deficiency, and will not have a jury trial; in the US District Court, the taxpayer pays the deficiency and sues for a refund, and he or she will receive a jury trial; in the US Court of Federal Claims, the taxpayer pays the deficiency, sues for a refund, and does not receive a jury trial. When cases remain unresolved, the taxpayer can appeal to the US Circuit Court of Appeals, and then may attempt to appeal to the Supreme Court. The steps to researching a tax question are gathering all the facts, diagnosing the problem, locating the authority, evaluating the authority, deriving the solution, and communicating the answer.

TAX COMPLIANCE
FILING REQUIREMENTS

Every individual US citizen and resident alien must file an income tax return so long as his or her gross income exceeds the standard deduction amount for the individual's filing status. Individuals who are claimed as a dependent do not have to file a claim unless their unearned income is more than $1000, or unless their total gross income is more than the standard deduction. Individuals will have to file a tax return even if their gross income is below the required amount if they: make more than $400 from self-employment; owe an alternative minimum tax; are nonresident aliens; are a member of certain religious organizations; must pay tax from an IRA or qualified retirement plan; have received tips from which Social Security tax was not withheld; or they have changed their country of residence or citizenship during the year.

AUTHORITY, AUDITS

The only individuals who have the authority to represent someone else before the IRS are certified public accountants, attorneys, and enrolled agents. Enrolled agents are those people who have been certified by passing a tax exam administered by the IRS. The IRS uses a few different ways to determine who will be audited. The Discriminate Functions System (DIF) screens all of the returns and assigns them a score assessing their audit-worthiness. The Taxpayer Compliance Measurement Program calculates the norms that will be used by the DIF, and so pinpoints where taxpayers are most likely to be cheating. Some audits are simply chosen at random. Most audits are conducted by telephone or mail, but some individuals will be required to go to the IRS district office or have an IRS officer visit their place of business.

PENALTIES

When taxpayers are late in filing their tax returns, they are penalized five percent of the balance of the tax due for each month that the return is late; after 5 months, the penalty increases 0.5% every additional month. Just because the government has cashed a taxpayer's check or mailed a refund does not mean that an audit is out of the question. In fact, the government has up to three years from the date on which the return was filed to examine it for mistakes. If the taxpayer has omitted an amount of gross income exceeding 25% of the gross income reported, the statute of limitations goes up to six years. For negligence, the IRS usually equals 20% of any underpayment of taxes, though the IRS has the burden of production and must assemble a preponderance of evidence to show that the taxpayer was negligent.

A taxpayer found to have committed civil fraud will be penalized 15% for every month or part of a month the return is late up to a maximum of 75%. Fraud, in this case, is any act that is designed to cheat the government. The IRS has the burden of proving that an individual has committed fraud and must provide clear and convincing evidence. In cases of criminal fraud, the IRS must prove guilt beyond a reasonable doubt. Criminal fraud is also known as tax evasion, and it is a felony punishable by fines of up to $250,000 for an individual and $500,000 for a corporation. If the preparer of an income tax return understates the amount of tax, then he or she may be hit with a $250 penalty; if the understatement is intentional, the penalty is $1,000.

SOLE PROPRIETORSHIP

The most common form of business is a sole proprietorship. Sole proprietorships are fairly easy to administrate. Unlike corporations, sole proprietorships are not legal entities separate and apart from the owner. This means that the owner's personal assets are subject to all liabilities incurred by the business. There are no special forms required to start a sole proprietorship. The owner of one will simply file a Schedule C in addition to his or her personal tax forms. Often, the owner of a sole proprietorship will minimize his or her tax burden by shifting income to other family members. Sole proprietorships have no flexible ownership, continuity of life, or capital structure because there is only one owner.

GENERAL PARTNERSHIP

A general partnership consists of multiple owners who perform the operations of the business together and split the income and profits. Often, partners will be bound together by a contract. Each partner will have fiduciary duties and the duty to act in good faith with one another. If a tort is brought against the partnership, all partners are jointly and severally liable, meaning that partners must be sued together and all partners are subject to being sued for the full amount of the claim. Partners are not entitled to any certain salary, though they are entitled to share in the profits. New partners cannot be admitted without the unanimous consent of the other partners. A partnership is dissolved automatically if a partner dies, if a partner goes bankrupt, or if the partnership is dissolved according to the termination provision in the partnership agreement.

LIMITED PARTNERSHIP AND LIMITED LIABILITY PARTNERSHIP (LLP)

A limited partnership is one in which there are one or more general partners and one or more limited partners. Limited partners cannot participate in managing the business, have no authority to bind the business, and cannot use their surname in the title of the business. A limited partner also has a limited liability. Limited partnerships can be terminated by court order, or by the withdrawal, death, insanity, or insolvency of a general partner. If any of the last four befalls a limited partner the partnership is not necessarily cancelled. A limited liability partnership (LLP) is one in which all partners have limited liability. Limited partners in an LLP may be held individually responsible for errors, omissions, and negligence. LLP partners are not usually held liable for any debts or obligations of the partnership.

LIMITED LIABILITY COMPANY (LLC)

A limited liability company (LLC) gives limited liability protection to all of its members but will still be treated as a partnership for income tax purposes. Unlike a limited liability partnership, the partners in a limited liability company are not responsible for the misdeeds of their subordinates. Also, unlike an LLP, a limited liability company does not have to reregister itself every time a partner leaves the group, so they are often less expensive to maintain. LLCs may choose to be taxed as a corporation, S corporation, sole proprietorship, or partnership. Most LLCs, however, will choose to be taxed as a partnership. LLCs have flexible ownership, capital structure, and centralized management. An LLC is a legal entity separate from its members.

S CORPORATION

Under federal income tax laws, an S corporation is treated as a pass-through entity, so shareholders may receive business profits as dividends. S corporations have limited owner liability, free transferability of ownership interests, centralized management, and continuity of life through stock ownership. There are strict eligibility requirements for S corporations: they must be domestic corporations, have no more than 100 shareholders, have no shareholders that aren't citizens, and have only one class of stock. If these requirements are not met, the business may be subject to double taxation. The disadvantages of an S corporation are limited flexibility in selecting a tax year, little ability to retain income at a lower current tax cost, and poor tax treatment of fringe benefits.

C CORPORATION

C corporations are artificial entities that are created when articles of incorporation are filed and a state issues a certificate of incorporation. There are a few different groups with roles in a C corporation. Shareholders are the actual owners of the corporation and vote on the members of the board of directors. These directors are charged with maintaining control over the basic operations of the business; they also select the officers, who oversee daily operations at a more specific level. C corporations are considered for tax purposes as a separate person, distinct from those who formed the corporation or those who own it at present. The shareholders of a corporation have limited liability and can only lose what they have put into the corporation. Typically, corporate tax rates are lower than the individual tax rates for individuals with a high level of income

C corporations are taxed separately from their owners. They give owners better tax treatment for owner fringe benefits, the ability to select a tax year, and the ability to take loans from qualified retirement plans. A C corporation may have continuous life and could theoretically continue after the deaths of all the shareholders. The income earned by a C corporation is subject to double taxation, meaning that the corporation has to pay a tax on earnings and shareholders' dividends will also be taxed. Any corporate tax advantages are also limited by the accumulated earnings tax, which strives to make sure that corporations do not hoard earnings and pretend that they are necessary to the maintenance of the business so as to avoid taxation.

PROFESSIONAL CORPORATION (PC)

Professional corporations operate much like any other commercial corporation, though their ownership is generally restricted to the members of a certain profession. A professional corporation will have continuity beyond the death of an owner; typically, that owner's share will either be transferred to another professional or bought up by the corporation itself. Running a business as a professional corporation instead of in an unincorporated form provides the advantage that all the members retain limited liability. Shareholders will remain liable for their own actions as well as for those of people directly under their supervision. Members of a professional corporation will also derive some benefit from the corporate tax structure.

ASSOCIATION AND A BUSINESS TRUST

An association is a group of people that are joined together for a particular purpose. Associations may operate under tax-exempt status under Section 501(a) if they have a written "Articles of Association" in which at least two people assert the creation of the association. In a business trust, on the other hand, a designated trustee takes legal title to a business and operates it on behalf of all other owners and beneficiaries. If a business trust is created for an entity with no economic reality, all of the tax liability will be placed on the individual who formed the trust. If the trust has only one trustee, it will probably be treated as a sole proprietorship. If there are two or more trustees, it may be treated as a partnership. Some business trusts are registered as corporations and treated as such.

TYPES OF ACQUISITION AND DISPOSITION

When a business is liquidated, all of the properties are distributed to the shareholders and the business' stock is cancelled. Many times, the tax treatment after liquidation may be disadvantageous, and so liquidation may not be the appropriate way to end a business. A corporation will have to pay a tax on capital gains when it distributes property to shareholders. In the taxable sale of a business, the sale of stock creates a taxable gain to the people selling stock, which will be equal to the difference between the selling price and their basis. This asset sale will create a taxable gain for the corporation should the selling price exceed the corporation's basis. In a tax-free disposition of a business, stock sale will qualify as long as 80% of voting power and at least 80% of the other stock in the seller are transferred to the acquiring firm in exchange for only voting stock in the buyer. In a tax-free sale, there is no tax to the seller or to the selling corporation at the date of sale.

PLANNING OF A TAXABLE SALE

When a taxable sale is set up as a payment over a series of installments, the seller's gain can be spread over the period in which these payments are made. The buyer's interest payments will be deductible when they are made and are taxable to the seller when they are received. The rules of imputed interest will apply here, meaning that the sale cannot be arranged in such a way that the tax on interest to the seller can be eliminated by understating interest at artificially low rates. In the case of a private annuity, payments will be made for the rest of the seller's life. Each annuity payment will be composed of three elements: tax-free return of basis, capital gain, and interest.

INCOME TAX FUNDAMENTALS
FILING STATUS

A taxpayer is considered single if he or she is unmarried or legally separated on December 31. Taxpayers are considered as married filing jointly if they are married and living together, married and living apart but not legally separated, or living in a common law marriage. Taxpayers are considered as married filing separately if they are married at the end of the year and elect to file separately to avoid joint liability or to pay lower total taxes. A taxpayer can file as a head of household if he was not married at the end of the year, if he paid more than half of the cost of the house, if he was a US citizen or resident for the entire year, and if the home was the main home for one or more family members. A taxpayer is a qualifying widower if his or her spouse died within the two years preceding the year for which the return is filed.

GROSS INCOME

Gross income that must be included in an income tax return includes: wages, salaries, commissions, and fees; taxable noncash fringe benefits; allocated and unreported tips; gains from real estate, securities, and other property; rents; interest from bank accounts, CDs, securities, loans, etc.; accrued interest from zero coupon bonds; dividends; royalties; alimony and separate maintenance payments; annuities, pensions, and IRA distributions; income from an estate or trust, but not from a gift or bequest; prizes and awards; all other cash and property received, so long as it is not specifically excluded by federal tax laws; and, for some taxpayers, up to 85% of Social Security benefits.

INCOME EXCLUDED FROM GROSS INCOME

The following sources of income may be excluded from gross income: gifts and inheritances; interest on certain municipal bonds and interest from mutual funds that hold such bonds; returns of capital; reimbursements for business expenses; exclusions of up to $250,000 in gain from the sale of a home ($500,000 if married filing jointly); some or all of Social Security benefits; compensation for injury and sickness, including worker's compensation and certain disability payments; employer-paid health coverage; employer-provided education assistance up to $5,250 (as of 2022); qualified foster care payments; proceeds of life insurance that are paid because of death or chronic illness; payments received under accident, health, and long-term care insurance policies; amounts contributed to a Medical Savings Account or Health Savings Account; employer-provided child or dependent care services; scholarships and fellowships; and employer-paid group life insurance up to $50,000.

ADJUSTED GROSS INCOME

Individuals are allowed to make the following deductions from their gross income to arrive at a figure for adjusted gross income: trade or business expenses; self-employed medical insurance premiums up to a limit; 50% of self-employment tax; amounts forfeited to a bank or savings institution for the premature withdrawal of funds from a deposit account; contributions to a tax-favored retirement plan for the self-employed; contributions to individual retirement accounts; deductions in connection with property held for the production of rents or royalties; deductions for interest on qualified education loans; contributions to a Health Savings Account; and losses from the sale or exchange of property.

STANDARD DEDUCTION

In 2022, the standard deduction for a taxpayer filing as married filing jointly, or as a surviving spouse, is $25,900; for one filing as married filing separately: $12,950; for single: $12,950; for head of household: $19,400. Dependents are those individuals whom another taxpayer has claimed as such. Dependents are not eligible to claim the regular standard deduction on their tax returns; they may claim the special standard deduction that is the greater of (a) $1,150 or (b) the dependent's earned income + $400—yet this deduction cannot exceed the individual standard deduction of $12,950.

ITEMIZED DEDUCTIONS

Itemized deductions are claimed on Schedule A. These are deductions from adjusted gross income in the calculation of taxable income. There are a few types of itemized deductions: medical expenses may be deducted when they are paid for the taxpayer, his or her dependents, and anyone who would have been a dependent if not for the income test. Deductions are allowed for medical expenses so long as they are for the purposes of maintaining or improving health; and unreimbursed expenses and insurance premiums paid for long-term care. Medical expenses that cannot be deducted include baby-sitting and child care, cosmetic surgery, costs covered by insurance, funeral expenses, health club dues, nonprescription drugs and medicines, nutritional supplements, and weight loss programs that have not been recommended by a doctor.

State and local taxes are deductible (capped at $10,000, $5,000 if married filing separately, according to the Tax Cuts and Jobs Act), but federal taxes are not. When a deduction is taken in the year of a payment and a refund is received later, the refund may be considered taxable income in later years. Real estate taxes will be deductible, even in cases where they are paid to a foreign country. These taxes will be deductible for all the properties owned by the taxpayer, though the mortgage deduction will be limited to two homes. If a particular property was only owned for part of the year, only that portion will be included as a deduction. Personal property taxes, too, will be deductible if they are based on the value of the property. Charitable contributions will be included when they are made to a qualified charitable organization.

Some mortgage interest on a primary (and one secondary home) may be tax-deductible. For acquisition debt, the deduction is limited to the interest on the first $750,000 of qualified debt. This was $1,000,000 prior to the Tax Cuts and Jobs Act, effective for tax year 2018. The TCJA also suspended the deduction of interest on home equity debt, unless it is taken for the purpose of buying, building, or improving a home. A deduction can also be made for casualty and theft, including any damage, destruction, or loss of property that results from a presidentially declared disaster (Prior to the TCJA, this applied to an identifiable event that is sudden, unexpected, or unusual, but the TCJA restricts casualty and loss deductions to presidentially declared disasters.) The figure for casualty loss will be whichever is less: fair market value before event minus fair market value after event or the adjusted basis. Of courses, losses will be reduced by any insurance recovery.

The deductions that can be made for investment interest costs are limited to the amount of investment income. A taxpayer may include capital gains in investment income if he or she chooses, but this means that any capital gain included in investment income will not be eligible for preferential long-term capital gain rates. Various miscellaneous deductions (e.g. unreimbursed employee expenses and tax preparation fees) used to be taken, subject to a 2% limit, but with the Tax Cuts and Jobs Act, effective in tax year 2018 these will be nondeductible. Other nondeductible expenses include: broker's commissions paid in connection with property or account; hobby losses; home repairs; lobbying expenses; capital expenses; home repairs, insurance, and rents; and capital expenses.

PERSONAL AND DEPENDENCY EXEMPTIONS

Prior to the Tax Cuts and Jobs Act, effective starting with tax year 2018, a taxpayer was allowed a personal exemption for himself, his spouse, and his dependents. In 2017 this was worth $4,050 per person, and individuals whom someone else claimed as a dependent could not also have taken the exemption for themselves. The exemption amount could be reduced, even to $0, if the taxpayer's adjusted gross income exceeded certain thresholds.

With the passing of the Tax Cuts and Jobs Act, these exemptions no longer exist. They will return in tax year 2026 according to current tax legislation.

TAXABLE INCOME TAX LIABILITY

Taxable income is simply adjusted gross income minus whichever is greater: allowable itemized deductions or the standard deduction. An individual's tax liability is determined by using the tax tables (if taxable income is under $100,000) or the tax rate schedules (if taxable income is greater than $100,000). Any tax credits, like childcare, foreign tax credits, and credit for the elderly, will be taken into consideration when determining the total tax due. The basic process of calculating tax liability is: determine total gross income; subtract deductions from gross income to find AGI; deduct either itemized deductions or standard deduction to arrive at taxable income; find tax amount from either tax tables or tax schedule; and subtract tax credits from this amount.

TAX CREDITS

Tax credits are one-for-one reductions in actual tax paid; these are in contrast to deductions, which only limit the amount of income subject to tax. Taxpayers may receive credits for each of their children; the credit amount increases per each child that can be claimed for a dependency deduction. A tax credit can also be received for child and dependent care; in order to qualify for this credit, the taxpayer must provide more than half of the cost of keeping up the home and must pay for child or dependent care so that he or she may work or look for work. Tax credits are also available for any individuals who reach the age of 65 before the end of the tax year, or who are under 65 but are retired with a permanent and total disability for which they receive income.

An earned income tax credit may be claimed if the individual has not earned a certain amount in the taxable year. The percentage of earned income that qualifies for the tax credit will change depending on the number of children the taxpayer has. An adoption credit may be claimed if the taxpayer has adopted a child that is either younger than 18 or unable to take care of him or herself. A foreign tax credit is allowed so that individuals do not have to pay both foreign and US income tax on the same income. This credit will usually be the lesser amount between the amount of foreign tax paid and the amount of US tax that would have been due on the foreign income. Taxpayers can treat the amount of foreign tax paid as either a deduction from income or as a refundable tax credit.

PAYMENT OF TAX AND ESTIMATED PAYMENT AND WITHHOLDING REQUIREMENTS

In almost all cases, individuals are required to file Form 1040 by April 15 of the following year. If individuals have adopted a fiscal year, they are required to file by the 15th day of the 4th month after the end of the taxable year. Individuals are permitted an automatic four-month extension, though the individual will have to pay interest on the delinquent payment to the IRS. Many self-employed taxpayers and taxpayers owing in previous years will make small estimated payments throughout the year. Tax law does not allow taxpayers to wait until the date for filing returns to pay all of their taxes. Employers will also be required to withhold a certain amount of money from paychecks for the purposes of paying taxes.

KIDDIE TAX

The kiddie tax is a series of tax rules aimed to keep parents from taking advantage of their children's lower tax rates. Basically, if a child has substantial investment ("unearned") income, it will be taxed at a higher rate. Prior to the Tax Cuts and Jobs Act, part of this income would be taxed at the parent's marginal rate. But with the Tax Cuts and Jobs Act (starting with tax year 2018), part of this income will be taxed at the same rates imposed on trusts and estates. This essentially boils down to three key features:

- It applies to children under the age of 19 and full-time students under the age of 24.
- It only affects unearned income, typically from investments held in the child's name. Earned income from jobs or self-employment is completely exempt from the kiddie tax.
- It only affects unearned income above an annual threshold: only unearned income above the annual threshold of $2,300 (as of 2022) is affected by the kiddie tax. All unearned "kiddie income" past this threshold is then taxed at the same rate as trusts and estates.

If your child is not subject to the kiddie tax, he or she is generally treated like any other unmarried taxpayer (assuming he or she is in fact unmarried).

IMPUTED INTEREST

The rules for imputed interest were created to keep taxpayers from transferring income from high to low tax brackets or from shifting interest income to capital gains income by raising purchase price and charging less interest. When the interest rate falls below a certain amount, the seller is required to add imputed interest. On the other hand, if the applicable federal rate should be above the rate charged at the time of the transfer, the seller can report the additional interest income and the buyer will be allowed an additional interest deduction. There are some exceptions to this rule, as when loans of up to $10,000 are made to purchase nonincome-producing property. The applicable federal rate is set every month by the federal government.

TAX ACCOUNTING METHODS
CASH METHOD, ACCRUAL METHOD, AND HYBRID METHOD

In the cash method of tax accounting, taxpayers recognize all income when it is received and recognize all expenses when they are paid. Taxpayers include all of the items of income that have been constructively received and deduct all bills that have been paid. Any expenses paid in advance are deducted when they apply. Service businesses or those with little or no inventory use this method most often. In the accrual method, income is recognized when earned; expenses are recognized when incurred; income and expenses are matched for the current year; items of income are included when earned; and all the events that set the individual's right to receive income must have happened. This method is used in businesses that are constantly purchasing inventory. A hybrid method of tax accounting is any one that includes elements of the cash and accrual methods.

LONG-TERM CONTRACTS AND INSTALLMENT SALES

For the purposes of tax accounting, long-term contracts are any for the building, installation, construction, or manufacture of buildings or products that are not completed in the year in which they were begun. Installment sales, on the other hand, occur when payments are received in a year other than the year of the sale. Each payment in an installment sale usually includes interest, gain on the sale, and the recovery of basis. It is mandatory for interest to be paid at a rate that is at least equal to the IRS minimum. Taxpayers may want to avoid installment sales if they will carry a net operating loss forward, if they carry a long-term capital loss forward, or if they have tax credits available. Installment sales offer the advantages of deferring tax, making property easier to sell, and notes that carry higher interest rates than a bank.

ACCOUNTING PERIODS AND METHOD CHANGES

In tax accounting periods, accounting periods are the annual time periods over which a taxpayer calculates his or her tax liability. Taxpayers typically file on the basis of the calendar year; in cases where a taxpayer wants to base his or her return on some other fiscal year, he or she must get the permission of the IRS. Also, businesses must receive the permission of the IRS if they want to change their accounting method, even if the original method was incorrect. It is not possible to make these kinds of changes by simply filing a corrected tax return. Some examples of possible changes to which these rules apply are switching from cash basis to accrual basis or changing from one method of inventory valuation to another.

TAXATION AT ENTITY LEVEL

Corporations are the only bodies that pay income tax at the entity level. They report their taxable income on Form 1120, are not subject to passive activity loss rules and their taxable income paid and the net income reported on financial statements will usually be different. Typically, the tax rates for corporations are more favorable than those for individuals, although this is then offset by the double taxation of corporation profits. If corporations receive dividends from another corporation, then they are entitled to a deduction. Starting in tax year 2018 with the Tax Cuts and Jobs Act, net operating losses may not be carried back, but they may be carried forward indefinitely in order to offset other income. Capital gains and losses recognized by corporations will be taxed at the same rate as ordinary income and will not be subject to the reduced capital gains rate. Only the deductions for capital losses can offset capital gains, and no amount can be used to offset ordinary income.

FLOW THROUGH OF INCOME
LOSSES TO CORPORATIONS

There are a couple of different ways to move cash out of a corporation. If shareholders are considered corporate executives, then they receive salary that is only taxed at the individual level, and a tax deduction is provided to the corporation; if they are treated as creditors, then the interest paid to the shareholder is a deductible expense for the corporation, and the shareholders receive rent payments for leasing property to the corporation. A constructive dividend is a distribution made by a corporation to shareholders that the corporation calls salary, interest, or rent, but that the IRS calls a dividend. Closely-held corporations are often used as tax shelters because they offer lower tax rates; because through the undistributed accumulation of earnings they can avoid double taxation; and because when the stock is sold or liquidated in the future, they recognize a taxable gain while indirectly paying a second tax, thus minimizing the present value of the second tax.

LOSSES TO PARTNERSHIPS AND S CORPORATIONS

In a partnership, a partner's initial tax basis will equal his or her initial investment of property plus the share of partnership debt for which the partner may ultimately be held responsible. In an S corporation, the shareholder's initial basis in stock equals cash plus the adjusted basis of any property transferred in exchange for the stock. As for reporting requirements, neither partnerships nor S corporations are considered taxable entities, and so their taxable income is measured at the entity level and then taxed directly to shareholders or partners. The shareholders of an S corporation will need to fill out a Schedule K-1 and add it to their individual tax return; the calculation of their cash flow from the corporation will not affect their tax liability. In some situations, shareholders will be considered employees of the corporation, and will have to fill out the appropriate W-2 form.

In a partnership, basis will be increased by ordinary business income, capital gains, and dividend income; basis will decrease from ordinary business loss, capital loss, and business distributions. When partners are given taxable income but no cash distribution from that income, they are essentially making a larger investment in the partnership: any future cash distribution can be considered as a return on investment. In an S corporation, the basis of a shareholder will increase by his or her share of the corporation's income or gain; he or she will see his or her basis decrease by the share in the losses of the corporation. Cash distributions are considered as a nontaxable return of investment that decreases the basis. Losses are deductible as far as the owner's equity investment and debt obligation.

SPECIAL TAXES AT ENTITY LEVEL FOR FLOW-THROUGH ENTITIES

The built-in gains tax is levied when a corporation that has purchased another corporation seeks to use gains from one of the corporations to offset pre-acquisition losses in the other. LIFO recapture is the amount of excess FIFO recovery over LIFO. S corporations that were formerly C corporations and owe a net passive income tax (that is, if the corporation's passive income is greater than 25% of gross income) owe excess net passive income tax. A personal holding company is a corporation in which five or fewer individuals own half or more of the value of stock. A personal holding company generates most of its income from investment or passive activities (for instance dividends, rents, or royalties).

A personal service corporation provides a service in the fields of health, law, engineering, architecture, accounting, actuarial science, performing arts, or consulting. These companies are, like all C corporations, subject to a flat tax rate of 21% (starting in 2018, down from 35% with the Tax Cuts and Jobs Act) and limitations on passive loss. An accumulated earnings tax will limit the tax advantage of corporate tax rates on earnings accumulated by the corporation. The purpose of this tax is to prevent corporations from avoiding tax. Corporations that accumulate more than $250,000 in earnings must demonstrate that this money is needed for the operations of the business, or else the IRS will impose a tax. As for using losses, partners and shareholders are allowed to deduct any losses that are passed through against income from other sources. Basis, however, cannot be reduced below zero.

INCOME TAXATION OF TRUSTS AND ESTATES

Trustees are required to file Form 1041 if the trust is not tax-exempt, and if the trust has any taxable income for the year, the trust has gross income of over $600, or if any beneficiary is a nonresident alien. The executor of a domestic estate must file Form 1041 if the estate has either gross income exceeding $600 or a beneficiary who is a nonresident alien Trusts and estates that operate on the calendar year must file on April 15; those that use a fiscal year must file by the 15th day of the 4th month after the end of the tax year. Trusts must use the calendar year unless they are tax-exempt, charitable, or grantor trusts. A beneficiary must pay income tax on his or her distributive share of income. The type of income distributed and taxed to beneficiaries is determined by the composition of the distributable net income (DNI).

INCOME TAXATION OF GRANTOR TRUSTS, SIMPLE TRUSTS, AND COMPLEX TRUSTS

For grantor trusts, the trust grantor and any other person with significant control over the trust can be taxed on his or her income. Grantor trusts are not treated as separate trusts for tax purposes; income from the trust is taxed to the grantor. Simple trusts, on the other hand, are required to distribute all of their trust accounting income to beneficiaries. There is a standard deduction of zero; no distributions are allowed for charity. Complex trusts are those that don't meet the requirements of simple trusts; in a complex trust, income can accumulate, charitable contributions can be made, and principal may be distributed to beneficiaries. These trusts have a standard deduction of zero and are allowed the same deductions as simple trusts.

INCOME TAXATION OF TRUST INCOME AND ESTATE INCOME TAX

Trust accounting income includes interest, dividends, royalties, rents, and other items. If allowed by state law, capital gains may also be included in the income of the trust. Unless indicated otherwise, taxable income for a trust is taxed in the same way as individual income; interest that is tax-exempt for an individual will also be so for a trust. Trusts and estates will be subject to at-risk rules and rules regarding passive activity loss. Trusts and estates may claim a deduction based on the amount of taxable income that is distributed to beneficiaries during the year. Estate income tax is calculated by determining adjusted total income, determining distributable net income (DNI), and subtracting DNI from adjusted total income. The amount left over is subject to tax.

ORIGINAL BASIS

The method of calculation used to assess the value of an asset will be based on the method through which the asset was acquired. For gifts, asset value is calculated as fair market value for losses or donor's basis for gains. For inherited assets, the value is fair market value on the date of death. For the assumption of debt, the buyer must include any debt that is assumed in the purchase price when calculating original basis. The adjusted basis is the cost plus capital additions minus capital recoveries. In situations where a long-term debt instrument has been issued at a price lower than its par value, the difference is referred to as original issue discount (OID). The interest income that is derived from OID cannot be deferred. The rules of OID do not apply to short-term debt.

Carryover basis can be calculated in a few different ways. If it is for the adjusted basis of purchased property, it is found by adding the purchase price, acquisition costs, and any improvements. If it is figured for the adjusted basis of a property acquired through inheritance, it is figured as the fair market value on the date of death (or an alternate valuation date). This is also called a "stepped-up basis." If carryover basis is figured as an adjusted basis from gifting, then the basis cannot be figured until the sale occurs. If the sales price is greater than both the donor's cost and the fair market value on the date of the gift, then the basis equals the donor's cost. If the sales price is less than both the donor's cost and the fair market value on the date of the gift, the basis is whichever item results in smallest loss. If the sales price is somewhere between donor's cost and fair market value on the date of gift, the basis equals the sales price.

STEPPED-UP BASIS

A stepped-up basis is calculated for assets that are included in the taxable estate of a decedent. The receivers of bequests will get a basis on those assets equal to fair market value on the date of death (or six months after the date of death). Stepped-up basis is only available for the assets in the taxable estate. In common law states, there is only a step-up basis for half of the assets; in community property states, there is a full step-up in basis. The property owned by a decedent will typically receive a full step-up basis for the person who acquires it. When there is joint tenancy with right of survivorship, either the husband and wife rule (half of fair market value included in decedent's estate, surviving spouse's new basis equals half of the total pre-death basis and half of the fair market value) or consideration furnished rule (each surviving co-owner's basis is old basis plus the fair market value divided equally) will apply.

STEPPED-UP BASIS (TENANCY IN COMMON)

When figuring a stepped-up basis for a situation in which tenancy is held in common, the surviving spouse's cost basis at death is the amount included in the estate of the deceased spouse. If it is left to a co-owner, the basis becomes his or her old basis plus an increase of the amount included in the estate of the deceased. Community property law allows couples to hold appreciated property as community property, whereas property that has decreased in value can receive a full step-down in basis at first death. For this reason, community property law is preferable to common law in the calculation of basis.

DEPRECIABLE PROPERTY, NONDEPRECIABLE PROPERTY, AND THE MODIFIED ACCELERATED COST RECOVERY SYSTEM (MACRS)

Property that is capable of depreciating includes property that is used in a trade or business; that is held to produce income; that loses its value over time; and that has a lifespan of usefulness that is greater than one year. Property that is used and disposed within one year, and equipment that is used for capital improvements, cannot be said to depreciate. Also, neither land nor inventory can be subject to depreciation. The modified accelerated cost recovery system (MACRS) is used to assess the depreciation of assets that have been placed in service after 1986. Here, the term accelerated means that the cost recovery method provides a higher deduction in the early years of the asset's recovery period than would be found in a deduction that was the same every year.

OPERATION OF THE MACRS

The modified accelerated cost recovery system (MACRS) does not consider the estimated useful life of an asset when computing tax depreciation. Assets that have a 3-, 5-, 7-, or 10-year recovering period are depreciated using a 200% declining-balance method. This method will be switched to a straight-line computation when the straight-line computation provides a greater reduction. Depreciation is an attempt to recoup the costs of the assets that are purchased for use in a trade or business. It reduces the cost basis of an asset, and therefore it increases future gains. At the same time, depreciation reduces current income by providing a deduction in the calculation of the business' net income.

COST RECOVERY CONCEPTS

REPAIRS, SPECIAL ELECTIONS, AND AMORTIZATION

When an expense on an asset will increase that asset's usefulness and longevity, the expense is considered betterment and must be added to the cost of the asset and depreciated over the life of the asset. If the expense only brings the asset back to its normal state of use, however, it is just a repair and may be expensed to reduce current income. Special elections are choices to deduct all or part of the cost of certain qualifying property in the year it is placed in service rather than taking depreciated deductions over a specified recovery period. An amortization is used only for intangible assets that have a definite life. Patents and copyrights are common examples of assets that may be amortized.

TAX CONSEQUENCES OF LIKE-KIND EXCHANGES

REPORTING REQUIREMENTS AND QUALIFYING TRANSACTIONS

When like-kind exchanges are made, Form 8824 must be filed in the year of exchange and for the following two years after a related party exchange. The property must be identified within 45 days from the date of transfer, and it must be received within 180 days after the old property is transferred, but not later than the due date for the tax return for the year of the transfer of the old property. Nontaxable exchanges are only possible when qualifying property has been disposed or received. No gain or loss may be recognized on property that is used in a trade or business or is held for investment. Gain can be recognized when cash or unlike property is received in addition to like-kind property. The gain will be whichever is less: either the gain realized or the fair market value of the nonqualifying cash or property received.

MULTIPLE PROPERTIES

When a like-kind exchange is made involving multiple properties, the exchange is considered as one of multiple properties if the transferred properties are separable into more than one exchange group, a group all the properties transferred and received within the exchange that are of the same asset class or product class. A typical three-cornered exchange will involve three parties and will qualify for Section 1031 treatment. The three parties are: the buyer, who wants to purchase the property; the trader, who wants to sell the property for other like-kind property for the purposes of avoiding taxes; and the seller, who wants to sell property, but owns no new property. Purchase, sale, and exchange are usually simultaneous, though this is not necessary.

LIABILITIES

Some special tax consequences apply to situations in which a property bearing a liability is involved in a like-kind exchange. In a situation where a taxpayer gives up property that is subject to a liability, and the transferee then assumes the liability, the taxpayer is treated as having received cash in the transaction equal to the amount of the liability that is transferred. If the taxpayer has a liability on the property that is assumed, and the taxpayer assumes a liability on the replacement property, these liabilities are netted together in order to calculate the cash received or paid.

BOOT

In a like-kind exchange, the boot is considered as all property other than the like-kind property, including cash. When mortgage properties are exchanged, the relief of debt is the boot received regardless of whether it is loan or mortgage. The assumption of debt is the boot given. In such situations, the basis of the assets received will be reduced by the cash received, loss recognized, and liabilities conveyed. The basis of assets received will be increased by the cash paid, gain recognized, and the liabilities assumed. When both parties are subject to a mortgage, only the net amount of debt is considered when calculating boot given and received; there will be a net cash boot when cash is both given and received.

RELATED PARTY TRANSACTIONS

Related party transactions are those that occur among parties who share an economic objective and are not dealing at arm's length. A like-kind exchange between related parties qualifies for nonrecognition treatment. If the property transferred is disposed of within two years after the date of transfer, the original property will not qualify for nonrecognition treatment, and any gain or loss that was not recognized will have to be recognized on the date of disposition. Nonrecognitions will not be affected by dispositions: due to death; for which the avoidance of income tax was not the primary reason; due to the involuntary conversion of property; of property in nonrecognition transactions; or that pertain to transactions that do not include the shifting of basis.

TAX CONSEQUENCES OF GAIN OR LOSS ON SALE OF ASSETS
HOLDING PERIOD

Capital gains and losses can be based on three different holding periods. Short-term capital gains and losses are taxed as ordinary income and result from the sale of securities that are owned for a year or less. Long-term capital gains or losses receive a preferential tax treatment, and result from the sale of securities owned for more than a year. Qualified five-year gain property for sales after December 31, 2000 of property held for more than five years receives a preferential tax treatment of 18%. Holding period generally begins the day after acquisition and extends through the date of disposition. If the property is received through a gift, and is later sold for a gain, the receiver's holding period will include the time the donor held the property.

SALE OF RESIDENCE AND DEFINITION OF CAPITAL ASSETS

Capital gains from the sale of a residence can be excluded from income, up to $500,000 for joint filers and $250,000 for individual filers. This exclusion can only be used once every two years and only applies when the taxpayer has lived at this residence two out of the five years before the sale. Capital assets are defined by indicating the things that do not count as capital assets. The following items are not capital assets: business inventories; business accounts or notes receivable; business supplies; real or depreciable business supplies or intangible business assets subject to amortization; creative assets; US government publications; commodities derivatives; and hedging transaction properties.

CAPITAL ASSETS

For businesses, capital assets are any that are held for long-term investment instead of active business use. Equity and creditor interests in other firms are considered to be capital. Capital losses can be deducted only to the extent of capital gains. Individuals may carry capital losses forward indefinitely, while businesses can only carry them forward five years and can only carry them back three years. When capital gains and losses are netted, short-term losses are used to offset short-term gains, and long-term losses to offset long-term gains. A net short-term loss offsets long-term gains, though if the net short-term loss is less than the long-term gain, the difference is taxed as long-term capital gain. Net long-term loss offsets short-term gains, and if it is less than the resulting amount is taxed as short-term capital gain.

DEPRECIATION RECAPTURE AND REAL OR PERSONAL PROPERTY

According to Section 1231, personal or real property used in trade or business are those that are held for more than a year and include both depreciable tangible and intangible personal property, as well as both depreciable and nondepreciable real property. This does not include inventory. When a taxpayer has Section 1231 net gain in a current year but has had a net loss in any of the previous five years, the previous year's loss must be recaptured by treating an equivalent amount of the current gain as ordinary income. The depreciation recapture rule states that gains that are attributable to previous year depreciation or amortization deductions must be characterized as ordinary income. Capital gains are always classified as Section 1231, never Sections 1245 or 1250. Ordinary income, on the other hand, is never 1231, but always either 1245 or 1250.

RULES FOR PERSONAL PROPERTY, RULES FOR REAL PROPERTY, AND EXCEPTIONS

Section 1245 of the Tax Code applies to personal property. Any gain on the sale of Section 1245 property is treated as ordinary income, insofar as it can be treated as such by depreciation and amortization. Section 1245 does not apply to losses; Section 1231 is used instead. Section 1250 applies to real property; when the property was held for longer than one year, there is no depreciation recapture assuming it was depreciated using a straight-line method. The exceptions to recapture under Sections 1245 and 1250 are gifts, death, charitable transfers, certain nontaxable transactions, like-kind exchanges, and involuntary conversions.

RELATED PARTIES AND WASH SALES

When assets are bought and sold among related parties, the gain on the sale is treated the same way as any other gain, but the loss will not be recognized for tax purposes until the related party sells the asset to an unrelated third party. In these instances, related parties include immediate family members, closely held corporations, sister corporations, etc. If shares are sold at a loss and then bought back within 30 days, the ability to deduct the losses on a tax return is lost. The amount of the disallowed loss can be added to the cost basis of the additional shares that were purchased. When these shares are sold, any taxable gain or loss will include the loss incurred on the original shares. This rule applies not only to stocks but also to bonds and mutual funds.

BARGAIN SALES AND SECTION 1244 STOCK

A bargain sale is one in which an asset is sold for an amount below the fair market value. In the case of individuals, the difference between the fair market value and the sale price will be treated as a gift. In the case of employees, the difference will be taxed as ordinary income. In the case of a shareholder, the difference is characterized as a constructive dividend and is taxable as ordinary income. In the case of a charitable organization, the difference is treated as part sale and part contribution. As for Section 1244 stock, otherwise known as small business stock, losses tend to be capital in nature. However, losses suffered by an individual who received the securities directly from the corporation may be characterized as ordinary.

ALTERNATIVE MINIMUM TAX

MECHANICS

The alternative minimum tax (AMT) is used when it creates a higher tax liability than the calculation of regular income taxation. The point of the alternative minimum tax is to make sure that individuals are not able to lower their tax liabilities through the use of various loopholes. The

AMT is a mandatory tax that must be paid only when it exceeds regular tax liability. There is a base exemption amount determined by filing status that reduces alternative minimum taxable income. The alternative minimum tax has two tiers, such that a slightly lower tax is levied on the first segment of income. Any capital gains distributions or reported long-term capital gains on Form 1040 may be taxed at a rate of 20% for both regular and alternative minimum taxes

PREFERENCES AND ADJUSTMENTS

Preferences are any tax benefits that have been restricted by the alternative minimum tax (AMT) system. They are always positive. Adjustments, on the other hand, may be either positive or negative. Children under the age of 14 may have substantial adjustments or preferences that are subject to the rules of the alternative minimum tax. In the AMT, no standard deduction is allowed; additionally, itemized deductions are not allowed for taxes, some interest, and most miscellaneous expenses. The rules for passive activities are basically the same for the AMT as they are for any other taxation. Gain or loss from the sale or exchange of property must be recomputed according to AMT rules, as will the gains and losses from conduit activities for which the taxpayer has basis or at-risk limitations.

EXCLUSION ITEMS VS. DEFERRAL ITEMS

Itemized deductions that may be deducted in full from the alternative minimum tax include casualty losses; returns on amounts included in income; estate taxes paid on income with respect to a decedent; charitable contributions; interest on debt that was created in acquiring or improving a qualified residence for the taxpayer; investment interest that is not in excess of qualified net investing income; and medical expenses in which the floor is 10%. Itemized deductions that are completely excluded by the AMT include state and local taxes and home mortgage interest that was not used to buy, build, or improve a primary residence or secondary home.

The Tax Cuts & Jobs Act eliminated miscellaneous itemized deductions. Consequently, prior to the TCJA, miscellaneous itemized deductions *not* subject to the 2%-of-AGI floor could be deducted from AMT, whereas such deductions subject to the 2% floor were completely excluded from AMT—but both of these are irrelevant to AMT for tax years 2018–2025.

CREDIT AND SMALL BUSINESS EXEMPTION

If the AMT is paid in a given year because of the deferral of deductions, it may be used to offset regular tax in the future when the deductions are used to reduce AMT below regular tax. A minimum tax credit can only be used against the regular tax liability, though it cannot reduce this below AMT liability for the year. The alternative minimum tax does not apply to S corporations and partnerships. C corporations are only exempt from AMT if they can qualify as small corporations. In order to be exempt from AMT, new corporations must have gross receipts of less than $5 million for the corporation's first three taxable years. After this, they are exempt from the AMT only if annual gross receipts are less than $7.5 million.

TAX MANAGEMENT TECHNIQUES
TAX CREDITS

Depending on a taxpayer's tax bracket, he or she may find a deduction/exclusion or a tax credit more advantageous. Though deductions or exclusions reduce the amount of taxable income that falls within a person's tax bracket, credits will reduce the amount of tax calculated on taxable income. Any child or dependent care assistance that is provided by an employer will also reduce the maximum amount computed for taxable income. Individuals will typically save more money, though, if they are able to pay for childcare expenses with money from a tax-advantaged account. Individuals may also claim tax credits for college tuition; taxpayers can reduce the amount of their federal income tax withholding based on the estimated tax benefits of education credits and deductions.

AMT Planning
Incentive Stock Options

The difference between fair market value and the exercise price of an option is an item of AMT tax and may trigger a significant AMT liability if the exercise of the option involves a large amount of appreciated stock. When this stock is sold, most of the AMT liability will be recovered as an AMT credit against the regular tax if the value of the stock has not decreased since the exercise of the option. AMT gain equals the difference between fair market value of stock at time of sale and exercise price. Regular tax gain equals fair market value at time of sale minus exercise price. Tax liability generally exceeds AMT tentative minimum, so most or all of the credit for AMT paid in previous years will often be claimed against regular tax in the year of sale.

Charitable Gifts and Stock Redemption Agreements

Appreciated property (like stock) can carry a substantial tax advantage if it provides a charitable contribution deduction for the full appreciated value and if this deduction can be applied to both regular and alternative minimum tax. Another consideration in planning AMT is the redemption of stock: an acquisition by a corporation of its own stock from a shareholder in exchange for property. The main point of a stock redemption is to achieve capital gain treatment instead of dividend treatment on the exchange of stock for money or other property. If the transaction is treated as a dividend distribution, redemption proceeds are taxable as ordinary income.

Constructive Dividends, Section 302, and Section 303 Redemptions

Corporations do not intend for constructive dividends to be treated as dividends for tax purposes. In cases where the economic effect of such a transaction is the same as if a dividend distribution had been made, though, the IRS may characterize the transaction as a taxable dividend. Dividends may be distributed in a property form other than money. Taxation will be measured by the fair market value of the property distributed. Under Section 302, there are four kinds of redemptions that may affect a shareholder's percentage of ownership: redemptions that are not essentially equal to a dividend; substantially disproportionate redemptions; complete redemptions; and distributions to noncorporate shareholders in a partial liquidation of the distributing corporation. Section 303 redemptions apply to those estates in which stock constitutes a substantial part of total assets.

Accelerated Deduction

When deductions are accelerated, or income is deferred, taxes will be reduced for the current year. This may be a good tax strategy if the marginal tax rate for that taxpayer is likely to be the same or less in the follow year. If the marginal tax rate is going to go up, though, it makes little sense to defer. Ways to accelerate deductions include: early payment of state income or property taxes; early payment of mortgage and qualified education loan interest; year-end charitable contributions; year-end expenses; year-end purchase of assets (as tangible assets may depreciate a half-year if they are purchased in the last month of the year); review of asset acquisitions; year-end purchases; education payments; and the purchase of supplies.

Deferral of Income

Individuals may want to defer some of their income to minimize their taxes in the current year. To do so, they may use a qualified retirement plan, through which the taxes on earnings may be deferred, and in which pretax income is used for contributions. Postponing the sale of investments until death can also create significant tax savings. Self-employed individuals who use the cash

method of accounting can delay billing late in the year so that collections will not be made until the next year. It is also possible to delay paying year-end bonuses until the beginning of the following year. In a nonqualified deferred compensation plan, some income may be deferred for selected employees for several years.

ESTIMATED TAXES AND WITHHOLDINGS AND NET OPERATING LOSS

For most taxpayers, the required annual payment will be whichever is lower: 90% of the tax shown on the current year's return or 100% of the tax shown on the prior year's return. A quarter of the required annual payment must be paid by the 15th of April, June, September, and January; if the tax on the return is less than $1,000, though, there can be no underpayment penalty. For corporations, estimated payment is either 100% of the past year's tax or 100% of the current year's tax. A net operating loss (NOL) is an excess of business deductions over gross income for a particular tax year. NOL deductions are allowed as either carrybacks or carryovers to other tax years in which gross income exceeded business deductions. NOL deduction is permitted for individuals, corporations, estates, and trusts, but is forbidden for partnerships and S corporations.

AT-RISK RULES

The at-risk rules are set up to limit the deductible loss a taxpayer claims to the amount that the taxpayer actually risks losing. The at-risk rules may apply to individuals, estates and trusts, partners, shareholders in S corporations, and most C corporations. The amount that is considered to be at risk is calculated as the sum total of: the cash amount and adjusted basis of other property contributed to the activity by the taxpayer; amounts borrowed to be used in the activity for which the taxpayer is liable; amounts borrowed to be used in that activity that are secured by property not to be used in the activity; and the taxpayer's share of qualified nonrecourse financing (loans from banks or credit unions, for instance) that is secured by the real property used in the activity.

PASSIVE ACTIVITY RULES

Losses that qualify for recognition under at-risk rules may also be subject to passive activity rules. Losses from passive activity may be used to offset passive activity income only. Passive activity rules may apply to individuals, estates, trusts, personal service corporations, closely held C corporations, publicly traded partnerships, and the owners of pass-through entity interests. All other corporations and partnerships are not subject to passive activity rules. Passive activity losses may either involve rentals or those businesses in which the taxpayer does not materially participate in a significant way. Income and losses from the following activities are considered passive: equipment leasing, rental real estate, limited partnerships (with some exceptions), and other partnerships or corporations in which the taxpayer does not materially participate.

NONPASSIVE ACTIVITIES AND RULES OF MATERIAL PARTICIPATION

The income and losses from the following activities are typically considered to be nonpassive: salaries, wages, and 1099 commission income; guaranteed payments; interest and dividends; stocks and bonds; sale of undeveloped land or other investment property; royalties from the ordinary course of business; business in which the taxpayer materially participates; partnerships, S corporations, and limited liability companies in which the taxpayer materially participates; and trusts in which the fiduciary materially participates. An individual is said to have materially participated if he or she: participates more than 500 hours per year to day-to-day activities; participates between 100 and 500 hours, but more than anyone else; has materially participated for any five of the past ten years; or has materially participated in a personal service activity for any three previous years.

Mometrix

AT-RISK LOSS AND PASSIVE ACTIVITY RULES
COMPUTATIONS, TREATMENT OF DISALLOWED LOSSES, AND DISPOSITION OF PASSIVE ACTIVITIES

When the deductibility of losses is calculated on Form K-1, follow these steps: first, it must be determined whether the partner has sufficient basis; second, it must be determined whether the partner has a sufficient amount at risk; third, it must be determined whether the passive activity rules apply; fourth , it must be determined whether the loss may still not be deductible because of limitations on either net operating loss or capital loss. If the deductibility of loss is limited by basis or amount of risk, suspended losses may be absorbed in subsequent years. The net passive activity losses are suspended and carried forward in order to offset future passive activity income, while the at-risk rules are applied before the passive loss rules. When all of the interest in a passive activity is disposed of, suspended losses are fully deductible against other income.

REAL ESTATE EXCEPTIONS

When an individual has a modified adjusted gross income of less than $100,000, then real estate losses up to $25,000 may be deducted in full. To qualify for this offset, the taxpayer must qualify as an active participant; in other words, he or she must have at least a 10% interest in any rental real estate activity and must substantially participate in management decisions. For vacation properties, in which customer use may be low, the $25,000 offset does not apply. A property is not considered a rental if: average customer use is seven days or less; average customer use is 30 days or less and the owner provides extraordinary services; or the property is used in a partnership.

TAX IMPLICATIONS OF MARRIAGE
FILING STATUS AND CHILDREN

If taxpayers are married on the last day of the year, they may elect to file jointly or separately, though filing jointly is usually more beneficial. If a taxpayer has children, the taxation policy depends on whether the child has earned income, unearned income, or both. If a child only has earned income, then the income up to the standard deduction is not taxable. If a child has only unearned income, and is under the age of 14, then his income may be subject to the estate and trust tax rates. Children over age 14 will generally have their unearned income taxed at the child's rate. When a child under 14 has both earned and unearned income, the unearned income is taxed as usual, and the earned income less the standard deduction is taxed at the child's rate.

COMMON LAW AND COMMUNITY PROPERTY

According to common law, a husband and wife split ownership of all property. In states that abide by common law, there is a stepped-up basis for half of the assets; this means a step-up in basis for the decedent's share of ownership, but not for the share of the survivor. Community property, which is recognized in nine states, is property that was acquired by either spouse during the marriage; ownership of this property is divided equally. Community property states have a full-step-up in basis. At death, the new cost basis is the fair market value at the date of death for both halves of the community property, even though only half is included in the estate of the decedent. Couples who reside in community property states should hold appreciated property as community property.

TAX IMPLICATIONS OF DIVORCE

Alimony is a series of payments made by one spouse to another, sometimes through an intermediary. Prior to the Tax Cuts and Jobs Act, the recipient of alimony would be taxed on the alimony, while the payor could deduct it, but the TCJA established that that applies only for divorces done before 2019. Alimony payments must be made in cash; must occur between two parties who do not live together; and must avoid front loading. Front loading is a method of property settlement

98

Copyright © Mometrix Media. You have been licensed one copy of this document for personal use only. Any other reproduction or redistribution is strictly prohibited. All rights reserved. This content is provided for test preparation purposes only and does not imply an endorsement by Mometrix of any particular political, scientific, or religious point of view.

in which payments are large at the beginning and then decrease quickly. Child support payments will be established by the courts, and will be based on a ratio of each parent's income, the percentage of time the child spends with each parent, and the amount of alimony. Child support is not deductible by the payor and is not included in the income of the recipient. The child can only be claimed as an exemption by one parent in each year.

QUALIFIED DOMESTIC RELATIONS ORDER AND THE TAX IMPLICATIONS OF DEATH

A qualified domestic relations order (QDRO) is a court order instructing a trustee or administrator of a qualified retirement plan how much to pay out to the nonowner spouse after a divorce. These orders ensure that property from a qualified retirement plan can be divided up without adversely affecting taxes. As for the tax implications of death, a tax return must be filed for an individual in the year of his or her death. Though the individual's tax year will have been shortened by death, all deductions, exemptions, and credits can be taken in full. Income that comes after death and becomes part of the estate of the deceased is called income in respect of decedent. A surviving spouse can file jointly in the year of his or her spouse's death.

CHARITABLE CONTRIBUTIONS AND DEDUCTIONS
QUALIFIED ENTITIES AND PUBLIC VS. PRIVATE CHARITIES

Qualifying public charities include: churches and educational organizations; hospitals and medical research organizations; government entities; and publicly supported organizations that receive a substantial amount of support from the general public or government (like the Red Cross). Qualifying private charities include: veteran's organizations, fraternal orders, and certain private nonoperating foundations. Contributions that are made to public charities may not exceed 60% of the taxpayer's adjusted gross income (per the TCJA), while contributions to private charities may not exceed 30% of AGI. For public charities, there is a 30% ceiling (20% for private charities) on long-term capital gain property.

CAPITAL GAIN PROPERTY

Any property that has been held for more than a year may be considered capital gain property for purposes of charitable contributions. There are two categories of capital gain property. Real and intangible personal property includes things like appreciated land and gifts of stock; tangible personal property includes things like cars or jewelry. For real and intangible personal property, the deductions on gifts to charity cannot exceed 30% of AGI if the entire value of the gift is deducted. For tangible personal property, there is a distinction between property that the charity can use directly and that which the charity must sell in order to obtain any value. For use-related contributions, there is a limit of 30% of AGI deduction assuming that the full price of the gift is deducted; for use unrelated gifts, the fair market value of the gift will be reduced by 100% of potential gain, meaning that the deduction is simply the donor's cost basis.

ORDINARY INCOME PROPERTY, CARRYOVER PERIODS, AND PARTIAL INTEREST GIFTS TO CHARITY

Ordinary income property is any piece of property that would have resulted in ordinary income had it been sold on the date of contribution. The deduction for ordinary income property is limited to the donor's cost basis. As for carryover periods for charitable contributions, individuals may carry over for five years any contributions that exceed the AGI for the current tax year. These carryover contributions are subject to the original percentage limits and will be deducted after deducting the allowable contributions for the current year. Typically, any contributions that are less than the entire interest in a property are not deductible. Two exceptions to this rule are gifts of a partial interest in a property if that is the donor's entire interest and property that is held in a charitable lead trust or a charitable remained trust.

NONDEDUCTIBLE CONTRIBUTIONS AND APPRAISALS

Contributions that may not be deducted include money given to: civic leagues, social and sports clubs, labor unions, and chambers of commerce; foreign organizations; groups that are run for personal profit; groups whose purpose is to lobby for law changes; homeowners' associations; individuals; and political groups or candidates. Also, taxpayers may not make deductions for: the cost of lottery tickets; country club dues; tuition payments; the value of donated blood; or contributions consisting of the right to use property. Appraisals are usually required if a contribution exceeds $5,000. Any charges associated with the appraisal may not be included in the deduction. Qualified appraisals are not required for securities that are publicly listed, so long as quotes are published regularly.

SUBSTANTIATION REQUIREMENTS

To claim deductions on cash donations of less than $250, individuals need to supply receipts or other written records with the date, amount, and name of the organization. Noncash donations of less than $250 do not require receipts unless they are easy to obtain. Cash donations of more than $250 in one day to one organization require written substantiations from that organization. Noncash donations of more than $250 require a written acknowledgement from the receiving organization. Non-cash donations of more than $500 require that the donor demonstrate the means through which the property was acquired, the date acquired, and the adjusted basis. Most noncash contributions of over $5000 will also require an appraisal.

Retirement Savings and Income Planning

RETIREMENT PLANNING

ASSUMPTIONS AND FINANCIAL NEEDS

Retirees must make a few assumptions in planning for their lives after work. For one thing, inflation tends to affect the prices of goods and services used by retirees to a degree slightly higher than the Consumer Price Index. Estimating costs and expenses for the retirement income also requires being able to estimate the years that will be spent in retirement, so a general idea of family longevity is helpful. Clients should also project their investment return and the future tax rate. In order to determine a client's financial needs in retirement, one should estimate their cost of living, anticipated medical costs, and any other extraneous costs that can be predicted.

TOTAL RETURN ASSUMPTIONS AND PROBABILISTIC ANALYSIS ASSUMPTIONS

In order to accurately plan for retirement, clients need to make some assumptions about their total returns in the future. Return assumptions must include qualified retirement plans, Social Security, and tax-deferred plans. There are a few different systems that try to predict future income by analyzing several factors. The Monte Carlo system takes an individual's age and investments and then makes certain assumptions about the future inflation rates, life expectancy, and investment returns for the individual. In order to compensate for a projected shortfall in cash-flow, individuals may: make the maximum contribution to a retirement plan; decrease current and future expenditures; make more aggressive investments; advance their retirement age; or consider making increasing annual payments instead of level annual payments.

SOCIAL SECURITY

ELIGIBILITY AND BENEFIT

Individuals are said to be fully insured with Social Security when they have received 40 quarters of coverage. They are said to be currently insured if they have 6 quarters of coverage during the entire 13-quarter period ending with the calendar quarter in which the person died, became entitled to disability benefits, or became entitled to retirement benefits. Individuals are entitled to retirement benefits if they are fully insured and at least 62 years of age. The retirement benefit at a normal retirement age will be equal to the worker's primary insurance amount. Some individuals may seek to take their retirement benefit before full retirement age: if this is done, the individual will collect benefits for a longer period of time, but the benefit will be permanently reduced.

Individuals are entitled to disability benefits if they: are insured for disability benefits; are under the age of 65; have been disabled for a year or expect to be; have filed an application for disability benefits; and have either completed a five-month waiting period or been exempted from this period. In order to be considered disabled, individuals must be so impaired that they cannot perform gainful work. Benefits may also be paid for the following types of survivors of a deceased insured individual: widows and widowers with the care of one or more children; children either under age 18, between 18 and 22 and disabled, or under age 19 and a full-time student; widows and widowers over the age of 60; disabled widows and widowers between ages 50 and 60; and parents over the age of 62 who were dependent on a deceased worker for support.

Though a spouse is entitled to as much as 50% of an employee's full retirement benefit, this benefit will end in the event of: the spouse's death; the worker's death; the termination of the worker' entitlement to disability; the spouse being under age 62 and with no child under age 16; or the spouse becoming eligible to receive retirement or disability benefits with a PIA at least half as large as that of the employee. Qualified children may receive monthly payments of up to 50% of an employee's full retirement benefit, though there is a limit on the amount that can be paid to the family as a whole. The child's benefit ends if: the child dies; the child marries; the child's parent is no longer eligible for disability benefits; or the child turns 18 and is neither disabled nor a full-time student.

FAMILY LIMITATIONS

Primary insurance amount, or PIA, is the fundamental unit that is used to calculate the amount of each monthly benefit. In order to determine an individual's PIA, one must know the average indexed monthly earnings (AIME), which is based on the lifetime earnings history of the individual. To figure Social Security benefits, one must know the average of 35 years of the worker's best earnings. AIME is determined by dividing the total earnings by 420. The formula for then finding PIA for persons who reached retirement age in 2022, or became disabled or died in 2022 before reaching retirement age, is found by adding 90% of the first $1,024 of AIME, 32% of the next $5,148 of AIME, and 15% of the AIME in excess of $6,172.

REDUCTION OF SOCIAL SECURITY BENEFITS

If individuals work after the full retirement age, they lose no benefits from collected Social Security. If individuals are younger than the full retirement age, they lose no benefits if they earn less than $19,560 (as of 2022). If they earn more than $19,560, one dollar of benefits is deducted for every two dollars earned in excess of $19,560. In the year when a person reaches full retirement age, the person can earn up to $50,520 in the months before his or her birthday without deductions; after he or she reaches $51,960 in income during those months, $1 of benefits is deducted for every $3 earned in excess of the $51,960 limit.

TAXATION OF SOCIAL SECURITY BENEFITS

Up to 85% of Social Security benefits can be included in AGI based on the IRS's complex formula. This percentage is ultimately a comparison of one's *provisional income* (PI) to two IRS-established thresholds. The calculation of PI = AGI + tax-exempt interest + 50% of SS income; and these thresholds are $32,000 and $44,000 for MFJ filers. (The thresholds are $25,000 and $34,000 for all other taxpayers, except MFS filers who have a $0 threshold.) For a MFJ filer, if PI < $32,000, then none of his SS benefits will be taxed, if PI is between $32,000 and $44,000, then up to 50% could be taxed, and if PI > $44,000, then up to 85% could be taxed (as of 2022).

CALCULATION OF TAXABLE SOCIAL SECURITY INCOME

If a MFJ taxpayer's SS benefits fall between the $32,000 and $44,000 thresholds, then he will take the lesser of (a) 50% of his total SS benefits and (b) 50% of the excess of his PI over the lower threshold ($32,000). For example, a MFJ has PI of $38,000 and SS benefits of $9,000. His PI exceeds the lower threshold by $6,000 ($38,000 - $32,000 = $6,000), 50% of which is $3,000. $3,000 is less than 50% of his total SS benefits ($9,000 x 50% = $4,500); therefore $3,000 of his SS benefits will be included in taxable income.

If a MFJ taxpayer's SS benefits exceed the $44,000 threshold, the calculation is more complex. First, take 85% of the excess of the taxpayer's PI over the upper threshold; call this the "first figure." Second, take the lesser of (a) 50% of his total SS benefits or (b) 50% of the span between the thresholds; call this the "second figure." Third, add the first and second figures together; call this the "third figure." The lesser of (i) the third figure and (ii) 85% of the taxpayer's total SS benefits is the amount of his taxable SS income.

For example, a MFJ taxpayer has PI of $46,000 and SS benefits of $10,000. His PI exceeds the upper threshold by $2,000 ($46,000 - $44,000 = $2,000), 85% of which is $1,700. 50% of his total SS benefits is $5,000, which is less than 50% of the span between the thresholds ($44,000 - $36,000 = $12,000 x 50% = $6,000). His "third figure" is therefore $1,700 + $5,000 = $6,700. 85% of his total SS benefits is $8,500 ($10,000 x 85%). Since $6,700 < $8,500, his total taxable SS income is $6,700.

WORKING AFTER RETIREMENT, TAXATION

Any individual who is older than 65 and is eligible for retirement benefits is eligible for Medicare Part A, as are those who have received disability benefits for more than two years, and others, including individuals requiring kidney transplants. If an individual is eligible for Medicare Part A, he or she is automatically eligible for Part B. Enrollment in Medicare Part B is voluntary, however. In order to receive benefits from Part B, an individual must make a monthly premium payment. Only people eligible for Medicare Parts A and B are eligible for Medicare Part C, also known as Medicare + Choice. Medicare + Choice provides managed care through contracts with Medicare.

MEDICARE

ELIGIBILITY

Under Medicare Part A, individuals are eligible to have their hospital expenses paid in full for 60 days during the period. An additional 30 days are provided with co-payment, and there is a 60-day lifetime reserve. The benefit period begins when the individual is hospitalized and does not end until the person has been out or 60 days. Individuals may have an unlimited number of benefit periods in their lifetime. Benefits in a skilled-nursing facility are only provided if the individual was forced to stay in a hospital for at least 3 of the last 30 days and if a doctor specifies that a stay in a skilled-nursing facility is required. These benefits will be paid for 20 days in full, and an additional 80 days will be covered with co-payment. In order for a facility to qualify, the individual must be under round-the-clock care and a doctor must be constantly available.

BENEFITS COVERED BY MEDICARE PART A

HOSPITALIZATION AND SKILLED-NURSING FACILITIES

Under Medicare Part A, individuals are eligible to have their hospital expenses paid in full for 60 days during the period. An additional 30 days are provided with co-payment, and there is a 60-day lifetime reserve. The benefit period begins when the individual is hospitalized and does not end until the person has been out or 60 days. Individuals may have an unlimited number of benefit periods in their lifetime. Benefits in a skilled-nursing facility are only provided if the individual was forced to stay in a hospital for at least 3 of the last 30 days and a doctor specifies that a stay in a skilled-nursing facility is required. These benefits will be paid for 20 days in full, and an additional 80 days will be covered with co-payment. In order for a facility to qualify, the individual must be under round-the-clock care and a doctor must be constantly available.

HOME HEALTH CARE AND HOSPICE; AND THE BENEFITS COVERED BY MEDICARE PART B

Recipients of Medicare Part A will have their home health care benefits paid in full. In order to receive these benefits, however, an individual must be confined to his or her home and must be treated according to a home health plan established by a physician. Individuals may receive benefits for hospice under Medicare if they are certified as terminally ill with a life expectancy of less than six months. Under Medicare Part B, individuals may receive coverage for physician and surgeon fees, diagnostic tests, physical therapy, medical supplies, prescription drugs that cannot be self-administered, rental of medical equipment, prosthetic devices, ambulance services, cancer screening, and bone mass measurements.

BENEFITS NOT COVERED BY MEDICARE, BENEFITS COVERED BY MEDICARE + CHOICE, AND COST OF COVERAGE

Medicare does not cover: custodial care; dental work; cosmetic surgery; routine foot care; eye and hearing examinations; prescription glasses and hearing aids; most prescription drugs; private rooms in hospitals or nursing homes; most chiropractic care; acupuncture; or most immunizations. Medicare + Choice, also known as Medicare Part C, covers everything covered by Parts A and B as well as services like prescription drugs. The prices charged for Medicare + Choice coverage, in addition to Medigap premiums, will vary between companies.

MEDICAID

While Medicare is publicly funded health insurance for the elderly (age 65 and older), Medicaid is publicly funded health insurance for the poor and disabled (including blind). Medicare is purely a federal program, but Medicaid is administered as a coordinated effort of both federal and state governments. Different state governments will accordingly have different names for their particular Medicaid program, with some not using the word "Medicaid" at all (e.g. Tennessee's is called TennCare). Furthermore, these different state Medicaid programs will have their own requirements for eligibility and for benefits, although always within certain limits that the federal government sets.

Medicaid can be for the poor of any age, and this includes elderly Americans with low income and low assets. In such cases Medicaid can sometimes assist the elderly poor with nursing home care and long-term care.

MEDICAID PLANNING

If the assets of a client exceed a certain amount, he or she will be ineligible for Medicaid. Strict rules have been established to prevent individuals from shifting assets solely for the purpose of becoming eligible for Medicaid. For instance, any assets that are transferred within 36 months of a request for Medicaid will be considered available. Assets in a revocable trust will also be considered as available, regardless of the date on which the trust was created. It is considered a misdemeanor for financial planners to assist clients in these suspicious asset transfers that are sometimes described as "Medicaid planning."

QUALIFIED RETIREMENT PLANS (QRP)

Some retirement plans are given special tax treatment because they meet certain requirements of the Internal Revenue Code. The tax advantages of such plans include: an immediate tax deduction for the employer for the amount contributed to the plan in that year; no current income tax for the employee on the amounts contributed by the employer; tax-exempt earnings; reduced income tax on lump-sum distributions; deferred income taxes on some distributions; and annuity or installment payments that are only taxed when they are received. Qualified plans may be defined benefit plans in which the maximum allowable benefit payable is the smaller of 100% of salary or $245,000 a year (as of 2022), in which the retirement benefit is certain, and in which deductible contributions may vary from year to year. Qualified plans also may be defined contribution plans, in which the maximum allowable benefit payable is either 100% of salary or $61,000 (as of 2022), which are not subject to the minimum participation rule, and in which the retirement benefit is uncertain.

NONQUALIFIED RETIREMENT PLANS AND GOVERNMENT RETIREMENT PLANS

Nonqualified retirement plans offer executives an alternative to qualified plans. They have few design restrictions as regard their structure of benefits, vesting requirements, or coverage, and are set up to defer the payment of income taxes until benefits are paid out. The employer deduction is deferred until payout, and it is matched to employer income. Nonqualified retirement plans may be either salary reduction plans, in which participants have the choice to defer compensation, bonuses, or commission, or they may be supplemental executive retirement plans, in which there are additional employer-provided benefits. As for government retirement plans, they are outlined in Section 457 of the Internal Revenue Code. In these plans, the decision to defer compensation must be made before it is earned, and the employer may discriminately choose any employee for coverage.

QUALIFIED RETIREMENT PLANS
MONEY PURCHASE

In the type of qualified retirement plan known as a money purchase, the employer must make contributions in an amount determined by a contribution formula: the contributions will be calculated as a percentage of income. Such plans will be subject to a minimum funding standard, regardless of whether or not the company made a profit. Any forfeitures can be allocated to the accounts of the remaining participants or used to reduce employer contributions. Investment in the stock of the sponsoring company is limited to 10%. Money purchase plans can be integrated with Social Security. Typically, younger employees will accumulate more with this kind of plan than they would with a defined benefit plan, though it will often not produce as large of a contribution for older employees.

PROFIT SHARING

In the type of qualified retirement plan known as profit sharing, the contributions made by employers must be significant and regular. It is not required that the company makes a profit for contributions to be made, and any forfeitures may be allocated among the remaining participants. In this kind of plan, the allocation of contributions is nondiscriminatory and there is no limit on the amount that can be invested in the stock of the sponsoring company. Profit sharing plans can be integrated with Social Security. They will tend to benefit younger employees more so than older ones and are common in new companies because they allow flexible contributions in times when earnings may fluctuate or not exist at all.

AGE-WEIGHTED, NEW COMPARABILITY, AND TANDEM PLAN

An age-weighted profit sharing plan allocates contributions based on age and compensation. This kind of plan tends to benefit older employees, since they have fewer years until retirement. In the profit sharing or money purchase plan known as a new comparability plan, the contribution percentage formula for one group of participants may be greater for one group than it is for another. In order to meet nondiscrimination requirements, these plans must be cross-tested. In what is known as a tandem plan, the employer uses both a money purchase plan and a profit sharing plan in order to maximize flexibility. In this plan, profit-sharing contributions are not required annually, though money-purchase contributions are. This plan is typical in businesses with young, highly paid employees.

SECTION 401(K) PLANS

Section 401(k) plans, also known as cash or deferred arrangements (CODA), cannot exist by themselves. These plans must be combined with a qualified retirement plan and may be combined with a salary reduction simplified employee pension or a savings incentive match plan for employees. In a traditional 401(k) plan, the set-up is much like that of a profit sharing plan: contributions can be funded entirely from an employee salary reduction and rules of nondiscrimination apply. In a SIMPLE 401(k) plan or safe harbor 401(k) plan there is no nondiscrimination regulation, though there are funding requirements for the employer. Employees may choose to have their contribution annually in cash as a bonus or they may defer it as a tax-deferred retirement plan contribution.

EMPLOYEE STOCK OWNERSHIP PLAN

In the qualified retirement plan known as the employee stock ownership plan (ESOP), the investment must be made primarily in employer stock. The portfolio for this plan is required to be 100% company stock, although there may be some diversification requirements for participants over age 55 and with more than ten years of service. It is possible to leverage one of these plans in order to buy company stock. These plans are good for corporations because they provide a market for company stock, give a tax deduction without in any way affecting cash flow, and protect company stock from hostile takeovers. ESOPs can be integrated with Social Security, though not if they have been leveraged.

STOCK BONUS PLAN, THRIFT OR SAVINGS PLAN, AND TARGET BENEFIT

In a stock bonus plan, benefit payments are made in shares of company stock, though it is possible for participants to receive cash in lieu of stock. These plans typically offer a diversified portfolio since individuals may choose not to buy company stock. Stock bonus plans are also capable of being integrated with Social Security. In a thrift or savings plan, contributions are made in after-tax dollars and earnings are tax-deferred. In these plans, employees are required to contribute so that they can receive a matching contribution. In a target benefit plan, the allocation of contributions is based on an age-weighted formula, which favors older employees. In these plans, the investment in the sponsoring company's stock is limited to 10%. These plans can be integrated with Social Security.

DEFINED BENEFIT PLAN

In a defined benefit plan, benefits can be determined by a formula. If the interest rate that is earned on plan assets is higher or lower than the actuarial assumptions, then the employer will increase or decrease future contributions to the plan in order to reach the target benefit. The formulas for these plans, which can be integrated with Social Security, are geared to retirement benefits rather than contributions. Forfeitures will always be used to reduce the employer's contribution, and benefits will always be paid, even if the plan is terminated. The plans give a larger benefit to employees who are closer to retirement. In such a plan, the investment risk rests on the employer. The benefits of such a plan are not portable, and the plan may have higher administration costs.

CASH BALANCE PLAN

In the qualified retirement plan known as the cash balance plan, a separate account with a hypothetical account balance will be established for each participant. Employee balance will grow based on hypothetical earnings (interest credits). The interest rate will vary annually and will be determined independently. The minimum interest rate cannot be more than the lowest standard interest rate, and the maximum rate cannot be less than the highest standard interest rate. An actuary will determine the required contribution for each year. Forfeitures must be used to reduce the employer's contribution, and the employer must pay out benefits in accordance with the provisions of the plan even in years in which profits are low or nonexistent. In these plans the investment risk rests on the employer, benefits are not portable, and there may be somewhat higher administration costs.

FEASIBILITY OF INSTALLATION
ADVANTAGES

In order to determine whether to recommend a qualified retirement plan, it is a good idea to review the objectives of the client that may be satisfied by such a plan. A qualified retirement plan may maximize personal tax benefits and personal retirement benefits, while at the same time it may provide protection for an estate. For a business, qualified retirement plans can reduce corporate income tax, reward important employees, reduce turnover, and increase employee job satisfaction. Moreover, qualified retirement plans provide employees with retirement income, promote employee savings, and provide employees with a share in ownership and a share in profits. These plans also provide flexible means of compensation for employers and employees alike.

CONSTRAINTS

In order to provide a qualified retirement plan that meets all of the needs of the client, a financial planner needs to know: the personnel characteristics and profile of the employee (age, service, compensation, etc.); the profits and cash flows of the business (that is, whether they are variable or stable); the profile of the employees (long- or short-term, full- or part-time); the profile of the business owner; the client's degree of sophistication and commitment (fiduciary responsibility, administrative costs, etc.); and the types of retirement plans that are available for specific kinds of businesses.

COVERAGE AND ELIGIBILITY REQUIREMENTS

In order to be included in the vesting schedule for a qualified retirement plan, an employee must have reached age 21 and have been in service for more than one year. In plans where full and immediate benefits are provided, the employee must have reached age 21 and have been in service for more than one year but less than two. Employers may exclude employees who are already covered by a collective bargaining agreement, nonresident aliens, part-time employees who have worked less than 1,000 hours in a year, employees who have worked less than a year, and employees who are under the age of 21. Coverage requirements ensure that highly compensated employees (HCEs) do not receive benefits at the expense of non-highly compensated employees (NHCEs). In order to receive favorable tax treatment, a plan must either pass the ratio percentage test or the average benefits test.

The standard for minimum participation in a qualified retirement plan is sometimes referred to as the 50/40 test. In defined benefit plans, minimum participation must benefit either 50 employees or 40% of all employees (whichever is less). Employers cannot combine different plans to satisfy this requirement. The actual deferral percentage test and the actual contribution percentage test are nondiscrimination tests for retirement plans that allow salary deferral and matching contributions. In the actual deferral percentage test, the deferral rates of NHCEs relative to their compensation are compared to that of HCEs. The actual deferred percentage of HCEs will be limited by that of NHCEs. The ADP of the HCEs cannot exceed the greater of: 125% of ADP of all other employees, or the lesser of ADP of all other employees plus 2% or ADP of all other employees multiplied by 2. The actual contribution percentage test is similar.

HIGHLY COMPENSATED EMPLOYEES

One will need both the look-back year and the determination year in order to measure whether an employee can be considered a highly compensated employee. In the look-back year, the employee must either own 5% of the employer or must have received compensation above $135,000 (as of 2022) and be among the top 20% of employees in that business in rank of compensation. Employers may choose to include an individual in this group of the top 20%, and if this is done then it may be possible for a company to have fewer HCEs. In the determination year, an individual only needs to own 5% of the company in order to be considered a highly compensated employee.

CONTROLLED GROUP

The IRS has set up rules that make it impossible for employers to set up two different businesses that have two different retirement plans. A control group, which indicates that the employer's retirement plans must be consistent, is said to exist when there is a parent-subsidiary relationship, a brother-sister relationship, or an affiliated service group. In a parent-subsidiary relationship, there is common ownership of 80% or greater by one or more companies in the group, and the parent owns 80% of at least one company. In a brother-sister relationship, five or fewer people own at least 80% of the stock value, and the same five or fewer people own more than half of the stock or voting power of each corporation. Affiliated service groups consist of a first-service organization (organization whose principal business is the performance of a professional service) and one or more "A" and "B" organizations. An "A" organization is an owner of an FSO and a "B" organization spends most of its time performing services for the FSO or "A" organization.

VESTING SCHEDULE

In a qualified retirement plan vesting schedule, employee contributions are entirely vested immediately. All of the employer-matching contributions that were made after 2001 must vest under a faster vesting schedule than in earlier years. In a three-year vesting, otherwise known as a Cliff vesting, 100% is vested after three years. In a two- to six-year vesting, vested is graded. Faster vesting schedules are also available for top-heavy plans. The portion of the benefit or account that is attributable to employer contributions other than the matching contributions will remain subject to five-year and three- to seven-year vesting standard. Both SIMPLE and SEP provide instantaneous 100% vesting.

INTEGRATION WITH SOCIAL SECURITY PLANS/DISPARITY LIMITS

For workers that make less than the taxable wage base, Social Security will provide greater benefit coverage. However, Social Security will provide no additional income to workers making more than the taxable wage base. This disparity in retirement benefits between high- and low-income workers can be corrected by integrating Social Security into a qualified retirement plan benefit. As long as it is not discriminatory and observes the regulatory limits, this practice is allowed by the IRC. In a defined benefit plan, one may want to use the excess method of integration with Social Security. In this method, a compensation level known as the integration level is defined by the plan, which then provides a higher rate of benefits for the compensation above this level.

When Social Security is integrated with a defined benefit plan, the percentage spread between the benefit as a percentage of compensation above and below the integration level will be restricted. There are a few terms that are used in such transaction. The base benefit percentage is the percentage of compensation that is provided for compensation below the integration level. The excess benefit percentage is the percentage of compensation that is above the integration level; excess benefit percentage cannot exceed the base percentage by three-fourths of a percentage point for any year or service. In the offset method of integration with Social Security, there is no integration level, and the plan formula is reduced by a fixed amount or some amount derived from a formula that is meant to replicate Social Security.

DEFINED CONTRIBUTION PLAN AND INTEGRATION WITH SOCIAL SECURITY

Defined contribution plans are only allowed to use the excess method to integrate with Social Security. In this method, a compensation level known as the integration level is defined and the plan then provides a higher level of benefits for compensation above this level. If the integration level is equal to the Social Security taxable wage base currently in effect, then the spread between the allocation percentages above and below the integration level can be no more than the lesser of: the percentage contribution below the integration level, or the greater of 5.7% or the old age portion of the Social Security tax rate. The following plans offer no integration with Social Security: LESOP, SARSEP, and employer-matching 401(k) elective contributions.

CONTRIBUTIONS AND BENEFITS

TAX CONSIDERATION, NATURE OF THE DEFINED BENEFIT, AND NATURE OF DEFINED CONTRIBUTION

When deciding on contributions or benefits in a qualified retirement plan, employers should determine the deductible expense to the employer in the year of the contribution. Contributions should be made from pre-tax dollars and should be excluded from the current income of both employers and employees. Earnings will be tax-deferred until they are distributed at retirement. As for the defined benefit, it should not exceed whichever is less, $245,000 (as of 2022) or the full amount of the participant's compensation averaged over three years of highest compensation. The yearly additions payable under the plan cannot exceed whichever is less, $61,000 (as of 2022) or the full amount of the participant's compensation.

COMPARISON OF DEFINED CONTRIBUTION AND DEFINED BENEFIT AND THE DEFINITION OF COMPENSATION

When calculating a plan's benefit or contribution formula, one can only take into account the first $305,000 of each employee's annual compensation (as of 2022). This limit is scheduled to be indexed for inflation in increments of $5,000. Compensation is defined as any wages, salaries, fees for professional services, and any other payments received for services rendered in the course of employment, to the extent that these amounts are able to be included in income. Compensation may also include the following: elective or salary contributions to a 401(k), 403(b), or SIMPLE plan; amounts either contributed or deferred under a 457 plan; and elective or salary reduction contributions to a cafeteria plan.

MULTIPLE PLANS AND SPECIAL RULES FOR THE SELF-EMPLOYED

Multiple plans are to be aggregated when calculating the maximum contribution or benefit. It is typical for the administrative cost of multiple plans to be higher than it is for single plans. Keogh plans are qualified retirement plans that cover one or more individuals in an unincorporated business. These plans are designed to provide coverage for self-employed individuals who are not considered to be employees, although really any retirement plan can be set up to cover the self-employed. Plans for the self-employed are usually set up as either money purchase or profit-sharing plans. In defined contribution Keogh plans in 2022, the maximum contribution is $61,000. When applying the rules of qualified plans for the self-employed, earned income will take the place of compensation.

TOP-HEAVY PLANS

A defined benefit plan is considered top-heavy when more than 60% of the current value of the accrued benefits has been allotted to key employees. A defined contribution plan is considered top-heavy when more than 60% of the total amount in the accounts of all employees is allotted to key employees. There are no top-heavy requirements for SIMPLE and safe harbor 401(k) plans. Key employees are those who have more than 5% ownership, are officers with compensation greater than $200,000, or are more than 1% owners and receive compensation in excess of $150,000 (as of 2022). When plans are top-heavy, they are required to provide 100% vesting after three years of service or after a six-year graded vesting.

When a qualified retirement plan is classified as top-heavy, it must also provide minimum benefits or contributions for non-key employees. In a defined benefit plan, non-key employees must receive benefits equal to 2% of compensation multiplied by the employee's years of service, up to 20%. In this formula, the figure for average compensation is based on the highest five years of compensation. In a defined contribution plan, in a top-heavy year the employer contributions must be at least 3% of compensation. When more than 90% of the total plan benefits are allotted to key employees, a retirement plan is considered to be super-top-heavy. In a defined contribution plan, contributions must be increased from 3 to 4% in a super-top-heavy year, whereas in a defined benefit plan they must be increased from 2 to 3%.

LOANS FROM QUALIFIED PLANS

As long as loans have been incorporated into the plan documents, they are allowed for all qualified plans. The stipulations for such loans are as follows: loans must be available to all participants and beneficiaries; loans cannot be available to highly compensated employees in greater proportions than they are for non-highly compensated employees; loans must be made in accordance with plan documents; loans must be made at a reasonable interest rate; and there must be adequate collateral given in exchange for loans. In order to avoid having a loan characterized as a distribution, the term of the loan cannot exceed five years and the loan amount must be whichever is less, $50,000 or 50% of the present value of the employee's vested account balance. Also, the plan documents may allow a $10,000 minimum loan, even when this is greater than half of the present value.

TRADITIONAL IRA

In the tax-advantaged retirement plan known as the traditional IRA, individuals are allowed to contribute up to the minimum contribution amount and are allowed to deduct this amount from current taxable income. In traditional IRAs, investment earnings are tax-deferred and premature withdrawals are subject to a 10% penalty. Typically, withdrawals are not eligible for the special averaging tax calculation that may apply to some lump sum distributions from qualified plans. Required minimum distributions (RMDs) must be made by April 1 of the year in which the individual reaches age 72. Loans are not available in a traditional IRA.

The following investments are prohibited in traditional IRAs: artworks, rugs, antiques, metals, gems, stamps, coins, and any other tangible property, although some exceptions are made for US gold, silver, and platinum coins. The deduction limit in a traditional IRA is the lesser of the maximum annual contribution amount or 100% of the individuals earned income. In 2022, the maximum contribution amount is $6,000. Traditional IRAs also have what are called active participant restrictions. Active participants are defined as those who have contributions and forfeitures made to a defined contribution plan, or those who are eligible but decline to participate in a defined benefit plan. For active participants, fully deductible contributions are only allowed if adjusted gross income is under a certain amount. This deduction will begin to decrease, or phase out, when income reaches a certain amount and will disappear altogether when it reaches a higher amount.

IRAs may be established any time prior to the due date of the individual's tax return, so for most taxpayers the cut-off date will be April 15. Since earnings will be tax-deferred, it is a good idea to make contributions as early as possible in order to maximize the benefit from compounding. Limited nonrefundable tax credits are available for low-income taxpayers who make contributions to a traditional IRA. Whereas nondeductible contributions can be withdrawn tax-free on a pro rata basis, deductible contributions and earnings will be treated as ordinary income and will be subject to federal income tax. When an individual contributes more than is allowed to a traditional IRA, there may be a 6% excise tax on the excess contribution.

ROTH IRA

In a Roth IRA, the contribution amount is limited for each year and will be eliminated beyond a certain amount of adjusted gross income. Qualified withdrawals are totally tax-free, but premature withdrawals in excess of contributions are taxed in full and are subject to a 10% penalty. Eligibility for contributions is not affected by active participation. Loans are not available in a Roth IRA; minimum distribution rules do not apply until the death of the owner. The maximum annual deductible IRA contribution is the lesser of the maximum annual contribution amount or 100% of the individual's earned income, minus the contributions to traditional IRAs. The nondeductible contribution will equal the after-tax contribution. In 2022, the maximum annual contribution amount is $6,000, or $7,000 for people over the age of 50.

In a Roth IRA, the adjusted gross income used for figuring phase-out limits excludes taxable income from the conversion of a traditional IRA to a Roth IRA. As of 2022, the phase-out limits are between $129,000 and $144,000 for unmarried individuals, and $204,000 to $214,000 for married joint return filers. The time limits and nonrefundable credit are the same as for traditional IRAs. Employers are allowed to sponsor Roth IRAs for employees as a limited alternative to qualified plans. As of 2005, employers were allowed to amend their Section 401(k) and 403(b) plans to transfer the elective deferrals of participants into a qualified Roth contribution program.

IRA ROLLOVERS (ROTH CONVERSIONS)

An individual is allowed to make a qualified rollover contribution to a Roth IRA from a traditional IRA. When this is done, the amount will become fully taxable as ordinary income. The conversion amount is not included in the assessment of AGI, so conversion will accelerate all the taxes on a traditional IRA that would have been deferred otherwise. If the individual has a qualified retirement plan, this must be rolled over into a traditional IRA before it can be converted to a Roth IRA.

CONVERSION ANALYSIS FOR ROTH CONVERSIONS

When deciding whether it is a good idea to convert a traditional IRA into a Roth IRA, there are a few things one should keep in mind. For one thing, it has been consistently shown that a Roth IRA will produce more money at retirement than a traditional IRA with the same investment and tax rates. This is mainly because when investors place the entire contribution limit, this whole amount is at work in a Roth IRA (whereas only the net investment is at work in a traditional IRA). It has also been demonstrated that conversion to a Roth IRA will produce better long-term results than leaving assets in a traditional IRA. The advantage held by the Roth IRA is even greater when taxes are not paid out of the amount converted. The advantage of conversion grows greater the longer assets remain in a Roth IRA before withdrawal.

DISTRIBUTION RULES

If a distribution from a Roth IRA is a qualified distribution, then it will not be included in the owner's gross income. Any distributions of earnings will be tax-free as long as the individual is at least 59.5 and the Roth IRA has been established for more than 5 years. Contributions are typically made with after-tax dollars and are never taxed. Any withdrawals from a Roth IRA must occur in a specific order. First will be withdrawals from excess contribution limits, which are generally free from federal income tax. Then next will be withdrawals from annual Roth IRA contributions, which can be recovered without tax penalty. Next, withdrawals are made from the taxed income component resulting from the first conversion contribution, and then from the conversion contributions made in later taxable years. Finally, withdrawals are made from the earnings from all contributions.

SIMPLIFIED EMPLOYEE PENSIONS (SEPS)

In a simplified employee pension (SEP), the annual employer tax-deductible contributions are limited to 25% of compensation for common-law employees; for owner/employees the limit will be

20% of net earnings. These pensions are subject to funding only by the employer. The rules for nondiscrimination and top-heavy plans will apply here. Also, it is possible to integrate a SEP with Social Security. When determining active participation status for a deductible IRA contribution, participation in a SEP will qualify an individual as an active participant. The controlled group/affiliated services group rules will apply to SEPs. All of the above mentioned characteristics are shared by the simplified employee pension with defined contribution plans.

A simplified employee pension (SEP) can cover all employees who are at least 21 years of age, have worked for three of the past five years (including the contribution year), and received compensation of more than $650 (as of 2022). Employees may be rendered ineligible if they are members of a collective bargaining unit or are nonresident aliens. Contributions to a SEP are fully discretionary, meaning that the employer has total control and flexibility. Loans are not permitted in a SEP. Small employer may decide to set up a SEP because the coverage rules are easier to work with than those of a qualified plan, shorter-term employees can be excluded from the plan, and the costs and administrative expenses are typically low. SEPs are not appropriate for businesses that have many long-term part-time employees.

SIMPLE IRAs
CHARACTERISTICS

SIMPLE IRAs are very easy to administer and offer benefits that are totally portable because the employees are always 100% vested. In a SIMPLE IRA, employees can get the benefit of a broad range of investments. The plans may be funded in part by salary reductions made by employees. Typically, qualified plans allow for a greater amount of annual contributions than do SIMPLE IRAs. Distributions will not be eligible for ten-year averaging. Employers who adopt such a plan cannot also maintain a qualified plan, SEP, 403(a) annuity, 403(b) plan, or 457 plan. Deferrals that are employee elected can be excluded from income, employer contributions are deductible, and earnings are tax-deferred. The rules for nondiscrimination testing and top-heavy plans do not apply.

CONTRIBUTIONS

When an employer establishes a SIMPLE IRA plan, all employees of the employer who received at least $5,000 in compensation from the employer during any 2 preceding calendar years (consecutive or not) and who are reasonably expected to receive at least $5,000 in compensation during the calendar year, must be eligible to participate in the SIMPLE IRA plan for the calendar year. An employee may defer up to $14,000 for 2022 (subject to cost-of-living adjustments for later years). Employees age 50 or over can make an additional catch-up contribution of up to $3,000 (also subject to cost-of-living adjustments).

SECTION 403(B) PLANS
ELIGIBILITY AND PLAN CHARACTERISTICS

Section 403(b) plans, also known as tax-deferred annuity plans or tax-sheltered annuity plans, cannot be offered without being available to all employees regardless of age, service, or union affiliation. In order to adopt such a plan, an organization must be either an educational organization or a tax-exempt employer as described in Section 501(c) (3) of the Code. These plans are funded by employee contributions and may be rolled over to traditional IRAs as well as other 403(b) plans, 401(k) plans, or 457 plans that are maintained by a state or local government. Although they are not considered to be qualified plans, they are subject to similar restrictions. These plans are subject to ERISA if an employer contributes but are exempt if employee participation is voluntary or if the participant controls all the rights under the annuity contract.

PLAN INVESTMENTS, CONTRIBUTION LIMITS, AND DISTRIBUTIONS

In a Section 403(b) plan, investments are limited to: annuity contracts, mutual fund shares, life insurance, and retirement income accounts maintained by churches or church-related organizations. The amount of employee salary reductions is subject to an annual limit. The limit on salary deferrals will apply in the aggregate of all elective deferrals under SIMPLE, SARSEP, 401(K), and 403(b) plans. The elective deferral limit may be increased if the employee has worked for 15 years for an educational organization, hospital, home health care agency, church, or other religious organization. Participants over the age of 50 may be eligible for additional elective deferrals. Distributions will be subject to the rules for qualified plan distribution. Loans may be given if they are allowed in the plan documents.

SECTION 457 PLANS
ELIGIBILITY AND FUNDING

Section 457 plans can be offered to all employees, to any group of employees, or to a single employee. These plans are available for employees of state and local governments, agencies of these governments, and other tax-exempt organizations. Governmental plans are required to be funded according to the requirements of the Small Business Job Protection Act: all plan assets and income are held in trust, or in custodial accounts or annuity contracts, for the exclusive benefits of participants and beneficiaries. The funded 457 plans of nongovernmental organizations are subject to ERISA. If a 457 plan is unfunded, then assets remain the property of the employer and are subject to the claims of the employer's creditors.

CONTRIBUTIONS

The amount of income that is deferred by an employee every year cannot exceed either 100% of compensation or the applicable dollar limit (whichever is less). There are additional salary reduction contributions for participants in the 457 plan of a government employer who are older than 50. A three-year catch-up provision will be applied in the last three years before the plan's retirement of eligible 457 plans; in these years, the limit of deferral will be increased to the lesser of twice the amount of the regularly applicable dollar limit, or the sum of the otherwise applicable limit for the year and the amount by which the applicable limit in preceding years exceeded the participant's actual deferral for those years.

DISTRIBUTIONS

Distributions cannot be made to a Section 457 plan before the employee is severed from employment, attains the age of 59.5, or has an unforeseen emergency that is defined in the regulations. One-time distributions by the participant are permitted so long as the total amount payable does not exceed $5,000, no deferred compensation has been made for at least two years, and the participant has not already used this option. There may also be a mandatory cash-out by the 457 plan if the account does not exceed $5,000, if no deferred compensation has been made for at least two years, and if there has been no previous use of the cash-out provision. In Section 457 plans, there is no forward averaging option, loans are permitted if allowed by the plan documents, and the participant may delay distribution one time if this choice is made prior to the start of distribution.

ERISA

The Employee Retirement Income Security Act (ERISA) defines a fiduciary as any person who exercises any discretionary authority or control over plan management, exercises any authority or control over management or disposition of plan assets, renders investment advice for a fee or other compensation, or has discretionary authority or responsibility over plan administration. According to this act, the IRS must approve all new plans. The IRS will also monitor existing plans, interpret existing law, issue regulations that must be applied to all plans, and judge matters of employer deductibility of plan contributions. The Department of Labor is charged with monitoring investment of plan assets and the actions of those who administer plans, as well as cooperating with the IRS on the oversight of prohibited transactions.

The Employee Retirement Income Security Act (ERISA) established the Pension Benefit Guarantee Corporation to provide mandatory insurance for defined benefit plans, as well as to plan termination insurance. This plan termination insurance guarantees retirement benefits, death benefits in pay status, survivor benefits in pay status, and disability benefits owed or in pay status. Qualified plan terminations are established for the benefit of the beneficiary and his or her family. These terminations cannot be made arbitrarily; they can only be made out of business necessity. Terminations may be either standard, in which a single employer terminates so long as he or she has sufficient assets for benefit liabilities, or distress, in which the employer does not have the assets to pay benefits.

The Pension Benefit Guarantee Corporation is allowed to terminate an underfunded plan for any of the following reasons: the plan does not comply with the minimum funding standard; the plan cannot pay benefits when due; the plan has unfunded liabilities following a distribution of more than $10,000 to an owner. Additionally, the plan can be terminated if not terminating the plan would lead to unacceptably high losses to the PBGC. In order to switch from a defined benefit plan to a defined contribution plan, the defined benefit plan must be cancelled and a new defined contribution plan created. This must be a voluntary standard termination, with 100% vesting for all the affected participants and all distributions of plan assets made in accordance with ERISA standards.

When a defined benefit plan is switched into a cash balance plan, all that is required is for the defined benefit plan to be amended. This means it is not necessary to undergo vesting, distribution, and plan termination. There is an order of priority established by ERISA for allocating plan assets: employee voluntary contributions; employee mandatory contributions; certain annuity payments in pay status; other guaranteed benefits; other nonguaranteed vested benefits; and, finally, all other plan-provided benefits. As for the reversion of residual assets to the employee, there will be a 50% penalty assessed. This penalty may be reduced to 20% if the employer either transfers 25% of the potential reversion amount to a replacement plan or increases the participants' accrued benefit by at least 20%.

DEPARTMENT OF LABOR REGULATIONS AND FIDUCIARY OBLIGATIONS

The Department of Labor (DOL) has established guidelines for qualified and nonqualified employee benefit plans that involve retirement income. The DOL has also established the nondiscriminatory rules for favored employee groups: highly compensated employees and key employees. Finally, the DOL has established vesting schedules for employees and requires sufficient funding for pension plans. According to ERISA, a fiduciary must act solely in the interest of the participants and their beneficiaries. More specifically, fiduciaries must: act for the purpose of providing benefits and defraying the expenses of administering a plan; act with the prudence and diligence of a responsible individual; diversify investments so as to minimize the risk of large losses; and act in accordance with the plan document and the instruments governing the plan

PROHIBITED TRANSACTIONS

There are six prohibited transactions between a retirement plan and a disqualified person/party: the sale, exchange, or lease of property; lending money or extending credit; furnishing goods, services, or facilities; transfer to or use of plan assets by a disqualified person; (if a fiduciary) dealing with plan income or assets in own account; and (if a fiduciary) receiving consideration for own account from a party involved in the plan transaction. Disqualified persons or parties include: fiduciaries; those providing services to the plan; an employer or employee organization whose members are covered by the plan; a 50% owner of such an organization; a family member of any of these people; a corporation, partnership or trust that is 50% owned by one of these people; or an officer, director, highly compensated employee, or 10% or more joint partner of one of these people.

REGULATION OF RETIREMENT PLANS
TAX CONSEQUENCES OF PROHIBITED TRANSACTIONS

When it is determined that a transaction has occurred between a retirement plan and a disqualified person or party, a two-tier penalty is imposed. First, there is a penalty tax equal to 15% of the amount involved in the transaction. This tax is levied on all the disqualified persons involved in the transaction for each year or part of a year in which the transaction remains uncorrected. And, since this tax may carry over from year to year, it may pyramid. Second, there is an additional penalty tax of 100% of the amount involved if the prohibited transaction is not corrected in a timely fashion.

EXEMPTIONS FROM PROHIBITED TRANSACTION RULES AND REPORTING REQUIREMENTS

The following transactions are exempt from the rules concerning prohibited transactions: receipt of benefits under the terms of the plan; distribution of plan assets according to the allocation provisions; loans that are available to plan participants and beneficiaries; loans made to an ESOP; purchase or sale of qualifying employer securities by an individual account, profit sharing, stock bonus, thrift or savings plan, or ESOP, without commission; and providing office space or services for the plan for reasonable compensation. As for reporting requirements for retirement plans, new plans are required to submit an Advance Determination Letter; plans that have been preapproved by the IRS must submit prototypes or model plans; and all plans must submit plan descriptions to participants and their beneficiaries.

PROCESS OF SELECTING A RETIREMENT PLAN FOR A BUSINESS
OWNER'S OBJECTIVES AND BUSINESS' OBJECTIVES

When deciding on which kind of retirement plan to establish for a business, the business owner must try to find the plan that maximizes his or her personal tax benefits, maximizes his or her own personal retirement benefits, and provides estate protection. From the perspective of the business, a good retirement plan should reduce the corporate income tax; provide a variable, stable, or increasing cash flow; and allow for adequate cash flow in the future. It is also important for a business to consider the needs of its employees; a good retirement plan will reward valued employees, motivate employees, reduce turnover, and increase employee satisfaction.

COMPARISON OF DEFINED CONTRIBUTION AND DEFINED BENEFIT PLANS (REWARDING HCES)

A good retirement plan will maximize the proportion of plan costs that benefit highly compensated employees. In a defined benefit plan, the maximum benefit is derived for key employees if they are older on average than other employees. Age-weighted plans use an allocation method to increase contributions to a QRP for older highly compensated employees by weighting for age and compensation. As long as this formula is applied universally, it is not considered discriminatory. When cross-testing is used, nondiscrimination in a defined contribution plan is calculated by looking at the projected benefits under the plan at various retirement ages. In 401(k) plans, there can be higher contributions to HCEs as long as there is maximum participation by NHCEs. Typically, integration with Social Security will discriminate against high-income employees.

115

COMPARISON OF DEFINED CONTRIBUTION AND DEFINED BENEFIT PLANS

A good retirement plan will provide a savings medium employees consider valuable. Defined contribution plans feature individual accounts, so employees will always know exactly how much they have saved. Cash balance plans, on the other hand, may be more attractive to younger employees. Any plans with employee participation, as for instance 401(k) plans, will allow employees to make before-tax salary reductions. Retirement plans should also seek to provide sufficient replacement income for each employee's retirement. If this is the main objective of the employer, a defined benefit plan is the best option because employer funding is mandatory, the plan provides maximum life insurance, and benefit is based on compensation rather than years of service.

CREATING INCENTIVE FOR EMPLOYEES, MINIMIZING TURNOVER, AND ENCOURAGING RETIREMENT

Profit-sharing plans, ESOP/stock bonus plans, and any other defined contribution plan or cash balance plan will give employees incentive to improve performance. As for plans that will minimize employee turnover, a defined benefit plan will give benefits that are based on years of service, while a defined contribution plan will give benefits that increase with each year of service. Defined contribution plans, however, are portable, meaning employees can transfer benefits to another job. Defined benefit plans seem to be the best at encouraging retirement, because they design a subsidized early retirement incentive and do not offer any additional benefits after the retirement age is reached.

INVESTMENT CONSIDERATIONS FOR RETIREMENT PLANS

SUITABILITY

There are a few terms one should be familiar with when considering whether the investment package offered by a particular retirement plan is suitable. The time horizon is the interval in which one expects to reach the specific financial goal. Liquidity is the ability to quickly convert an investment into cash without the loss of principal. Marketability is the degree to which there is an active market for the investment. It is always a good idea to compare the expected return on various investments on a before-tax basis when selecting asset classes and investment vehicles. Retirement plan assets should be exempt from income taxes before distribution. It is important that investment strategies are appropriate for tax-exempt growth.

UNRELATED BUSINESS TAXABLE INCOME (UBTI)

Unrelated business taxable income (UBTI) is any gross income above $1,000 generated by a qualified retirement plan trust that is carrying on a trade or business not related to the purpose of the trust. According to the IRS, a qualified retirement plan in which funds are invested into a common trust has unrelated business taxable income in the same amount as it would have if it made the same investment directly. The income generated either by a common trust fund operating a business or an IRA purchasing a limited partnership interest will be considered UBTI when it is passed through to a qualified retirement plan or IRA. Passive income is not considered UBTI. Dividends from stocks purchased on the margins, as well as income from non-real-estate partnership interest, are considered UBTI.

RISK TOLERANCE AND DIVERSIFICATION

The selection of asset classes and investment vehicles in a retirement plan may depend on the investor's tolerance of risk. The required liquidity and marketability will have a big influence on the risk assumed by the portfolio. In a defined benefit plan, the participant's benefits are fixed and the employer assumes the investment risk; in a defined contribution plan, benefits are variable and the employee assumes the investment risk. It is sound policy, and policy mandated by ERISA, for a portfolio to contain diversified investments that are not all subject to the same amount of risk. It is also standard policy for the asset classes and investments to be monitored periodically, and for the plan to be required to submit detailed plans.

LIFE INSURANCE

As long as the benefits are incidental to the overall plan, life insurance is allowed in qualified retirement plans. There are some restrictions on the premiums that can be paid for life insurance in a qualified retirement plan. In an ordinary policy (whole life) defined contribution plan, the premiums paid by the plan cannot be more than half of the contributions made to the plan on the participant's behalf. In a nonordinary policy (term or universal life), the premium is not allowed to exceed a quarter of the contribution made to the plan on behalf of the participant. Upon retirement, the contract must either be converted to a payout option of the start of benefits or distributed to the participant. In a defined benefit plan, the insurance benefit cannot be 100 times greater than the expected monthly retirement benefit.

RETIREMENT PLANS
PREMATURE DISTRIBUTIONS AND HARDSHIP WITHDRAWALS

Individuals will be subject to penalties for premature distributions if they receive a distribution before the age of 59.5. These distributions will be subject to a 10% nondeductible penalty and will be taxed as ordinary income. Of course, the participant is always given 60 days in which to undo the distribution. In qualified plans and 403(b) plans, an individual must experience some triggering event in order to qualify for a hardship withdrawal. Safe harbor triggering events include: medical care for the participant, a spouse, or dependent; purchase of principal residence; tuition and related fees; or the prevention of eviction or foreclosure. Clients will still have to pay the 10% tax and the distribution will still be taxed as ordinary income.

IRC SECTION 72(T) FOR QUALIFIED AND TAX-ADVANTAGED PLANS

According to IRC Section 72(t), early distributions from qualified plans are not subject to the 10% penalty if they: are made to a beneficiary after the death of the participant; are made because the participant becomes disabled; are part of a series of equal payments made for life; are made to an employee after the end of service after age 55; are made on account of an IRS levy; are made to pay higher education fees for the participant, spouse, or a dependent; or are corrective distributions. Early distributions may be made from tax-advantaged plans if: they are made after the death of the participant; are attributable to the participant becoming disabled; are for medical expenses in excess of 10% (or sometimes 7.5%) of adjusted gross income; are made for expenses related to the first home purchase; are made on account of an IRS levy; or are corrective distributions.

SUBSTANTIALLY EQUAL PERIODIC PAYMENTS

Individuals may be allowed to make take early distributions from a qualified or tax-advantaged retirement plan if they are part of a series of substantially equal periodic payments made for the life of the individual or the joint lives of the participant and a beneficiary. There is no minimum age requirement for these, and the IRS does not have to find out why the withdrawals are made. It is necessary for the payments to be made at least annually. There are three ways to calculate these payments: the life-expectancy method creates the exact annual payment required and will result in the smallest payment; the amortization method will simply amortize the account balance using a reasonable interest rate; and the annuitization method will divide the account balance by an annuity factor based on a reasonable interest rate.

ELECTION OF DISTRIBUTION OPTIONS
LUMP SUM DISTRIBUTIONS

There are four conditions that must be met by lump sum distributions: they must be distributed in one taxable year; they must represent the full account balance to the participant's credit from all the qualified plans of a single type; they must be payable in a lump sum; and they must be made from a qualified pension plan, a profit sharing plan, or a stock bonus plan. Lump sum distributions will be taxed as ordinary income, though taxes may be deferred if the distribution is rolled over to another qualified retirement plan, to a traditional IRA, or to a conduit IRA. A lump sum distribution may qualify for ten-year forward-averaging treatment if the participant was born in 1935 or before and has been a plan participant for at least five years.

ANNUITY OPTIONS

Qualified pension plans are required to provide two kinds of survivorship benefits for spouses. There must be an automatic lifetime survivor benefit in the form of a qualified joint and survivor annuity that provides an annuity between 50-100% of the annuity payable during the joint lives. Qualified pension plans are also required to offer an automatic lifetime survivor benefit in the form of a qualified preretirement survivor annuity that will provide a survivor benefit if the participant should die before retirement. The nonparticipant spouse may opt for a different benefit form. A life annuity is an automatic form of benefit for an unmarried employee. A period certain annuity provides payments for a predetermined period of time. Annuity payments will either be taxed on a noncontributory basis, in which the full amount of the payment is includible in gross income and is taxed as ordinary income, or on a contributory basis, in which the payment consists of taxable and nontaxable components of gross income.

ROLLOVER AND DIRECT TRANSFER

When benefits from a retirement plan are distributed through a rollover, the participant is said to have constructive receipt of the money. Only one rollover per account per year is allowed. The following distributions are not eligible for rollover: amounts that are part of a series of equal periodic payments; nontaxable portions of a distribution; hardship withdrawals; corrective distributions of excess contributions and excess deferrals; and the cost of life insurance coverage. The form of distribution known as direct transfer occurs when the assets of a qualified retirement plan or IRA are transferred from a custodian/trustee to another custodian/trustee. When this occurs, the participant does not have constructive receipt of the funds, and he or she avoids the 20% mandatory withholding.

REQUIRED MINIMUM DISTRIBUTION
RULES AND THE LIFE EXPECTANCY METHOD OF CALCULATION

A required minimum distribution (RMD) will apply to qualified plans, IRAs, SEPs, SIMPLE IRAs, and Section 457 government deferred compensation plans. The calculation base for RMD is the balance as of the end of the previous calendar year to the distribution. Required minimum distribution will be calculated separately for each IRA, though distributions may be taken from any account in order to satisfy the minimum. In the life expectancy method of calculating RMD, the owner's account balance is divided by the appropriate life expectancy. In order to satisfy the rules of RMD, the entire interest must be distributed by the required beginning date, or interest must be distributed over the lifetime of the participant, or the life of the participant and beneficiary.

DESCRIBE THE REQUIRED MINIMUM DISTRIBUTION
THREE LIFE EXPECTANCY TABLES

The Uniform Lifetime Table is used to determine the minimum required distributions during the lifetime of the participant if the retirement benefit is in the form of an account balance. This will be used in situations in which the employee's spouse is either not the sole designated beneficiary or is the sole designated beneficiary but is not more than ten years younger than the employee. The Joint and Last Survivor Table is used in situations where the employee's spouse is either the sole designated beneficiary or is more than ten years younger than the participant. If the designated beneficiary should be changed to anyone other than the spouse, this table can no loner be used. Designated beneficiaries, including a spouse, can use the Single Life Table. While a spouse can recalculate this every year, nonspouse beneficiaries cannot.

PENALTIES

If a certain amount of money that should be distributed is not, there is a 50% tax on this amount. If the value of the account has decreased below the calculated minimum based on the December 31 balance, then this 50% penalty will not apply. The 50% penalty on any shortfalls in required minimum distribution will apply to traditional IRAs and may apply to Roth IRAs. Since Roth IRAs are not subject to minimum required distributions during the lifetime of the participant, there is no required beginning date during the lifetime of the participant. However, Roth IRAs may be subject to minimum required distributions after the death of the participant.

DESIGNATED BENEFICIARY

A designated beneficiary must have been a beneficiary as of the date of death and must have been labeled as a designated beneficiary by September 30 of the year following the year of death. Beneficiaries can only be eliminated by a qualified disclaimer, which will be in writing, will be received by the transferor of the asset no more than nine months after the death, is made by someone who has not already accepted any assets of the deceased, and is made by a person who is not directing where the assets should go. Neither executors nor trustees have the ability to choose a beneficiary after the date of death. If a beneficiary should die in the interval between the owner's death and the date of designation of beneficiaries, required distributions will be made using the life expectancy of the beneficiary.

DEATH OF OWNER PRIOR TO REQUIRED BEGINNING DATE

If the owner of a retirement plan should die before the required beginning date, the entire benefit must be distributed within five years. The only exception to this "five-year rule" occurs when the owner already has a designated beneficiary; in this case, distributions will be made over the life expectancy of the designated beneficiary. If the designated beneficiary is not the surviving spouse of the participant, then the entire interest of the participant must be distributed over the life expectancy of the designated beneficiary. Also, the minimum required distributions will begin by December 31 of the year following the year of the participant's death. If the designated beneficiary is the surviving spouse of the participant, the entire interest of the participant must be distributed over the life expectancy of the spouse.

DEATH OF OWNER AFTER REQUIRED BEGINNING DATE

If the owner of a retirement plan should die after the required beginning date, then the entire balance must be distributed at least as rapidly as it was before the participant died. This rule is commonly followed by using whichever is longer, the life expectancy of the designated beneficiary or the remaining life expectancy of the participant minus one. If the sole designated beneficiary is the surviving spouse, distributions are made based on his or her life expectancy. If the designated

119

beneficiary is not the surviving spouse, the "at least as rapidly" rule and method described above will apply. If no designated beneficiary was named, the distribution period will be the deceased owner's life expectancy calculated in the year of death with one year subtracted for each subsequent year.

MULTIPLE BENEFICIARIES AND TRUST AS BENEFICIARY

If a retirement plan has more than one designated beneficiary, the required distributions must be made based on the age of the oldest beneficiary. Although each beneficiary can set up an individual account at any time, in order for a beneficiary to use his or her own life expectancy to calculate distributions, these separate accounts must have been set up by December 31 of the year following the owner's death. If the beneficiary of a retirement policy is a trust, then it is possible to designate an underlying beneficiary of the trust as the beneficiary whose age will be used to calculate the required minimum distribution. If the trust is the beneficiary and the plan owner's spouse is the sole beneficiary of the trust, the spouse cannot roll over the account into his or her own IRA account.

QUALIFIED DOMESTIC RELATIONS ORDER (QDRO)

A domestic relations order is any judgment, decree, or order that is made according to state domestic relations law and related to the provision of child support, alimony, or marital property rights. A qualified domestic relations order (QRDO) is a domestic relations order that concerns the rights of an alternate payee to receive all or part of the benefits payable from a retirement plan. Before a property settlement can be a domestic order under ERISA, a state authority must first approve it. QDRO rules do not apply to IRAs or nonqualified plans. A legitimate QDRO will include the name and address of the participant and alternate payee, the amount of the benefit to be paid to alternate payee, the number of payments or the period to which the order applies, and the retirement plan to which the QDRO applies.

TAXATION OF RETIREMENT PLAN DISTRIBUTIONS
WAIVER AND COST BASIS RECOVERY

If a nonparticipant spouse wants to consent to the waiver of a qualified pre-retirement survivor annuity or a qualified joint and survivor annuity, then this consent must be in writing, must acknowledge the effect of the waiver, and must be witnessed by either a notary public or a plan representative. As for the recovery of cost basis, no tax will be paid on distributions until those distributions are made. Moreover, the tax is paid on net distribution, and the cost basis is recovered tax-free. Cost basis consists of: all employee contributions that have not been considered deductions to federal income taxes; any loans included in the employee's income; any employee contributions included in the employee's income; and any life insurance costs that were included in the employee's income.

CAPITAL GAINS TREATMENT AND NET UNREALIZED APPRECIATION

Lump sum distributions from qualified retirement plans may be eligible for capital gains treatment. However, there are a couple of conditions that must be met: the employer contributions must be from before 1974, and the participants in the qualified retirement plan must have been 50 years old by January 1, 1986. The long-term capital gains tax rate is 20%. If the value of securities includes net unrealized appreciation, it will not be taxed to the employee at the time of distribution (that is, if a lump sum distribution includes employer securities). The amount of appreciation is taxed when the employee sells the securities at long-term capital gains tax rates. However, the employee may choose to pay the tax on the amount of appreciation at the time securities are distributed by including this amount in income.

OLD-AGE, SURVIVORS, AND DISABILITY INSURANCE

Old-Age, Survivors, and Disability Insurance, also known by the acronym OASDI, is a form of social insurance in the United States that is designed to help retirees pay expenses when their income has been reduced because they have entered into retirement. OASDI is more commonly called Social Security. For many retirees, Social Security income is an important part of their retirement income, and their financial planner should assist them in managing their benefits to take the most advantage of it. It is important that planners also discuss Social Security with their clients who are still in the workforce, as it is funded with taxes that are withheld from the worker's paycheck. Additionally, the planner should be able to discuss with self-employed individuals that their part (the self-employed) of the Social Security tax is higher than a person working for someone else, as the company pays half of the Social Security tax.

BUSINESS SUCCESSION PLANNING

A substantial aspect of retirement for business owners is determining how their business should be passed on. While this can be as simple as choosing a relative, friend, or other associate and teaching him the ropes before one retires, it also can involve more complex scenarios. If a business owner wishes to sell his ownership interest, he can choose to sell it to other owners (e.g. in a partnership) or to an outside party. In either case, he will likely need to have his business undergo an official valuation (i.e. appraisal) to determine a fair price.

This may sometimes involve life insurance, so that unexpected business successions can occur more smoothly. For example, partners in a business may arrange a *cross-purchase agreement*, where each partner has a life insurance policy on every other partner. Then if any partner unexpectedly dies, each other partner receives sufficient cash to buy out a portion of the deceased partner's share in the partnership. (The death benefit on such life insurance policies can either be a set number or a formula, to reduce the need for updating death benefits whenever the business's value changes.)

A less complex arrangement is an *entity-purchase agreement*, where the company itself (rather than the individual partners) purchases life insurance on each partner.

Estate Planning

PROPERTY TITLING
COMMON LAW VS. COMMUNITY PROPERTY

The body of law that is based on tradition and general principles is called common law. Common law is not covered by statute; it is based on particular cases. Under common law, a husband and wife have equal ownership of all property. Community property, then, is any property that has been acquired through the efforts of either spouse during a marriage and while living in a community property state. This does not include any property gained by one spouse through a gift or inheritance. In California, the income from community property is considered to be community property, as is anything purchased with that income. According to the Texas rule (which also applies in Idaho and Louisiana), the income earned from separate property during marriage is community property, but the gain on sold separate property remains separate.

SOLE OWNERSHIP, JOINT TENANCY WITH RIGHT OF SURVIVORSHIP, AND TENANCY BY THE ENTIRETIES

When property is titled as belonging solely to one person, that person has total ownership with all the rights attending. In cases where property is titled for joint tenancy with right of survivorship (JTWROS), the interest of one owner will automatically pass to the other at death. This arrangement will take precedence over other ways of dividing property, including wills and trusts. In most states, though, one tenant may sever the tenancy without the knowledge of the other. Joint tenancies are most commonly created between family members. The arrangement known as tenancy by the entireties is similar to joint tenancy, except it may only be created between a husband and wife. Neither spouse is allowed to sever the tenancy without the knowledge of the other.

TENANCY IN COMMON, TRUST OWNERSHIP, UGMA, AND UTMA

As with the case of joint tenancy, two or more people hold interests that are held with a tenancy in common, and each person has the right to possession. Property held in this way may be held unevenly; that is, one party may own more than another. In the case of a trust ownership, a trustee is obliged to hold onto the property and maintain it on behalf of him or herself and a beneficiary. Trusts are arranged by a written agreement in which the trustee and settler set forth the terms and duration of the trust. A trust passes property outside of a probate. The Uniform Gifts to Minors Act allows securities, cash, life insurance, and annuities to be transferred as gifts to minors. These gifts may still be held in custodial form. The Uniform Transfer to Minors Act allows property interest, including real property, to be transferred.

PROBATE PROCESS

In probate, the court validates the will of a deceased individual. Testate succession is when a person dies and has left a will, obligating the executor named in the will to dispose of the decedent's property. Intestate succession is when a person dies without having left a will. The court will appoint an administrator to dispose of property, and the state will determine how the assets are conveyed. In a per stirpes distribution, larger distributions are given to those that have a closer family relationship to the deceased; in a per capita distribution, all eligible descendants will receive an equal share of property. Probate is good in that it protects creditors, provides clean title for heirs or legatees, makes the distribution of property an organized process, and establishes title in cases where it may be questioned. However, probate can be expensive, time-consuming, and controversial.

The following assets are subject to probate: assets in which the decedent has sole title, assets held by tenancy in common, assets held as community property, assets disposed of by will, and contract proceeds that are payable to the estate. Probate may be avoided by: establishing joint tenancy with right of survivorship; using trusts; establishing a funded revocable living trust; creating a tenancy by its entirety; or establishing a beneficiary to transfer by contract, as for instance life insurance contracts and retirement plans. Ancillary probates may occur when a person who lives in one state and owns property in another die; a probate hearing in the state of the property will be held.

OPERATION OF LAW (TITLE)

Operation of law refers to the rights to a property being passed from one individual to another in accordance with the established laws. In the case of joint tenancy with the right of survivorship, for instance, the law states that there will be equal ownership and automatic survivorship, as well as an undivided right to possess the property. This type of ownership is not subject to probate; neither are interests by the entirety, an ownership arrangement that can only be set up between a husband and wife, and in which neither party can transfer property without the consent of the other. In the case of tenancy in common, ownership may be unequal and will not include automatic survivorship. This arrangement can be subject to probate, as can the decedent's share of a community property arrangement, which can only exist between spouses and in which there is no automatic survivorship.

TRANSFERS THROUGH TRUSTS

There are three parties involved in a trust: the trustor, who creates the trust and who funds it; the trustee, who has legal title and manages the trust assets; and the beneficiary, who enjoys the beneficial interest in the trust. In an inter vivo (living) trust, the trust is activated immediately after it is created and is funded during the lifetime of the trustor. In a testamentary trust, the creation of the trust is written into the will and activated upon the death of the trustor. There are five main reasons for transfers through trusts: to provide for more than one beneficiary, to manage property in the event that the trustor is incapacitated, to protect beneficiaries, to avoid probate, and to reduce transfer taxes. Trusts are said to be transferred by contract if they are passed through life insurance contracts, annuities, qualified retirement plans, buy-sell agreements, or prenuptial agreements.

WILLS

A will gives the testator the chance to direct the passing of his or her property and thereby avoid intestacy. Wills are revocable, and may be revised or amended by codicils. A holographic will is written entirely by the testator and may be valid without witnesses. A nuncupative will is one the testator spoke before death in the presence of a number of witnesses. A living will is a legal document that describes which medical procedures are to be used in the event that the testator becomes unconscious or incompetent. Joint wills are two separate wills that have reciprocal provisions in case of the death of one party. Pour-over wills distribute the probate assets to a previously created trust upon the death of the testator. In order to avoid controversy over a will, the testator may choose to include an in terrorem clause, which asserts that beneficiaries who unsuccessfully contest a will should have their bequests eliminated.

POWERS OF ATTORNEY

The power of attorney is a right that one individual grants to another to act on his or her behalf. This power is typically witnessed and accredited. The person who provides the power is known as the principal, and the person who is appointed is called the attorney-in-fact. A durable power of attorney will not be terminated if the principal is disabled or incapacitated. A springing power of attorney will not be effective until the occurrence of some specified event. Power of attorney will apply in any situation in which the principal is unable to give an informed consent on medical decisions. In the case of property management, a durable power of attorney gives a person the right to make decisions regarding the other person's assets. Powers of attorney may be either special, in which case they are limited by the desire of the principal, or general, in which the principal has every right the principal would have.

ADVANCE MEDICAL DIRECTIVES

Testators may establish an advanced medical directive to establish the protocol for their medical treatment in various situations. Living wills are considered to be medical life-support directives. Advance medical directives do not designate an agent to make medical decisions. Living wills are notorious for being vague and only covering situations that have to do with sustaining life. Of course, it is impossible for a living will to cover all possible medical outcomes, and so most living wills only apply to patients who are terminally ill. In some states, individuals may deem it necessary to construct both a living will and the durable power of attorney so that they will be covered in all situations.

ESTATE PLANNING DOCUMENTS
TRUSTS

Clients may want to create trusts in order to manage property in the event that they should become incapacitated or incompetent. If this individual was serving as the trustee, he or she may want to name a successor trustee to take over in the event of impairment. These trusts may be either living or testamentary. A living trust is similar to a will in that it serves as a guide for the disposition of property, has a fiduciary, and is revocable and amendable. On the other hand, a living trust will appoint a trustee rather than nominate an executor, and the formal execution requirements will be stricter for a will. Testamentary trusts, on the other hand, will take effect at the end of the probate process, will contain all of the provisions commonly found in a will, and must both appoint a trustee and nominate an executor.

SUITABILITY OF GIFTING AS A PLANNING STRATEGY
TECHNIQUES FOR GIFT GIVING

In order for a transfer to be seen as a valid gift: the donor must be capable of transferring property, the donee must be capable of receiving a possessing property, there must be acceptance by either the donee or the donee's agent, and the donor must not have any interest in the property. The designer of a gifting program should try to give assets that have a high rate of return in order to avoid a buildup of revenue that would be taxed at the donor's tax rate. If growth assets are given, then post-gift appreciation will not be taxed in the donor's gross estate. A gift of income-producing property will eliminate the income tax payable by the donor on the property. In general, one should avoid giving installment obligations, since one would then have to recognize the entire untaxed proceeds at the time of transfer.

GIFT PROPERTY AND STRATEGIES FOR CLOSELY HELD BUSINESS OWNERS

The following kinds of property are appropriate to be given as gifts: income-producing property (rental property, e.g.); property that will probably increase in value; property that the donor owns in a state other than his or her own state of residence; and property that has already appreciated, assuming that the donee is in a lower tax bracket than the donor. Although the stock of a closely held corporation can be ideal for gift giving, one must be sure not to give too much away. This is because estates must retain a certain percentage of stock (35% of the adjusted gross estate should consist of the closely held stock) in order to qualify for privileged tax treatment.

GIFTS OF PRESENT AND FUTURE INTEREST

Gift tax exclusion only applies to gifts of present interest. In order for a gift to be considered of present interest, the donee must have the immediate right to use, possess, or enjoy the gift. If this right is delayed, then the gift is said to be of future interest. Gifts made to a trust are considered to be of present interest only if the beneficiary can immediately claim custody of the property. The most common types of future interests are reversions, in which the transferor retains a future interest in the property, and remainders, which grants the right to own and enjoy property after all previous owners' interests end. Income beneficiaries will receive a life estate for years in the trust income, while remaindermen will receive the remainder upon the termination of the income interests.

There are a few statutory exceptions to the present interest requirement. A so-called minor's trust [also called a Section 2503(c) trust] is considered a present interest gift and qualifies for the annual exclusion. In these arrangements, the property will pass to the minor when he or she reaches the age of 21. Gifts that fall under the Uniform Gift to Minors Act or Uniform Transfer to Minors Act will be considered as gifts of present interest and will receive the annual exclusion. In Section 529 plans, the donor is allowed to donate the annual exclusion for this year and the next four years while still qualifying for the annual exclusion. If the donor should die before the completion of the years for which the gift was made, the leftover portion of the original transfer will be included in the donor's estate.

GIFT TAXATION
ANNUAL EXCLUSION AND SPLIT GIFTS

In 2022, donors were allowed to exclude the first $16,000 of gifts of a present interest from the amount of the donor's taxable gifts; this annual exclusion amount could be doubled through the practice of gift splitting with a spouse. Gifts in trust are treated as gifts to the trust's beneficiary in determining the number of allowed exclusions. If the trustee has to distribute the income annually, the amount of income interest in the trust will qualify for the annual exclusion. Gift splitting is only available to married couples that file a joint return; one taxpayer will file the return and the other will sign consent for the gift splitting. If gift splitting is selected for a particular year, every gift is considered to have been split.

PRIOR TAXABLE GIFTS, EDUCATION AND MEDICAL EXCLUSIONS, AND MARITAL AND CHARITABLE DEDUCTIONS

If an individual has had no prior taxable gifts, then he or she may apply the tax rates from the unified federal estate and gift tax rate schedule to the taxable gifts of the current year. If the individual has had prior taxable gifts, then the tax on gifts will be cumulative, and once the lower tax rates have been used up it will be necessary to use the progressively higher rates indicated in the Code. Any qualified payments that are made to an educational institution for tuition, to a provider of medical care, or to a political organization are fully excluded from being taxable gifts. Any gifts made to a spouse who is a US citizen are fully deductible, as are any charitable gifts.

TAX LIABILITY

Gifts are taxable when made during the donor's lifetime and when they exceed the donor's annual exemption or are not a present interest. The taxpayer must make use of unified credit to the extent that the tax is due, and the taxpayer must pay the tax to the extent that unified credit is not available. Any gift tax that is paid without the use of unified credit in the three years following the donor's death is included in his or her taxable estate. Net gifts are situations in which the donee has agreed to pay whatever gift tax is due. When a net gift is made: the actual gift tax liability decreases, since the gift taxes paid reduce the value of the taxable gift; the donor's unified credit is used to calculate the donee's gift tax liability; only the net amount of the gift is included in the estate tax calculations as an adjusted tax gift; and the gift is treated as a part sale and part gift to the degree that the gift tax paid by the donee exceeds the donor's basis in the property.

INCAPACITY PLANNING

GUARDIANSHIPS

In financial planning, we may define incapacity (or disability) as the inability to act on one's own behalf. There are numerous means of caring for an individual, his or her dependents, and his or her property if that individual should become incapacitated. A guardianship is an arrangement established by the state after an interested party brings an action. Guardianships are established to care for an individual's dependents when that individual has been declared incompetent, mentally ill, etc. In a typical guardianship, there will be a ward (the protected person), a guardian (also known as a conservator), and a state administrating body. In a voluntary guardianship, the ward may choose his or her guardian. These are typically just interim arrangements until more permanent solutions can be made.

CARE OF PERSON AND PROPERTY

In order to be prepared in the event that a client becomes incapacitated, a financial planner should establish provisions for long-term health care, for protecting property from the claims of the state or others, for changing taxes, and for managing the financial affairs of a client. If, rather than having a conservatorship, a financial planner has durable power of attorney, he or she will be able to: avoid public proceedings over the status of the principal, avoid delays and legal hang-ups, and keep ownership vested in the principal. The advantages of a living trust over a conservatorship are that it is more flexible, it has smaller administrative costs, and it grants broader management authority. The advantages of a living trust over durable power of attorney are that it assures that transactions will be completed, and management and distribution terms are typically more specific.

DISABILITY INSURANCE AND LONG-TERM CARE INSURANCE

A good disability insurance policy will: provide partial rather than total disability; apply specifically to an occupation; be renewable and noncancelable; cover disability from both accident and illness; pay at least 60% of take-home pay; pay at least through age 65; offer cost-of-living adjustments; offer standard-of-living adjustments; and have a three-month waiting period. A good long-term care policy will: be guaranteed renewable for life; have a three-month waiting period; provide coverage for both skilled and intermediate care; provide long-term coverage for Alzheimer's disease; provide a favorable benefit period; and will not require the insured to be hospitalized before entering a nursing home.

BUSINESS DISABILITY COVERAGE

If a business' owner or one of its key employees becomes disabled, the business could be seriously damaged. This scenario is especially dangerous in small businesses. Disability insurance is often procured to cover business overhead, key person disability, salary continuation for owners and key employees, or a disability buy-sell agreement. Business overhead policies are those that cover the business' ongoing operations costs while the owner is disabled. Key person insurance helps a business find a temporary replacement for a key employee, replace the revenue lost by the disability of this employee, and fund a search for a replacement. A buy-sell plan shifts ownership from the disabled individual to a group of other employees.

Mometrix

ESTATE TAX CALCULATION
GROSS ESTATE

According to Section 2033, gross estate includes the value of "all property to the extent of the decedent's interest therein." Section 2034 includes dower and curtesy interest in the gross estate, and Section 2035 includes any gift tax paid on gifts within three years of death. Section 2036 includes in the gross estate the value of any interest in property the decedent transferred if the decedent retained for life the right to earn income from or the enjoyment of that property, and any property in which the decedent has designated the persons who shall enjoy the property or the income from that property. Section 2037 covers transfers that occur at death, and asserts that the decedent must have retained a reversionary interest in the property that exceeds 5% of the value of the property. This reversionary interest must include the possibility that the property transferred by the decedent may return to the decedent, or his or her estate, or that the decedent may retain a right of disposition.

Section 2038 of the Code includes in the gross estate those transfers that contain the power to alter, amend, revoke, or terminate. Section 2039 includes in gross estate the value of any annuity or other payment that is received by the beneficiary, and Section 2041 includes any property that is subject to a general power of appointment at the time of the decedent's death. Interests arising at death may be excluded from gross estate. It is a common practice to create an irrevocable life insurance trust so that the proceeds may be kept out of the estate. It should also be noted that any power of appointment that is limited by an ascertainable standard relating to health, education, support, or maintenance is not a general power of appointment.

DEDUCTIONS, ADJUSTED GROSS ESTATE, AND TAXABLE ESTATE

The following items may be deducted from the value of gross estate: funeral expenses; debt and mortgages; certain taxes payable at death; administrative expenses regarding the disposition of assets; and losses incurred while administering the estate. Adjusted gross estate is calculated by subtracting expenses, debts, and losses from the gross estate. Both charitable contributions and transfers made to a surviving spouse may be deducted from the adjusted gross estate. Taxable estate, then, is calculated by subtracting the charitable deduction and the marital deduction from the adjusted gross estate.

ADJUSTED TAXABLE GIFTS RULE AND TENTATIVE TAX BASE

An individual's adjusted taxable gifts are the taxable portions of all gifts that occurred after 1976. Gifts are taxable to the extent that they exceed any allowable annual gift tax exclusion, gift tax marital deduction, and gift tax charitable deduction. The only reason for adjusted taxable gifts entering into the estate tax equation is so that they will move the decedent's taxable estate up into the appropriate marginal rates. If a gift is added to the gross estate, the value of the gift is the fair market value of the property as of the date of death. Gifts that can be included in a decedent's gross estate are not considered to be adjusted taxable gifts. If a taxable gift should be added to a taxable estate, the value on the date of the gift will apply. In order to derive the tentative tax base, simply add adjusted taxable gifts to the taxable estate.

CREDITS

An individual's tentative tax payable will be decreased by the amount of gift tax that is either paid or payable on gifts included in the tax base. The gift tax is not a credit. Instead, it is a reduction of estate tax--the dollar amount of the unified credit after application. As for the unified credit, it has to be used the first time a gift tax or estate tax must be paid. Taxpayers cannot pay tax in lieu of using a unified credit. The total tax on the net gift will be computed, and then some or all of the credit will be applied against the total tax due. The balance will be the net tax due. If the credit isn't

127

fully used in one transaction, the balance will carry over to the next transaction. Credit that remains after calculating the tax due at death, however, cannot be used.

If a piece of property has been taxed in the estate of another person either ten years before or two years after the death of the decedent, it may be eligible for the credit for taxes on prior transfers. This credit is limited to whichever is less: the amount of the federal estate tax attributable to the transferred property in the transferor's estate, or the amount of federal estate tax attributable to the transferred property in the decedent's estate. If the transferor died either within two years before or within two years after the death of the decedent, the credit will be the smaller of the two limitations. If the transferor died more than 2 years before the decedent, the credit will be reduced by 20% for every 2 years by which the transferor's death preceded, up to ten years. As for the state death tax, it does not reduce the total estate tax; it merely divides the total death taxes between the state and federal governments.

SATISFYING LIQUIDITY NEEDS
SALE OF ASSETS DURING LIFETIME

There are a few basic guidelines to remember when considering the sale of various assets during one's lifetime for the purpose of satisfying liquidity needs. Typically, it is best to sell assets that have a built-in loss. Death will eliminate this potential tax benefit by stepping down the basis of the value on the date of death. It can also be a good idea to sell high-basis assets, since the sale of these will create little or no taxable gain. On the other end of the spectrum, low-basis assets are not a very good option for sale. The tax on these assets will be eliminated if they are held until death, and the beneficiary will receive a new basis at the fair market value.

POWERS OF APPOINTMENT
USE AND PURPOSE

The power of appointment is the power to appoint some other person to receive a beneficial interest in some piece of property. The person who grants this power is called the donor, and the person who receives the power is known as the donee. The people to whom the holder gives power are the appointees. When the power of appointment is allowed to lapse, the people who receive the power are known as the takers in default. A power of appointment is general if there are no restrictions placed on it, and special (or limited) if restrictions are placed on it. A power of appointment will be used when the owner of estate wants someone else to make decisions concerning the estate, when the estate owner does not know the estate's future needs, when the assets would be subject to the generation-skipping transfer tax, or when the estate owner seeks to qualify assets for the marital deduction but would like to retain the right to control who will receive the property.

5 OR 5 POWER

The so-called "five or five power" is used to avoid both estate and gift taxes. Right of invasion will have to be made noncumulative. The property that is subject to the general power of appointment will be included in the estate of the holder only to the extent that the property that could have been appointed by the exercise of the power (but has lapsed) goes over whichever is greater, $5,000 or 5% of the total value of the funds subject to the power at the time of the lapse. The failure to exercise will result in gifts to the remainderment of the trust, with a yearly reduction by the amount of the holder's life estate in the lapsed amounts. If a beneficiary has 5 or 5 power and fails to exercise it in a given year, the beneficiary will become the grantor of that portion of the trust over which the power has lapsed.

CRUMMEY PROVISIONS

Even though gifts placed in an irrevocable trust are considered to be gifts of a future interest, if a lapsing power to withdraw, otherwise known as a Crummey power, is placed, then the future interest will be converted into a present interest. In such a scenario, the beneficiary will have a noncumulative right to withdraw a certain amount of property that has been transferred to the trust within a certain predetermined period. If this right is not exercised, the annual transfer amount remains in the trust to be managed by the trustee. The taxable gift made by a Crummey trust beneficiary will be a transfer subject to gift tax, which uses up a bit of unified credit. For the purposes of calculating estate tax, the property subject to the lapsed power will be included in the beneficiary's estate as a transfer in which interest has been retained.

TAX IMPLICATIONS

Section 2514 states that the exercise or release of a general power of appointment shall be deemed a transfer of property by the individual possessing such power. Section 2514(e) states that the lapse of a power will be treated as a release only to the extent that the property to which it pertains exceeds whichever is greater, $5000 or 5%. According to Section 2041, the donee's gross estate will include all property subject to a power of appointment at the time of the death of the decedent. On the other hand, the existence of a special power of appointment or the exercise, release, or lapse of that right will not force inclusion in the power holder's gross estate. The exercise, release, or lapse of such a special power will trigger the imposition of any gift tax.

TRUSTS
CLASSIFICATION

Simple trusts are simply conduits through which income is forwarded to beneficiaries, though no principal is distributed. The trust will pass its income through to the beneficiaries, who will then report the income in the same category as it was held in the trust, and then pay taxes on it according to their own tax bracket. Complex trusts are those irrevocable trusts that neither distribute principal nor accumulate some fiduciary accounting income. Revocable living trusts are subject to the right of rescind and amend, become irreversible upon the death of the grantor, are includible in the estate, and do not trigger any gift tax at the time they are created. Irrevocable living trusts cannot be revoked by the grantor after their creation unless with the consent of all beneficiaries. Also, they may be subject to a gift tax at the time of transfer and may have both income and estate tax benefits.

RULE AGAINST PERPETUITIES

The rule against perpetuities requires a time period for a trust to terminate and distribute its property. In order to meet the requirements of this rule, an interest must vest within 21 years after the death of someone at the moment of the transferor into an irrevocable trust. Violations of the rule against perpetuities will cause the interest concerned to become void, and the interest will revert to the transferor or to the transferor's successors. The provisos of the rule do not allow us to wait and see whether any grandchildren will be born. These arrangements typically allow the transferor to control a property for his or her life, and for the lives of his or children and grandchildren, but no longer.

SELECTED PROVISIONS

If trust documents contain a spendthrift clause, it is to protect the assets of the trust from the "spendthrift" ways of the trust's beneficiaries. A provision of this kind might prevent a trust beneficiary from assigning his or her interest in the trust corpus. Also, these kinds of provisions can prevent creditors from getting at trust assets by any legal or equitable process. A perpetuity clause prevents interests from being invalidated under the rule against perpetuities. This provision will usually identify all of the people in a trust that are to be calculated. Sprinkling provisions give the trustee the authority to allocate income and corpus among trust beneficiaries in accordance with their need. Support provisions limit the trustee's right of distribution to the amount of the trust's assets needed to discharge the obligation of support to one or more specified beneficiaries.

TAXATION OF TRUSTS AND ESTATES

When property is transferred to a revocable trust there is no resulting taxable gift, since there has not been a completed gift. When property is transferred to an irrevocable trust, a taxable gift is created, and the grantor will be subject to a gift tax liability on the actuarial value of both the income stream and the remainder interest transferred to the beneficiaries of the trust. As for federal estate taxes, the assets of a revocable trust will be included in the gross estate of the deceased grantor. All of the assets transferred to an irrevocable trust will avoid probate and inclusion in gross estate, provided that the grantor does not retain: a life income interest or right to enjoy the property, a reversionary interest of more than 5%, a right to determine the beneficial enjoyment of trust assets, a right to change the beneficiary designation, or a right to change the trustee.

QUALIFIED INTEREST TRUSTS
GRANTOR RETAINED INCOME TRUSTS (GRITS)

In a grantor retained income trust (GRIT), property is transferred into an irrevocable trust, in which the grantor will retain the right to income for a period of years, and after which time the trust will end and the property will be transferred to the remainderman. If the transferor is still alive at the end of the income period, all the beneficial interest in the trust will cease, and the asset will be out of the transferor's estate. However, taxable gift value will be included in the estate tax base as an adjusted taxable gift. The main reason for setting up a GRIT is to leverage the applicable exclusion amount to avoid estate tax (not gift tax). To calculate the value of the gift, take the fair market value of the property and reduce it by the retained interest. This will equal the retained interest that is considered a gift. This is a future interest, which is discounted.

GRANTOR-RETAINED ANNUITY TRUSTS, GRANTOR-RETAINED UNITRUSTS, AND QUALIFIED PERSONAL RESIDENCE TRUSTS

Grantor-retained annuity trusts are arranged to make fixed payments to the grantor at least every year. In a grantor-retained unitrust, the required payment will be determined every year as a percentage of the fair market value of the trust property, and the value of the assets will be recalculated every year. A qualified personal residence trust is allowed to hold an interest in only one residence. If a grantor survives the term of a qualified personal residence trust, he or she does not have to leave the residence: instead, he or she can rent it as a remainderman. This transaction must be arranged arm's length and at a fair rental value. It is not permitted for the settler, the spouse of the settler, or some entity that is controlled by the settler or the spouse to purchase the residence from the trustee.

TANGIBLE PERSONAL PROPERTY TRUSTS AND LIMITATIONS ON THE VALUATION OF REMAINDER INTERESTS

Many individuals will resist setting up a tangible personal property trusts because it can be difficult to value a term interest for tangible personal property. The zero valuation rule of Section 2702 will not apply to tangible property in situations where the failure of the interest holder to exercise those rights would not substantially affect remainder interest. Also, no depreciation deduction is allowed. Meanwhile, Section 2702 can limit the advantage of a grantor-retained trust by valuing the income interest at zero when the transfer is made to a family member. The entire value of the transferred

130

property will immediately be subject to a gift tax. In order to be qualified, a retained income interest must be paid annually and there has to be an exact way of calculating interest.

CHARITABLE GIVING

CONSIDERATIONS FOR CONTRIBUTIONS AND TRANSFERS

It is possible to transfer an unlimited amount of property to qualified charities without incurring any federal gift taxes. There is no limit to the size of the gift tax charitable deduction. Charitable organizations will incur no income tax liability as the result of the gift, and they will not be subject to any income tax on the income derived from the transferred property. The transfers made during the individual's life will not only provide an income tax deduction, but will also subtract property from the estate of the taxpayer. Most people consider making a lifetime gift to charity so that they can use the unlimited charitable deduction to either reduce or avoid gift tax liability while removing the value of the asset from the donor's potential gross estate.

QUALIFYING FOR A CHARITABLE INCOME TAX DEDUCTION

Public charities are any publicly supported charitable, scientific, religious, medical, or educational nonprofit organizations. Any groups that prevent cruelty to children or animals, as well as any governmental groups that use donations specifically for public purposes, may be included in this category. In order to make a contribution that qualifies as a charitable deduction for the purposes of income taxes, the contribution must: be made to a qualifying organization; be a gift of property, rather than time or service; be made before the end of the year in which the deduction will be claimed; have a value greater than any value received from the qualifying organization; and must be claimed by the taxpayer as an itemized deduction.

INCOME TAX CHARITABLE DEDUCTION LIMITATIONS

Any charitable contribution to a qualified charity will reduce current income taxes. Regardless of the size of the gift; however, no federal gift tax will be due on a gift to a qualified charity. Gifts made to qualified charities may also make an individual eligible for a deduction from the federal estate tax up to the value of the gift. The qualified charity will not be required to pay tax on the receipt of either lifetime gifts or bequests. In general, no income tax will be payable by qualified charities on the income earned by donated property. As for federal income taxes, the type of property transferred will determine the percentage limitations on the amount that can be claimed as a charitable contribution deduction.

CHARITABLE REMAINDER TRUSTS (CRTS)

In a charitable remainder trust (CRT), the donor retains a limited right to enjoy the property, but still receives an income tax deduction and reduces his or her federal estate tax. A CRT must have at least one noncharitable income beneficiary, and it must have an irrevocable remainder interest to be held for or paid to a charity. The grantor will retain the right to change the charitable remaindermen without this resulting in inclusion in the grantor's estate. If a trust is not funded, assets will be included in the estate and it will be impossible to claim the income tax charitable deduction. In a CRT, the beneficiary will receive income for a period of life or no more than 20 years, and the remaining amount will go to charity.

CHARITABLE REMAINDER UNITRUSTS (CRUTS)

In a charitable remainder unitrust (CRUT), the amount of the income tax deduction will equal the total value of the property less the present value of the retained interest income. In a CRUT, the income recipient is a noncharitable beneficiary (most often, the donor). The noncharitable beneficiary will receive a fixed percentage of the net fair market value of the principal; this percentage cannot be less than 5% or more than 50% of the annual value. The remainderman is the charity, and additional contributions are allowed. The remainder interest at inception must be greater than or equal to 10% of the original value of the property transferred to the trust. CRUTs may have sprinkling provisions and they may hold tax-exempt securities.

CHARITABLE REMAINDER ANNUITY TRUSTS (CRATS)

In a charitable remainder annuity trust (CRAT), the income tax deduction equals the total value of the property less the present value of the retained interest income. As with the other CRTs, the income recipient will be a noncharitable beneficiary (the donor, typically). Either a fixed amount or a fixed percentage of the initial value of the trust must be paid to the noncharitable beneficiary; the annuity percentage cannot be less than 5% or more than 50% of the initial fair market value of all the property transferred in trust. At inception, the remainder interest must be greater than or equal to 10% of the original value of the property transferred to the trust. The remainderman is the charity, and additional contributions are not allowed.

CHARITABLE LEAD TRUSTS

Unlike in a charitable remainder trust, in a charitable lead trust the donor gives away an income stream and receives a remainder interest. In a charitable lead trust, the donor will place an income-producing property in a reversionary trust and will direct that the income from the trust be directed to a designated charity for a period of time no greater than 20 years. At the end of this period, the property will revert back to either the donor or to some other noncharitable beneficiary. Through this process, the donor will receive a large income tax deduction for the year in which the trust is funded, with the value of the deduction being the present value of the total anticipated income during the period in which the charity receives the income. These trusts will typically be set up as grantor trusts with annual income taxable to the donor.

CHARITABLE LEAD UNITRUSTS (CLUTS) AND CHARITABLE LEAD ANNUITY TRUSTS (CLATS)

In a charitable lead unitrust (CLUT), a fixed percentage of the net fair market value of the principal will be payable to the charitable beneficiary. This percentage can be no less than 5% and no greater than 50% of the annual value. Additional contributions are allowed in a CLUT, and the donor can pay up to income and then make up the deficiency in subsequent years. In a charitable lead annuity trust (CLAT), either a fixed amount or a fixed percentage of the initial value of the trust must be payable to the charitable beneficiary. The annuity percentage can be no less than 5% and no more than 50% of the initial fair market value of all the property transferred in trust. In a CLAT, additional contributions are not allowed, and the trust must invade the corpus when the income is insufficient for payout.

POOLED INCOME FUNDS

Pooled income funds will be created and managed by a public charity rather than by a private donor. The donor is required to contribute an irrevocable, vested remainder interest to the charity. It is called a pooled income fund because the properties are commingled with properties transferred by other donors. These funds are not allowed to invest in tax-exempt securities, and no donor or income beneficiary is allowed to be a trustee. Donors must retain a life income interest, and each beneficiary must receive a pro rata share of income, every year, based on the rate of return earned by the fund. Sprinkling provisions are not allowed in these funds, though additional contributions are.

PRIVATE FOUNDATIONS AND OTHER TYPES OF CHARITABLE GIFTS

Private foundations, which are typically arranged by a family in order to meet some charitable goals, can be established by either a corporation or a trust. These foundations allow individuals to make contributions, gifts, and bequests, which can then be distributed to public charities. Many of these family foundations are designed to promote the family name; if they are organized properly, they may be exempt from federal income tax and any gifts or bequests made to the foundation may be deductible. In a net income with makeup CRUT, any payments to a beneficiary are limited to whichever is lower, the set percentage or the actual income of the trust. These always contain provisions for "make up" if the income is less than the set percentage. In a wealth replacement trust, charitable remainder trusts are combined with irrevocable life insurance trusts to replace the asset the heirs of the donor would be losing.

LIFE INSURANCE IN ESTATE PLANNING

Using life insurance as part of estate planning will provide income for the family of the decedent, will fund business continuation agreements, and will provide cash for the payment of the decedent's debts, estate expenses, and taxes. However, if these arrangements are set up poorly, it may result in the death proceeds being included in the gross estate. If the owner and beneficiary are being selected while the estate is less than the applicable exclusion amount (AEA), then no transfer taxes will be expected, and the selection is easy and flexible. If the spouse is chosen as the owner and beneficiary at a time when the estate is likely to exceed AEA, the proceeds will probably be subject to transfer taxation on the second death, and a taxable gift will occur when the noninsured spouse is named owner and someone else is beneficiary. When a child is named as the owner and beneficiary, he or she may turn over assets to provide liquidity, or may purchase estate assets to avoid making a gift.

LIFE INSURANCE TRUSTS

Life insurance trusts are considered to be irrevocable trusts. Usually, an irrevocable life insurance trust is the best choice. If the trust is not irrevocable, IRC Section 2038 will draw insurance proceeds into the estate of the trustor. It is not possible for the trustor to be named as a beneficiary, so the trustee will be both the owner and the beneficiary. If the purpose of the trust is to pay estate taxes upon the death of the second spouse, then a second-to-die policy is appropriate; if the purpose is to replace the financial contribution of the deceased spouse, then a term policy will be more appropriate. Irrevocable life insurance trusts will exclude insurance proceeds from income and estate taxation for both spouses, exclude insurance proceeds from the probate estates of both spouses, and ensure that the responsible party will have the necessary liquidity after death.

ESTATE TAXATION

The adjusted taxable gift of the decedent will include the value on the date of the gift minus the annual exclusion for any life insurance policy the decedent transferred after 1976 and more than three years before death. The replacement cost of any policy owned by the decedent on the life of another person is included in the gross estate of the decedent. The life insurance proceeds on the life of the decedent will also be included, assuming that the decedent made a transfer of any incidents of ownership in the policy within three years of death. The proceeds of life insurance receivable by a representative, as well life insurance receivable by any other parties, will be included in the gross estate if the decedent possessed any of the incidents of ownership at death.

GIFT TAXATION
TRANSFER OF LIFE INSURANCE

Any transfers of ownership during the life of the insured will trigger a gift in the approximate amount of the cash value of the policy. If the owner and the beneficiary of the policy are different, the gift tax may be applied upon the death of the insured. Should a donor give a life insurance policy and then die within three years, the value of the proceeds are brought back into the estate of the donor. Any premiums paid within three years by the insured for a policy that he or she does not own will not be pulled back into the estate as per Section 2035. If these premiums exceed the annual exclusion, they may constitute a taxable gift. Any transfer of a policy by gifting can be subject to the gift tax; this tax will be based on the valuation of the policy at the time of the gift and not on the value of the proceeds at the time of death.

ESTATE TAXATION
VALUATION OF GIFTS OF LIFE INSURANCE

When a gift of life insurance is not a paid-up policy, it will be valued at the replacement cost for a comparable contract with the same company. When the gift is a new policy that is either transferred immediately after purchase or is purchased for another person, the gift is valued as the gross premium paid by the donor. If the gift is an already-existing policy for which future premiums will be payable, it will be valued as the policy's interpolated terminal reserve plus the unearned portion of the paid premium; in other words, the value of the policy's reserve at the date of the gift, plus the amount of gross premium paid, which is not yet earned by the insurer. Life insurance policies that are transferred into irrevocable trusts are gifts of future interest to the beneficiary of the trust.

USE OF LIFE INSURANCE IN ESTATE PLANNING
INCOME TAXATION

The proceeds of any life insurance policy paid by reason of death cannot be included in the deceased's gross income, or in the beneficiary's gross income, for federal income tax purposes. The only exception to this rule is the transfer for value rule: when a life insurance policy is acquired by another person for a valuable consideration, the difference between the death proceeds of the policy and the cost basis of the purchaser can be included in the gross income of the beneficiary. This rule does not apply to gifts of policies, or to the following purchasers: the insured, the insured's partner or partnership, a corporation in which the insured is a shareholder or officer, the insured's spouse, or a purchaser whose adjusted basis is determined by reference to the transferor's adjusted basis.

MINORITY DISCOUNTS

Minority discounts are valuation discounts that are allowed on the interest in a business when that business is not a controlling interest. In almost every situation, more than 50% of the voting shares will constitute a controlling interest and less than 50% will constitute a minority interest. The discount afforded for a minority interest will depend on a few factors, for instance the minority owner's degree of control over corporate policy, or the minority owner's ability to realize his or her own pro rata share of the entity's net assets by liquidating his or her interests in the entity. It is possible to obtain minority discounts between 15 and 50% percent for transfer tax valuation. Some of the factors that will influence the size of the discount include the quality of management, size of business, history of profitability, and the degree of the company's financial leverage.

MARKETABILITY DISCOUNTS

The lack of an established market will make it more difficult to sell certain stocks than those business stocks that are publicly traded. Some examples of stock that may have poor marketability include restricted stock, stock in a closely held business, and partnership interest. It is possible to obtain a marketability discount between 15 and 50% for transfer tax valuation. Marketability discounts may apply to both minority and majority interests. There are numerous factors that will influence the size of a marketability discount, including the extent of resale restrictions, SEC restraints on marketability, dollar value of the sale, the growth expectations of the firm, and the size of the company's total assets and equity.

BLOCKAGE DISCOUNTS AND KEY PERSON DISCOUNTS

It may be possible for large amounts of stock on a certain exchange to be given a blockage discount if it is determined that the simultaneous sale of this stock would have a depressing effect on the market price. If the block of stock represents a controlling interest in the corporation, then a premium may be attached to its value. It may also be possible to obtain blockage discounts for massed amount of other valuable property. A key person discount may be given to a business that has lost some significant person who was responsible for its goodwill. Typically, the IRS will require an executor to prove that it would not have been possible to avoid the loss, even with the purchase of key employee insurance.

VALUATION TECHNIQUES AND THE FEDERAL GROSS ESTATE TAX
FAIR MARKET VALUE AND VALUING REAL ESTATE

The valuation date for an estate account may either be the date of death or some alternate valuation date. Tax will be imposed on the fair market value of the property on the date of transfer. Fair market value is defined as the price a willing buyer would pay a willing seller under normal circumstances. There are a few special cases in which this definition of fair market value must be qualified. When valuing real estate, the value will depend on location, size, shape, condition, and any other factors particular to the land. A co-ownership discount may be applied if one of the co-owners declines either to sell his or her interest or to buy the interest of the estate, thereby impairing the marketability (and hence the value) of the property.

VALUING INSURANCE POLICIES, ANNUITIES, AND BONDS

If the donor of an insurance policy is not the insured, the value of the gift will be the replacement cost of the policy. Annuities, meanwhile, will be valued differently depending on whether they are commercial or private. Since commercial annuities are contracts offered by companies constantly in the business of selling annuities, they can be valued at the price at which the company will issue a comparable contract. The value of a private annuity contract is determined by the present value of the future payments required under the contract. The fair market value of publicly traded bonds is simply the mean between the highest and the lowest quoted selling price on the date of death. In cases where there was no trading on the valuation date, the mean price from the closest trading date is weighted inversely by the number of days from the valuation date.

VALUING STOCK

The valuation of publicly traded stock is accomplished by finding the mean between the highest and lowest selling prices on the applicable valuation date. If the stock was not traded on the valuation date, one must use the mean of the high and low prices on the nearest trading date and then weight that mean according to the number of days from the valuation date. The valuation of closely held stock is a much more complicated process and involves such factors as: the nature and history of the business, the book value of the stock, the earning capacity of the company, the company's capacity for paying dividends, the outlook for the industry in which the business operates, and the fair market value of the stock of comparable companies.

VALUING LIFE ESTATES, REMAINDERS, AND REVERSIONS

The valuation of life estates, remainders, and reversions is quite simple. For all of these, fair market value is the same as present value. In order to determine present value, one must look at the appropriate IRS tables to find the present worth of an annuity, of an income interest, or of a remainder interest. The IRS tables will show the factors for these three present worth calculations at various interest or discount rates. There will also be a distinct table that can be used to adjust for situations in which annuity or income interest is for a certain term, and when the annuity interest is payable over the life of a certain person. Still another table will give the factors used when the annuity or income interest is payable for the joint lives of two parties.

MARITAL DEDUCTION (ESTATE TAX)
CHARACTERISTICS AND TERMINAL INTEREST RULE

Any amount of property may qualify for the marital deduction, though it may not be applied to a terminable interest. The 100% marital deduction is simple, inexpensive, and gives the surviving spouse total control over assets. On the other hand, the unified credit of the decedent will go unused, and this may cause the estate tax between the two spouses to be slightly higher. A terminable interest is one that ends upon some event or contingency. A terminal interest, on the other hand, is a property interest subject to a future absolute or contingent termination of the surviving spouse's interest. Moreover, it is an interest in which the possibility of termination is created by the decedent, and in which some other person or entity will possess or own the property.

QTIP PLANNING AND THE PRIOR TRANSFER CREDIT

Individuals may elect for a prior transfer credit if they want the spouse who dies first to have power over the ultimate disposition of qualified terminable interest property (QTIP). In order for a property transfer to receive QTIP treatment: one spouse must make an irrevocable election for QTIP and the surviving spouse must receive a qualified income interest for life. A qualified income interest is one in which income is paid at least annually, the value of the property may be subject to federal estate tax as gross estate, and the surviving spouse is entitled to receive all income from the property. If a property is treated as QTIP and qualifies for the marital deduction, it must be included in the surviving spouse's gross estate.

SPECIAL PLANNING FOR NONCITIZEN SPOUSES AND BYPASS PLANNING

According to IRC Section 2506(d), the marital deduction cannot be used if the surviving spouse is not a US citizen. The marital deduction is allowed, however, for property that is placed in a qualified domestic trust that passes to a surviving spouse who is not a US citizen. Bypass trusts are used to take advantage of the unified credit. They are funded with assets equal to those of the exemption, and the leftover property can be divided in any proportion between a trust and the qualified terminable interest proper (QTIP) trust. The assets in a bypass trust will be taxed upon the death of the first spouse, even though the use of the unified credit will mean no tax is due. It will bypass the estate of the surviving spouse for tax purposes. Bypass trusts give a spouse the right to some income, without that income being included in his or her estate at death.

DEFERRAL AND MINIMIZATION OF ESTATE TAXES
DEDUCTIONS AND CREDITS

Significant estate tax savings may be obtained by interspousal gifting. Any contributions to qualified charities will also be fully deductible for both the estate and gift taxes. The cost of a funeral, the debts of the decedent, and any losses incurred during the administration of the decedent's estate may be fully deductible. There is also a credit for pre-1977 gifts, though the amount of this credit is limited to whichever is less, the gift tax or the estate tax on property included in the estate. The prior transfer credit will be allowed for property that is included in the transferor's estate provided that the transferee dies within 10 years of the transferor. Credits are also allowed for most of the foreign death taxes that are paid on property included in the US gross estate but located in a foreign country.

LIFETIME PLANNING TECHNIQUES

The Certified Financial Planner Board of Standards has outlined the following steps in estate planning. First, the planner must explain to the client the estate planning process; the planner must also explain the role of the planner and the role of the client in this process. The planner should then obtain the information about the client that will be necessary to make estate-planning decisions. The planner should then review these facts and make some preliminary recommendations to the client. The planner should then establish a plan that distributes the wealth of the client to the appropriate people, in the appropriate amounts, and at the appropriate times. When a plan has been decided upon, the planner and client should begin implementing the plan. Finally, the planner needs to constantly monitor the progress of the plan, making any adjustments necessitated by performance or changes in the law.

POSTMORTEM PLANNING TECHNIQUES
QUALIFIED DISCLAIMERS

Postmortem estate planning includes filing the right tax returns, making the right elections, planning estate distributions, determining whether any disclaimers can and should be made, and selecting the appropriate valuation date for assets. A disclaimer is a way of changing an estate plan. Specifically, it is the formal refusal of an inheritance of property from a decedent. In order to be a qualified disclaimer, which will not be a taxable gift, the disclaimer must be: irrevocable and unqualified; in writing; delivered to the grantor or to the grantor's legal representative within nine months of the date of transfer; and must be one in which the disclaiming person receives no benefit from the property disclaimed.

ALTERNATIVE VALUATION DATE

Sometimes, an executor will choose to value an estate six months after the date of death if this will reduce the value of the estate for tax purposes. The kinds of properties that can decline in value after the death of the owner are most commonly securities, or closely held business stock. Any assets that are disposed of between the date of death and the alternative valuation date will be valued on the date of disposition. Any wasting assets will be valued as of the date of death, no matter whether an alternative valuation date has been selected. These wasting assets include annuities, leases, patents, and installment sales.

DEFERRAL OF ESTATE TAXES AND CORPORATE STOCK REDEMPTIONS

When an estate tax is deferred, it may then be paid over the next 14 years; the first four payments are interest-only payments beginning the year after the due date, and the next ten are payments of the estate tax. In order to defer an estate tax, the value of the decedent's interest in the business must be at least 35% of the value of the adjusted gross estate and it must be an interest in a closely held business. As for corporate stock redemptions, in most cases in which a closely held corporation buys back stock from shareholders, the proceeds must be treated as dividend income. However, a corporate stock redemption may be claimed under Section 303, in which case proceeds are classified as long-term capital gain.

POSTMORTEM USE VALUATION

According to Section 2032(a) of the Code, executors may elect for special use valuation for any real estate that is used in a closely held business or for farming. This reduced valuation will be made on the basis of current actual use rather than on highest and best use. There are five requirements that must be met in order for a property to receive special use valuation: it must be held for qualified use and actively managed by the decedent for most of the past eight years; the value or real and personal property must be 50% or more of the gross estate after deduction of secured debt and mortgages; the real property portion must be at least 25% of gross estate after deduction of secured debt and mortgages; the qualifying property must pass to qualifying heirs; and on the date of the decedent's death, the property must be used as a farm or in a closely held business.

QUALIFIED FAMILY-OWNED BUSINESS EXCLUSION AND OPTIMAL QTIP PLANNING

Under Section 2057 of the Code, a family-owned business deduction can be coordinated with a unified credit, such that as the unified credit increases, the deduction decreases. This deduction may not exceed $675,000. In order to claim this deduction, the decedent must have been a US citizen and must have materially participated in the business for most of the past eight years; the interest must be a qualified family-owned business; and the net value of the business passing on to qualified heirs must be at least 50% of the decedent's adjusted gross estate (AGE). As for electing to classify property as qualified terminal interest property, this can help property qualify for the marital deduction. This is not a good idea if the surviving spouse is already in possession of a large estate, however, because adding more property will only increase his or her estate taxes.

MONETARY SETTLEMENT PLANNING

When an individual receives monetary payments in a structured settlement, the payments are spread out over time. Money paid in a legal settlement can either be paid as lump sums or as structured settlements. Big financial windfalls, like lottery winnings, are subject to income taxes and may be disbursed over time. Retirees may receive a lump sum distribution from a qualified retirement plan if they have held the plan for at least five years, but they may suffer from having all the income tax assessed in one fiscal year. Insurance proceeds can either be received as a lump sum or as an annuity; lump sum payments are not taxed. In a systematic withdrawal plan, the client can slowly transfer money to an IRA account.

DISPOSITION OF ESTATE

TAX IMPLICATIONS OF VARIOUS ESTATE PLANS

Any income generated by the property will be taxed to the donee after the transfer. The basis of the donee will be whichever is less: fair market value or the donor's basis (adjusted for paid gift tax). Transfers in which the donor can unilaterally retrieve the property will not trigger the gift tax. Completed gifts, however, will give the donor a gift tax liability for however much fair market value on the date of the gift exceeds available annual exclusion and/or any permissible charitable or marital deductions. Whereas a donor doesn't have to pay the gift tax on funds used to pay the gift tax, an estate will have to pay taxes on the funds used to pay estate taxes. Completed gifts that do not involve a retained interest typically affect the calculation of a decedent's potential estate tax by either decreasing the value of the gross estate, increasing the value of the adjusted taxable gift, or decreasing the tax base.

SECTION 2503 (C) MINOR'S TRUST AND CRUMMEY TRUST

Any income derived from custodial property will be taxed to the minor at the kiddie rate, regardless of whether it is distributed. It will not be taxed to the extent that it is used to discharge a parental obligation of support (in this case, it will be taxed to the parent). An irrevocable transfer will trigger a gift-tax liability. The gift will be one of present interest, which qualifies each dollar of gifted custodial property for a dollar of annual exclusion. As for a Section 2503(b) mandatory income trust, it will be subject to income tax as an entity separate from the beneficiaries. And, since income must be distributed to the income beneficiaries, it will also be taxable to them at the appropriate tax rate. The irrevocable transfer will also create a gift tax liability.

ESTATE PLANNING FOR NONTRADITIONAL RELATIONSHIPS

If an individual has children from another relationship and wants to make sure that they receive part of an estate, one can establish a trust, place the property in a joint tenancy with the right of survivorship, or perform lifetime gifting. As for adopted children, for probate purposes adopted children are allowed to inherit property from the adopted parent but not from the natural parent who gave them up. Partners in a same-sex relationship, individuals in a communal relationship, or cohabiting partners of different sexes are not eligible for the marital deduction, so estate taxes cannot be deferred. In such relationships, it is important to include very specific bequests in the will.

GENERATION-SKIPPING TRANSFER TAX (GSTT)
BASICS AND DIRECT SKIP

When a deceased individual's property is passed to someone two generations younger than the individual, the generation-skipping transfer tax (GSTT) is applied. This tax exists because the IRS wants property to be taxed for each generation and does not want people to avoid taxation by passing property to their grandchildren. The tax will be imposed at the highest federal estate and gift tax rate. A direct skip is a transfer made directly to a person two generations away. In such a case, the transferor will pay the GSTT at the time of transfer. In a direct skip, the GSTT is tax exclusive, meaning that the taxable amount does not include the amount of GSTT.

TAXABLE DISTRIBUTIONS AND TAXABLE TERMINATIONS

For the purposes of determining GSTT, a taxable distribution is any distribution of income from a trust to a skip person that is not otherwise subject to estate or gift tax. In such a case, the transferee will have to pay the GSTT if it is a taxable distribution. If the trust is to pay the tax for the transferee, the payment will be treated as an additional taxable distribution. The tax payable on a taxable distribution is tax inclusive. A taxable termination, on the other hand, is a situation in which the end of an interest on property held in a trust causes all of the interest in the trust to be in the hands of the skip person. In this case, the trustee will pay the GSTT, and the tax payable will be tax inclusive. Taxable terminations cannot occur as long as one nonskip person has a present interest in the property.

GENERATION-SKIPPING TRANSFER TAX ON LIFETIME TRANSFERS
OUTRIGHT TRANSFER OF CASH OR PROPERTY

An individual will be considered two or more generations away from another if he or she is a grandchild, great niece or nephew, or any generation beyond. The GSTT is a separate tax from the unified gift and estate tax, and is levied in addition to these taxes. To each generation-skipping transfer, there is applied a flat tax equal to the highest gift and estate tax rate. The GSTT applies to: property placed in trust; transfers involving the creation of life estates; remainders; and insurance and annuity contracts. The GSTT is subject to the predeceased ancestor exception: if the parent in a line of descent dies before the transfer, then lower generations will move up a generation.

TRANSFER IN TRUST

It is possible for a gift that qualifies for the gift tax annual exclusion to still be subject to the generation-skipping transfer tax. This gift in trust will only qualify for the annual exclusion from generation-skipping transfer tax if it meets two requirements: first, the trust must state that it will make no distribution to any person other than the beneficiary during his or her lifetime; and second, upon the death of the beneficiary, the trust assets must be includible in the beneficiary's gross estate for federal tax estate purposes. In order to fulfill these requirements and qualify for the exclusion, grandparents will often set up a Section 2503 (c) or Crummey trust for their grandchild.

EXEMPTIONS AND EXCLUSIONS

Any outright lifetime gifts that qualify for the gift tax annual exclusion will be automatically excluded from generation-skipping transfer tax. There is also such a thing as generation-skipping transfer tax exemption. In married couples, each spouse will have a GSTT exemption. Thus, each spouse can use this exemption to avoid the generation-skipping transfer tax, and so the exemption can be doubled. Also, qualified medical and educational payments may be excluded from the GSTT; in other words, the payments of medical expenses, tuition, or other school expenses can be excluded from the generation-skipping transfer tax.

INCOME IN RESPECT OF A DECEDENT (IRD) ASSETS

The phrase "income in respect of a decedent" refers to amounts that were due to a decedent but which were not included in taxable income in the year of his or her death. IRD, then, could be salary that was earned but never paid. If the taxpayer was not paid until after his or her death, this amount may not be included on his or her final income tax return. Some other examples of IRD include the forgiveness of debt on an installment note, distributions made after death from a qualified plan or IRA, dividends on stocks paid after the death of the stockholder, the posthumous completion of a decedent's contingent claim to sales proceeds, or the posthumous collection of sale proceeds.

INCOME IN RESPECT OF A DECEDENT (IRD) INCOME TAX DEDUCTION

Income in respect of a decedent (IRD) will be subject to both estate and income tax. However, the holder of IRD will be entitled to an income tax deduction for the portion of estate taxes attributed to owning IRD in the gross estate. Also, an income tax deduction will be allowed for the generation-skipping transfer taxes that are ascribed to IRD items included in a taxable termination, or in direct skips caused by the death of the transferor. A deduction will be allowed for each year the IRD is included in income. In order to compute this deduction, all items treated as IRD in the gross estate are aggregated, and the total is reduced by all the deductions in respect of a decedent in order to arrive at a total. The value of the IRD will then be whichever is less: the lesser of the amount included in gross estate or the amount included in income. Estate taxes are then recalculated by excluding the net value from the gross estate. The difference between the original estate tax and the recalculated estate tax is the IRD deduction.

USE OF INTRA-FAMILY TRANSFERS OF ASSETS IN ESTATE PLANNING

The most common use of intra-family transfers in estate planning strategies is to pass assets to other members of the family to reduce or avoid taxes. While the gift tax may not be avoided altogether, this strategy may help the advisor transfer income from one family member in a higher tax bracket to another family member in a lower tax bracket. It should be noted that the gift tax exclusion is $16,000 (as of tax year 2022) for single filers, and $32,000 for those filing as "married filing jointly." Intra-family transfers are also useful for transferring capital assets with low cost bases to others as well. The most common types of transfer relationships are spouse to spouse, child to child, and grandparent to grandchild.

WILLS AS THEY PERTAIN TO ESTATE PLANNING

The estate planning will is a document that assists individuals (usually referred to as grantors) in distributing their property after their death. The will is not valid until after the grantor dies. To be legally recognized, the grantor must be at least 18 years old, be of sound mind, sign and date the will in the presence of at least two witnesses, appoint an executor, name the beneficiaries, and declare that they intend to create a will. Legal wills will help prevent a decedent's estate from being held up in probate, where the estate of the decedent may be subject to more taxes. The most common type of will is the simple will. This written document is more likely to hold up in court than verbal wills.

DURABLE POWER OF ATTORNEY

The power of attorney document is a document that may be prepared to allow another individual, also known as the attorney in fact or AIF, to act and transact on behalf of the individual for whom the document is prepared (the principal). The purpose of this document is to assist elderly people who may not be able to travel, or United States citizens living abroad who need a presence in the U.S. to assist with legal matters. Occasionally, they are drafted for convenience sake, in the event that the individual does not want to deal with such matters. A *durable* power of attorney document will persist to be valid in the event that the principal becomes incapacitated. Durable power of attorney may be either immediately effective, or springing, meaning that the AIF's powers do not come into effect until the principal is incapacitated. Powers of attorney cease to be valid at the death of the principal.

MEDICAL POWERS OF ATTORNEY AND LIVING WILLS

Often people confuse medical powers of attorney with living wills. While they share a common use, they differ radically in content. A living will is a document that states a person's wishes regarding certain life-and-death medical matters. With a medical power of attorney, however, the principal appoints an attorney in fact (AIF) to be able to make other and more general healthcare decisions for them. This is most useful when caring for a friend or relative who suffers from dementia, and may not be able to make coherent decisions about their health on their own. In short, living wills provide directives to medical personnel about an end-of-life event, whereas medical powers of attorney provide the attorney in fact with the power to make general healthcare decisions for the principal.

AVOIDANCE OF ESTATE TAXES THROUGH THE USE OF LIFETIME GIFTING STRATEGIES

Gifting money from an estate is an effective way to reduce taxes before it comes time to settle the estate. The maximum amount that an individual may gift per year without incurring the gift tax is $16,000 (per recipient) as of 2022. For taxpayers who file "married filing jointly," the maximum for the couple is $32,000. Alternatively, the taxpayer can pay qualified college expenses or medical expenses on behalf of another to reduce the estate. There is no limit to these strategies. There is also no limit to the transfer of assets between spouses. This helps when one spouse is in much poorer health but may have many more assets than the other. As long as there exists a qualifying relationship between the giftor and giftee, these are legal and useful strategies for reducing the taxpayer's estate taxes.

INTER-VIVOS AND TESTAMENTARY CHARITABLE GIVING IN REDUCING ESTATE TAXES

The use of the terms inter-vivos and testamentary differentiate the time period in which the charitable giving is performed. Inter-vivos giving means that the charitable gift was given while the taxpayer was alive, and testamentary gifts are those gifts given after the person has passed away. The ways in which inter-vivos gifting is accomplished are through the use of charitable trusts (i.e., charitable remainder trust), the establishment of private charitable foundations, setting up donor-advised funds, and just giving cash or non-cash donations. Through the use of appropriate estate planning techniques, decedents may establish charitable trusts and private charitable foundations after their death. They may also give directly from their estate through instructions contained in their will, or establish that spousal disclaimers be passed to charity.

Marital Deduction and Bypass Trusts

The marital deduction and bypass trusts are used for estate planning when a person dies and leaves a surviving spouse. In the event that the decedent chooses the marital deduction option, his or her spouse must inherit all of the deceased's property, but the deceased's estate receives the full marital deduction when settling the estate's taxes. This may be helpful at the time, but it creates a large tax consequence at the death of the second spouse. Bypass trusts are set up to address this problem. If a bypass trust is used, the marital deduction may not be taken. When the taxes for an estate are settled using a bypass trust, the executor may apply a "unified credit" and take the applicable tax reduction. This amount is set aside, and the surviving spouse does not receive this amount but may use it for health, education, maintenance, and support without tax consequences. The most effective strategy is to put the most highly appreciated assets in the trust so that they are not taxed at fair market value.

Satisfying Liquidity Needs

Through Life Insurance

Having quick and easy access to cash is essential in the expedient settlement of estates for expenses such as funeral costs and debts owed by the deceased. Life insurance is often regarded as the best and most efficient means of providing liquidity to assist in estate settlement. Life insurance proceeds are paid tax-free, so there will be no additional tax at the liquidity event. The proceeds are made immediately available so that expenses may be paid in a timely fashion. Having life insurance also prevents the decedent's heirs from having to take loans to pay expenses. Additionally, the typical life insurance plan will be purchased for much less than the death benefit. This assists in paying expenses associated with the estate without having to pay a larger portion of the estate's assets, which would have been necessary if the decedent had not purchased the life insurance policy.

Using an Installment Plan Through IRC Section 6166

Having quick and easy access to cash is essential in the expedient settlement of estates for expenses such as funeral costs and debts owed by the deceased. In the event that life insurance proceeds are not available to cover expenses, the heirs may have to take loans or apply for installment plans to cover expenses. If the estate taxes are from a closely held business interest (must be greater than 35 percent of the estate), then the heirs may pay the taxes from the estate in 10 equal installments under Internal Revenue Code 6166. The payments may be made over 14 years, and interest-only payments may be made during the first four years. To qualify under Code 6166, the business must have been a sole proprietorship, partnership, or corporation, and continue to operate after the decedent's death. The interest paid on IRC 6166 tax installments may not be deducted from the payers' adjusted gross income.

Psychology of Financial Planning

CLIENT AND PLANNER ATTITUDES, VALUES, BIASES
RISK TOLERANCE

Objective risk tolerance is the objective or quantitative measurement of a client's financial capacity to withstand the impact of a potential financial loss when considering a decision that involves risk. **Subjective risk tolerance** is the subjective or qualitative measurement of a client's risk tolerance, regardless of their financial capacity to withstand a financial loss. It measures a client's emotional tolerance for risk and their perceptions surrounding taking risks. Both measurements play an important role in determining where a client's risk tolerance falls on the spectrum between risk-averse and risk-seeking parameters.

By understanding not only a client's *financial capacity* (objective tolerance) to withstand a financial loss in the short term but their *emotional capacity* (subjective tolerance) to withstand the loss as well, financial planners can find the right balance between a client's reported risk tolerance and their assessed risk tolerance. This leads to improved recommendations and better adherence to the fiduciary standard.

RISK CAPACITY

Risk capacity is the level of risk that a client's individual financial circumstances can withstand when evaluating the impact of a financial decision that involves risk. A client's risk capacity can constrain the level of risk a client is willing to accept when faced with a potential for loss. A potential loss that could result in a significant loss of wealth will generally limit the amount of risk a client is willing to take.

Clients will begin to constrain their risk tolerance levels at the point when the loss is perceived to negatively impact their present financial well-being. Clients with a higher capacity for risky outcomes who don't perceive the loss to impact their present financial well-being will be less likely to constrain their risk tolerance. Understanding a client's risk capacity and how it impacts the client's decisions can help financial planners improve how they approach conversations regarding risk with their clients.

ASSESSING A CLIENT'S OVERALL RISK TOLERANCE

A client's **risk perception** is the perception a client has about a specific financial risk that is based on the client's beliefs and attitude toward risk. A client's **risk preference** is established based on the client's risk perception without regard for the risk factors involved in a specific financial decision. It is a measure of a client's overall attitude toward risk. **Risk literacy** is a measure of a client's proficiency in comprehending and responding to risk-related information and making risk-related decisions.

Risk perception, risk preference, and risk literacy are useful qualitative measures for assessing a client's overall risk tolerance. They enhance a financial planner's understanding of a client's tolerance for risk by providing qualitative information about a client's true risk tolerance beyond quantitative and objective assessments. Planners can use these concepts to help drive qualitative conversations with their clients to gain perspective on how clients perceive and respond to risk. Planners can help clients shift their risk perception, preference, and literacy through explanation, framing, and education.

143

ASSESSING SUBJECTIVE RISK TOLERANCE

Financial planners often rely on various methods to assess a client's subjective risk tolerance, such as using the planner's professional judgment, **heuristics**, **risk tolerance scales**, and **triangulation**. As planners gain experience in their practices, they can recognize certain behaviors or responses from clients surrounding conversations that concern risk, building the **planner's professional** knowledge and judgment of commonly occurring subjective risk factors. **Heuristics** are mental shortcuts that a financial planner uses, consciously or subconsciously, to frame a client's risk tolerance based on other activities in a client's life such as their career or leisure activities.

Planners often use established **risk tolerance scales** that ask clients questions about their risk tolerance but limit the answer choices to a handful of predefined responses. Planners then use scoring methods established with the risk tolerance scales to determine a client's risk tolerance. Oftentimes, planners use a combination, or **triangulation**, of subjective risk tolerance assessment methods to gain a better understanding of the client's risk tolerance instead of using just one method.

FRAMING

Planners' conversations with their clients on the topic of risk can create stress responses in a client. Clients often struggle to put risks in a perspective that allows them to understand the risk they are taking. **Framing** is a method of tying risks to familiar outcomes to help clients orient themselves so they can better understand the potential risk and reward of risk-related decisions.

Financial planners can use the concept of framing by providing clients with insight regarding the potential outcomes of a risk-related decision. This creates a framework for clients to evaluate the trade-off between the potential risk and reward of each outcome by comparing the outcomes to each other. By framing risk-related decisions in terms of their outcomes, financial planners can improve their understanding of a client's risk tolerance by observing how the client evaluates and chooses risk options.

PSYCHOLOGICAL ELEMENTS IN THE FINANCIAL PLANNING RELATIONSHIP

The financial planning relationship goes beyond the process of mathematical projections and the recommendation of financial-based solutions. Clients and planners both bring into the relationship psychologically driven perceptions, biases, and belief systems that can impact the relationship. Financial planners have a responsibility to get to know their clients in personal ways that help the planner understand a client's underlying motivation for financial decisions and behaviors. To achieve this, planners must ensure that they don't let their personal values and belief systems cloud their judgment of their clients' needs.

To build a lasting, personal relationship with a financial planner, a client needs to feel heard and understood. Financial planners can build trust with their clients by seeking out shared values that help the planner and client connect on a more personal level. These connections can help a planner gain insight into the client's values and belief systems, which can help facilitate conversations regarding risk management, wealth growth, and wealth decumulation through retirement income and estate planning.

MASLOW'S MOTIVATIONAL THEORY

Maslow's hierarchy of needs theory offers a pyramidal illustration that shows the extrinsic and intrinsic motivations for needs universal to all humankind. Starting from the base and moving to the tip, it shows that basic physiological needs such as food and water must be met before the need for safety can be fulfilled. Once these extrinsic, or externally motivated, needs are met, clients can focus on intrinsic, or internally motivated, psychological and self-fulfillment needs. Clients must fulfill the need for belongingness and love before they can focus on their self-esteem through prestige and a feeling of accomplishment. The pinnacle of the pyramid is the need for self-fulfillment or self-actualization, where people can focus on achieving their full potential.

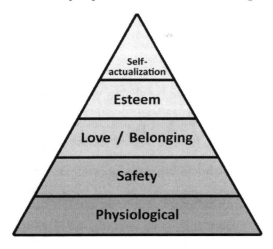

Planners can use Maslow's hierarchy of needs model to drive conversations with clients about meeting these needs in their present and future. Not until clients have reasonably secured their physiological and safety needs for their present and future should they consider spending financial means to achieve their intrinsic needs. Financial planners can help clients consider nonfinancial means for fulfilling these needs, allowing clients to focus their financial means on extrinsic needs while also being able to strive to fulfill intrinsic needs.

FAMILY FINANCIAL SOCIALIZATION MODEL

The **family financial socialization model** was developed to provide a framework for planners to understand how clients are socialized around money by their families. As we grow up, we develop attitudes, values, and beliefs about money that tie back to our childhoods and our experiences with our families. Our money stories can reveal our **money scripts**, which are unconscious beliefs developed around money that influence how we think about money. These money scripts can be related to how we feel about money, such as when we have it and when we don't, and how we feel about others when they do or don't have money.

The model explains how our attitudes and beliefs surrounding money don't only come from money lessons taught to us purposely by our caregivers but are also learned through our observations of how others around us react to financially related matters. By having clients tell their money stories, planners can learn about their clients' money scripts by recognizing patterns of behavior and decision-making outcomes surrounding financial matters revealed in the stories. Planners can use this information to gauge clients' financial literacy and provide a starting point for helping clients fill in their financial knowledge gaps.

FINANCIAL SELF-EFFICACY

Financial self-efficacy is measured by the confidence level a client has in understanding financially related matters and handling financially related tasks. A client with higher financial self-efficacy is more likely to persevere during financially uncertain times and is also more likely to be better financially positioned to focus on achieving self-actualization. Research shows that clients with higher self-efficacy are better able to meet their needs up and down the Maslow's hierarchy of needs model.

145

There are some universal strategies that planners can use to help clients increase their financial self-efficacy. Planners can help clients establish small, tangible tasks that clients feel are achievable. Planners should also strive to understand a client's preferred learning style. Planners can also provide frequent positive feedback to encourage clients to remain on track and help them practice self-empathy when making financially related mistakes.

SELF-DETERMINATION THEORY

Self-determination theory states that clients are more likely to achieve their goals when they feel confident in their ability to make autonomous and competent financial decisions that result in positive outcomes. The theory supports the view that frequent positive feedback provided by planners can help clients build confidence in their ability to competently make financially related decisions and to feel that they have some control over their financial lives. This positive feedback creates a stronger working relationship between the client and planner.

To maintain a strong relationship with a planner, a client has to feel as though the planner has faith in the client's ability to achieve their goals. Planners can use frequent positive feedback to set the stage for **positive expectancy**, where they use positive reinforcement to help clients build confidence in their own abilities. This increased confidence in their ability to create positive outcomes helps clients remain motivated to achieve their goals.

TRANSTHEORETICAL MODEL OF CHANGE

The **transtheoretical model of change (TTM)** was developed to help assess an individual's willingness to accept and make a change. This willingness to change is contingent upon where the individual is in the decision-making process. The TTM outlines the five stages of decision-making, which are pre-contemplation, contemplation, preparation, action, and maintenance.

The **pre-contemplation stage** is the stage in which an individual is not ready to make a change. This may be due to a lack of awareness or concern for the need for change. In the **contemplation stage**, an individual recognizes the need for and benefits of change but is not able to take action due to ambivalence, anxiety, or fear about an uncertain outcome. At this stage, the individual believes they will make the change sometime in the future. In the **preparation stage**, an individual is ready to make a change in the near future and is preparing for the change. When individuals are ready to make a change currently, they are in the **action stage**. The TTM recognizes that change is hard and thus includes a **maintenance stage** in which an individual must take active steps to maintain the change.

CULTURAL BELIEFS AND VALUES

Studies show there is a link between goal attainment and well-being. A client's values and goals are the deepest manifestations of the culture they grew up around. For a planner to help a client achieve their goals effectively, the planner must gain an understanding of the client's culture and how the attainment of their goals ties into that culture. A client's culture can have an impact on the financial planning relationship and trust between the client and the planner. A client must sense from the financial planner that they are being heard and understood by the planner and are in an environment of acceptance and understanding.

Planners can gain an understanding of a client's culture through qualitative assessments and having meaningful conversations with clients about their past experiences and observations surrounding money. Clients may reveal social norms and obligations they are beholden to in their culture that could influence how they view achieving their personal goals. Differences in cultural values within a family can also create barriers to goal setting and the financial planning process.

COLLECTIVIST VS. INDIVIDUALIST CULTURES

Clients' values and goals are deeply tied to the social culture they are a part of. For planners to effectively help clients attain their goals, they must gain an understanding of their clients' cultures and their impact on the financial planning process. **Collectivist cultures** prioritize well-being at the community level and expect members to act with unity and selflessness. **Individualist cultures** focus more on independence and personal identity.

When a client is part of a collectivist culture, their financial goals can be impacted by the needs of their community. Members may be required to support other family members or send money to relatives in another country. A client may not prioritize saving for retirement because they come from a culture that depends on the able-bodied members of the community to care for the elder and disabled members of the community, and thus they have an expectation that they will be cared for in their retirement years. Couples and families from individualist cultures may have conflicting attitudes and beliefs about money that can impact goal congruence and goal setting. Planners have a responsibility to understand how clients' cultures can impact the financial planning process.

NONVIOLENT COMMUNICATION

The financial planning process can reveal conflicts and power dynamics that impact goal congruence between couples, families, and even between the client and planner. Goal congruence often cannot be achieved when there is a power imbalance between parties, because the party with the least power is less likely to assert their needs and wants in the goal-setting conversation. Planners have an obligation to make recommendations that are in the best interest of all the parties involved in the financial planning process.

To level a power imbalance in a conversation about goals, a planner can use the **four-step method of nonviolent communication**. The first step is for the client(s) and planner to share their **observations** about an issue without blame, criticism, or exaggeration. The second step is to discuss the **feelings** that each party experiences when they discuss the issue. In the third step, the parties each discuss their **needs** or values surrounding the issue. Finally, each party makes their **requests** to take action or have an action taken by another party. This communication process creates a framework that allows each party an opportunity to express their concerns and wants equitably in order to build goal congruence.

BEHAVIORAL FINANCE

COGNITIVE BIASES AND HEURISTICS ON DECISION-MAKING

Cognitive biases and **heuristics** are mental algorithms relied upon by individuals when they don't have access to, or lack the ability to process, relevant information when facing matters of uncertainty. These biases can occur when a client relies on recently learned information (**availability bias**) or prominent information (**recency or persuasion bias**) that may seem familiar (**familiarity bias**), without knowing the validity or relevancy of the information. A client may use stereotyping (**representative bias**) to decide if they wish to work with a planner or rely on **mental accounting** (compartmentalizing cash flows and assets) when discussing financial goals.

These biases can impact a client's ability to make rational decisions, which can negatively impact the outcome of the financial planning process. When a client has conflicting thoughts about a decision (cognitive dissonance), they look for ways to resolve the conflict. This can lead them to look for ways to resolve the conflict by taking no action (**status quo bias**), finding validation for their beliefs (**confirmation bias or sunk cost fallacy**), or overweighting the value (endowment effect) of something related to the decision. Planners can also negatively impact the financial planning process if they are not aware of their own cognitive biases.

SYSTEM-BASED DECISION-MAKING THINKING PROCESSES

In financial planning practices, a dual process of thinking has been observed in the decision-making process. **System 1** thinking uses an intuitive process that produces quick decision-making that often relies on cognitive biases and heuristics, which are prone to producing cognitive errors. When System 1 thinking (fast thinking) is engaged, there is very little mental processing of information. **System 2** uses a reflective decision-making process that is slow, deliberate, and more logic-based. System 2 thinking (slow thinking) requires more energy and mental processing of relevant information when making decisions.

The system engaged by a client when goal setting can have a significant impact on the financial planning process. If a client depends on System 1 thinking when discussing financial goals, they may not give the planner correct or complete information, making it difficult for the planner to help a client achieve their goals. Planners can help clients engage their System 2 thinking by asking questions that challenge the client to think deeply about their perceptions and goals and how they relate to each other.

OVERCOMING DECISION-MAKING BIAS AND PSYCHOLOGICAL BARRIERS

To facilitate the financial planning process, it is important for financial planners to help clients reduce biases in their decision-making. Before planners can achieve this, they need to be aware of four factors that can impact the decision-making process: **distraction effects**, **fatigue**, **individual differences**, and **visceral influences**. If a client is distracted, tired, or experiencing a mental or emotional block, they are less likely to engage in System 2 (slow) thinking when discussing financial planning matters, which can lead to cognitive errors in decision-making.

One method a planner can use to help a client reduce cognitive biases and psychological barriers to the financial planning process is called **modifying the decision maker**. A planner can help shift a client from System 1 thinking to System 2 thinking by providing education and checklists of specific actions, which can improve a client's cognitive engagement in the process. A second method is called **modifying the environment**. This method aims to change the way a client sees a situation, such as presenting savings recommendations in weekly or monthly amounts as opposed to annual amounts. By creating small nudges that shift a client's perspective on their situation, planners can improve their clients' responsiveness to recommendations.

COGNITIVE BIASES

Clients are not the only ones susceptible to cognitive biases. Financial planners can fall victim to **stereotyping** clients based on their wealth, profession, gender, or age, which can lead the planner to make assumptions that influence their recommendations in suboptimal ways. A planner may lack **situational awareness** of their client if they don't take time to get to know their client's personal circumstances or risk tolerance. A planner could be guilty of applying **herding behavior** to their clients' portfolios if they recommend investments used by other investment professionals without personally researching those investments.

Financial planners have a fiduciary duty to provide advice in the best interest of their clients. Planners can better ensure they meet this requirement by recognizing that they themselves can also fall prey to cognitive biases. Planners can reduce their cognitive biases by using questionnaires, assessments, and checklists to gather information and by having meaningful conversations with their clients with a focus on the clients' individual needs.

WILLINGNESS TO ESTABLISH GOALS

A client's willingness to establish goals is often contingent upon how they perceive their financial well-being. Planners can evaluate a client's perceived well-being by learning about the client's financial comfort zone, financial socialization, and money beliefs. By discussing with clients their past financial experiences and behaviors, planners can gain an understanding of how a client's perception has developed over time.

A client's **financial comfort zone** refers to the client's familiarity and comfort with frequently occurring financial matters. The further a financial matter is outside of a client's comfort zone, the more resistance a planner may experience from a client when establishing goals. A client's **financial socialization** is the development of their financial values, attitudes, and behaviors over their lifetime. Clients who have greater socialization and comfort with their financial status are more inclined toward goal setting. Having conversations about a client's **money beliefs**, which are notions or patterns of beliefs surrounding money, can help a planner understand a client's patterns of behavior surrounding money and provide intervention through guidance and recommendations that can help a client improve their perception of well-being and willingness to set goals.

PATHOLOGICAL FINANCIAL BEHAVIORS

Certain pathological financial behaviors have been associated with poor financial socialization and negatively related money beliefs and generally result in poor financial outcomes. These behaviors can have a major impact on a client's finances, narrowing the client's financial comfort zone. Five common pathological financial behaviors are:

- **Compulsive buying disorder**—obsessive spending that leads to financial hardship
- **Gambling disorder**—persistent and recurring betting or financial risk-taking behavior that impacts an individual's ability to meet financial obligations
- **Hoarding disorder**—excessive accumulation of belongings over a period of time without decumulation, which can result in reduced quality of life and living space
- **Financial dependence**—reliance on others for nonwork income that leads to fear, anxiety, or a lack of motivation to work or achieve goals
- **Financial enabling**—an inability to say no to financial requests from family or friends, even to one's own financial detriment

A client's financial comfort zone is closely tied to their financial status. When a client's financial status becomes incompatible with their financial comfort zone, decision-making can become impulsive and be impacted by cognitive errors.

MONEY SCRIPT CATEGORIES

Four major money script attitudes that lead to predictive behavior have been commonly identified in financial planning practices. Money scripts are subconscious beliefs held by individuals about money that are deeply rooted in childhood experiences and family financial socialization.

- **Money avoidance**—clients with a money avoidance script associate wealth with greed and power and negatively associate money with bad outcomes.
- **Money worship**—clients with a money worship script believe that money provides power and happiness and is the solution to all problems.
- **Money status**—clients with a money status script tie their personal worth to their financial wealth.
- **Money vigilance**—clients with a money vigilance script tend to be more frugal and vigilant when it comes to saving but frequently suffer from anxiety about running out of money.

149

Clients with higher levels of debt and lower levels of income and net worth have been associated with money avoidance, money worship, and money status scripts. Clients with these scripts have also been shown to be associated with pathological financial behaviors such as compulsive buying, gambling, hoarding, financial dependence, and enabling. Planners should use money script assessments to help them determine a client's money script.

HELPING CLIENTS OVERCOME PSYCHOLOGICAL BARRIERS

Planners frequently come up against common psychological barriers with clients that impact the financial planning process and planners' ability to provide guidance in the best interest of their clients. There are numerous tools and strategies that planners can use to identify these psychological barriers and help clients move past them. During the data-gathering step of the process, planners can employ assessments and questionnaires designed to determine clients' risk tolerance and attitudes about money, as well as information about clients' cultural backgrounds and values.

Planners have access to psychometrically designed questionnaires and scales that can measure clients' feelings of well-being and risk tolerance. Planners can also engage in motivational interviewing, which is a type of therapeutic communication technique to help clients recognize their own problematic financial behaviors and associated attitudes about money. Planners can also use nudging and framing techniques to help clients shift their perspectives on psychological barriers. Providing checklists of small, actionable tasks can also help clients recognize their progress in the financial planning process.

SOURCES OF MONEY CONFLICT

MOTIVATION

Motivation to solve a financial problem or achieve financial goals is the primary reason that clients seek out financial planners and financial advice. Depending on a client's individual financial situation, they are generally motivated to meet physical or material needs and work toward self-actualization. Once a client reaches out to a planner, it is the planner's obligation to understand the client's motivation to seek out advice as well as their motivation to follow recommendations and achieve their goals.

Planners can use their understanding of a client's motivation to help their client establish goals and keep them on track to achieve those goals. Clients' motivation stems from two financial perspectives: *exterior* or traditional financial concerns for physical needs and security, and *interior* or personal motivation to achieve goals or solve a problem. A client's overall motivation is to achieve well-being. Planners can help their clients achieve their goals by helping clients understand the "why" or meaning behind their motivation. Clients are more likely to achieve goals that are congruent with their motivations.

WELL-BEING

Well-being is defined as the state of being comfortable, healthy, or happy financially, physically, and emotionally/spiritually. When clients are unwell in any of these areas, they will likely experience psychological barriers to the financial planning process. **Financial well-being** is the ability to meet present needs and prepare for future needs. **Physical well-being** is tied to the ability to live and act with independence. **Emotional/spiritual well-being** is a state of relative peace with oneself. To be effective in guiding a client through the financial planning process, planners need to conduct assessments to determine a client's well-being in all three areas.

Planners may find that while a client's financial and physical well-being may not be directly related to each other, a client's emotional/spiritual well-being is often deeply tied to their physical and financial well-being. A client who lacks the physical or financial capability to meet their essential needs will find it difficult to achieve their goals and attain well-being overall. Planners must recognize that they are essentially in the well-being business, and part of their role is to help clients transition to improved well-being.

TRANSITIONS

Transitions are steps of change a client may go through or need to go through when progressing toward their goals. Clients can experience transitions when they achieve a personal or professional milestone, lose a loved one or an income source, receive an inheritance, or face disability or retirement, to name just a few events that can trigger the necessity for transition. Planners who sustain long-term relationships with clients often witness and support clients, and sometimes even generations, through multiple periods of transition. Nine common emotions and behaviors associated with the transitioning process are:

- Loss of identity (with marriage, retirement, or a death)
- Feelings of confusion or overwhelm (due to lack of understanding or amount of information)
- Feelings of hopelessness (in face of uncertainty)
- Feelings of euphoria or invincibility (due to financial improvement)
- Inability to focus or preoccupation with a particular issue (psychological barrier)
- Behaving inconsistently (saying one thing and doing another)
- Feelings of anger or behaving combatively
- Feelings of exhaustion
- Numbness or indifference toward an issue (lack of interest in process)

It is important for planners to exercise awareness of and alertness to these emotions and behaviors and help their clients become aware of and work through them.

WILLINGNESS AND MOTIVATION TO CHANGE

A large part of a financial planner's role is to be an agent for change. The challenge planners face is that research shows that only 20 percent of clients are in the action stage of the transtheoretical model of change when they engage a planner. For these clients, the relationship between their willingness to change and their motivation to change is positively correlated. These are relatively easy clients. For the other 80 percent, it is important for planners to be able to assess clients' willingness to change and help them develop motivation to change.

A client's lack of motivation to change may be related to the client's money script or financial trauma. The client may demonstrate a willingness to change, but because of psychological barriers, the client cannot align their willingness to change with their motivation for change. Planners must work with clients to identify and change the problematic behavior in order for clients to align their willingness and motivation to change. By developing an internal awareness and attunement of their own challenges and deploying deep listening skills when working with clients, planners can strengthen their skill set in recognizing and helping clients build their motivation to change.

SOURCES OF MONEY CONFLICT

Because money is a scarce resource that needs to be effectively managed to optimize its use, conflict can arise when two or more individuals are involved in deciding the allocation of financial resources. Money conflicts can occur between couples, parents and children, adult siblings, and even between a client and planner. These conflicts arise due to perceived differences between the parties and their desires for how financial resources should be allocated.

Major sources of money conflict are money script differences, cultural differences, power imbalances, and lack of financial transparency. Differences in attitudes and beliefs about money (**money script differences**) can be a significant source of conflict in a relationship. **Cultural differences**, like money script differences, stem from parties' backgrounds, histories, and financial socialization and can be major sources of conflict. **Power imbalances**, which can occur because of differences in income, education, age, or other disparities, may cause conflict due to one party's sense of unfairness or entitlement. When there is a lack of **financial transparency,** conflict is inevitable due to one party hiding debt or resources from another interested party. These conflicts can cause significant barriers to the financial planning process and must be resolved to move forward.

FINANCIAL TRANSPARENCY

Financial transparency is the act of being open and honest about financial matters and is imperative for effective financial planning. When a client is not transparent with a financial partner or with a financial planner, the result of the financial planning process will be impacted. If a source of debt or income is not disclosed during the process, then the goals in the plan may not be achievable or the recommendations suitable.

Being financially transparent can be seen as risky. The disclosing party may fear being shamed or hearing demands for retribution. They may fear that someone may lose respect for them or that they will lose influence over others. If they are hiding income or assets, they may feel they will lose some autonomy or reveal a perceived power imbalance or be seen as untrustworthy. Financial transparency requires trust, and it can create trust when it is reciprocated. Lack of financial transparency is a source of money conflict that financial planners must uncover and work to resolve to ensure that the plan is congruent with a client's actual situation.

FINANCIAL CONFLICT

Financial conflict exists when there is a lack of financial alignment or goal congruence between parties. The conflict is less about money or even the communication about money, but rather the emotional responses the conflict elicits. These emotional responses create psychological barriers that prevent the parties from resolving the issue. Since a planner's objective is to help clients achieve well-being, recognizing and resolving conflict are necessary skills for success.

In the absence of a client stating verbally that they have a conflict, planners may observe more subtle cues of conflict on the horizon. Visible agitation, sighing, fidgeting, or other signs that the client's mind or focus is not fully present during an interaction can indicate that a client is not receptive to the conversation. A planner may observe where clients sit in juxtaposition to each other or sense tension between them. There may be physiological signs such as cold, clammy hands (felt during a handshake), sweating, or developing red patches on the skin. To resolve conflict, planners can use communication techniques that display empathy, active and responsive listening, and assertive messaging.

AREAS OF FINANCIAL CONFLICT

- **Differences in values**—clients from different cultures, backgrounds, and financial socialization.
- **Differences in spending habits**—how interested parties manage their personal and joint financial resources can lead to conflict. These differences can be reflected in credit scores, debt or savings balances, and financial and nonfinancial asset accrual.
- **Power imbalances**—differences in assets, income, income stability, or even a perception of financial unfairness.
- **Gender differences**—women continue to earn less than men and generally do not have a pathway to sustainable income and asset growth.
- **Lack of financial transparency**—when a lack of financial transparency is revealed, trust is broken. Transparency can lead to feelings of exposure and vulnerability.
- **Acts of financial infidelity**—related to a lack of financial transparency, acts of financial infidelity are acts of financial deception which lead to mistrust by others.
- **Holistic well-being**—good mental health is as important as physical and financial health. Individuals who are depressed or anxious will have difficulty engaging in conflict resolution or efforts toward goal congruence.

Studies show that goal congruence in a relationship is predictive of relationship satisfaction. Planners who can identify and effectively resolve conflict will better succeed in helping clients achieve goal congruence and overall well-being.

GOAL CONGRUENCE

Studies show that goal congruence in a relationship is predictive of relationship satisfaction. Goal incongruence has been likened to two people facing each other in a canoe, each paddling as hard as they can, going nowhere fast. When people work against each other it creates conflict, and they cannot come to an agreement on how to achieve a goal or manage scarce financial assets. Goal incongruence can also exist when only one person wants to take an action and the other wishes to preserve the status quo.

Planners can help clients reduce anxiety about conflict by letting them know that conflict is normal. Planners can also use principles of positive psychology to help clients recognize the value of working together and the potential positive outcomes of doing so. Planners can have clients discuss their money scripts with each other to gain a better understanding of the underlying source of conflict. Goal congruence requires trust, understanding, communication, and collaboration between parties. To achieve goal congruence, planners must know how to reduce conflict to help clients face the same way in the canoe and paddle together toward a common goal.

SHOWING BIAS OR FAVORITISM

Financial planners have an obligation to act in the best interest of their clients. When planners show bias or favoritism toward one client over another or even toward a planner's own value system over a client's value system, planners cannot meet their obligation and may impact the goal congruence between joint clients. Planners must be able to recognize feelings of bias in themselves and take steps not to act on bias or show favoritism.

One way planners can mitigate their risk of bias is to divide their focus equally between each client in the conversation. Planners should try not to engage more with a vocal client than a less vocal client. Planners should also avoid showing favoritism toward a client whose values may align with the planner's values or recommendations. To avoid bias and favoritism, planners should engage in active listening and encourage all parties to make their needs and wants known. Planners should

153

focus on helping clients find the best solution for them and not just the solution that the planner supports.

AMBIVALENCE

Goal ambivalence is a type of goal incongruence, but instead of there being conflict between the clients, there is conflict *within* the clients themselves. Clients who are experiencing goal ambivalence are conflicted with opposing emotions about an action they want to take or maybe feel they should take. The pull of the polarizing emotions keeps the client from taking any action, including setting goals. Ambivalence can lead to missed opportunities or poor outcomes if the client doesn't take action. Planners need to try to help clients get past their ambivalence to help them establish and achieve congruent goals.

Planners can take steps to help clients break their ambivalence. Planners can encourage clients to be curious about the emotions causing the ambivalence. Planners can also help clients realize that they are not defined by their mistakes or behavior, but rather that their mistakes and behavior are a source of learning and personal growth. One method is to have a client have a dialogue with themselves about each side of the conflict and recognize the feelings the dialogue initiates. Planners can also introduce clients to the value of meditation to access their emotions more deeply.

FINANCIAL MANIPULATION
MANIFESTATIONS OF FINANCIAL MANIPULATION

Financial manipulation is defined as financial enabling, financial control, or financial abuse for personal gain. This type of abuse can occur in different types of relationships, such as between spouses or romantic partners, family members (often from different generations), and possibly even between a client and a planner.

Financial enabling is the repeated act of lending or giving money to a family member or friend that the giver (enabler) knows won't be reimbursed or returned by the receiver. Financial enabling does not necessarily start out as abuse or intent to abuse. Financial enabling can turn into **financial abuse** if the receiver becomes financially dependent on the enabler, or the enabler begins to feel entitled to dictate demands. An imbalance of power, particularly a financial imbalance, can lead to conflict if one individual controls most or all of the financial decisions in a relationship. This **financial control** can lead to resentment or sabotage of joint financial goals by the individual not in control. Financial abuse is emotionally charged, as well as being highly correlated with or a prominent sign of domestic abuse. An abuser uses financial control to prevent their target from leaving the relationship or to force them to follow demands.

SOURCES OF FINANCIAL MANIPULATION

Money is a scarce financial resource and thus a common source of conflict. It drives competitive behavior, can create power imbalances, and invites temptation and envy. When money is used as a source of power, that power can be used for **financial manipulation**. The underlying behavior of financial manipulation can be driven by childhood experiences, such as mimicking observed behavior, expecting a partner to replicate childhood experiences (such as becoming a stay-at-home mom), or in retaliation for behavior inflicted upon them in their past (e.g., treating others how they felt they were treated).

Planners are in a particular position to spot and identify financial manipulation, given their access to client financial information. It is important for planners to know that clients may not intend to manipulate or even realize they are being manipulative. Planners can use communication and listening skills to look for patterns of behavior and engage clients equally to allow for all parties to express themselves. Planners should look for signs that manipulation has turned abusive, as can occur between spouses or romantic partners, or in cases of elder abuse, between generations. Financial manipulation becomes abuse when it's used to restrict another's financial independence.

PRINCIPLES OF COUNSELING

DEVELOPING COUNSELING SKILLS

Financial planning is more than just an exchange of services for money. Financial matters are personal and emotional. Revealing their finances can lead to clients feeling vulnerability, shame, ineptness, resistance to change, or fear of being reprimanded for their past or current financial behaviors. It is essential for planners to establish counseling skills to help clients recognize these emotional barriers if they are going to help clients transition through change to well-being.

Planners must be able to provide a space and environment to their clients that breeds trust and feels safe if they wish clients to be open with them. Planners must also be equipped with communication techniques that can reveal and resolve a lack of transparency, conflict, and goal incongruence. Planners must also internalize these skills to gain a better understanding of how different values, lived experiences, and financial socialization can impact the financial planning process. A planner who does not recognize their own cultural and personal biases will likely not be able to recognize these biases in clients. Thus, the planner not only risks being unable to effectively help their clients achieve well-being but also violating their sworn-to code of ethics and fiduciary obligation.

VERBAL AND NONVERBAL COMMUNICATION

Effective communication is the cornerstone for building trust and developing a good working relationship with clients. Communication comes in many forms that we don't necessarily recognize consciously but react to subconsciously. How the client and the planner sit can send **nonverbal communication** cues. If clients are slouching, arms crossed, eyes down, or focused on fumbling with papers or technology, these may be *nonverbal cues* that they are not actively engaged in the exchange. Planners can send their own cues to a client by being attentive, open, and engaged in the exchange.

Verbal communication is more than just words. There is pacing, which is the quickness or slowness of someone's speech. Planners can match the pacing of a client's speech and then slow the pace if needed, which the client will then match. A planner can also *re*state, paraphrase, or summarize back to a client what was heard to communicate attentiveness and understanding. The type of questioning used can also improve communication engagement. Close-ended questions yield yes/no or single-word answers, essentially ending the communication. Planners can use open-ended questions to engage the client and encourage openness to facilitate the financial planning process.

SPATIAL ARRANGEMENT AND ACTIVE LISTENING

Financial planning is a very personal experience that clients may approach with resistance, fear, and lack of transparency. It is the planner's goal to help clients get motivated toward change and help them transition through the stages of change. This requires building trust between the planner and client that will invite a more open exchange of information and ideas. Planners need to consider how the environment they design facilitates that open exchange.

The **spatial arrangement** of the meeting place can impact the openness of a conversation. If a planner is sitting behind a desk and a computer, this puts a barrier between the client and planner that can impact a client's openness toward the planner. Virtual meetings can be particularly difficult due to being in different locations. Creating a comfortable, engaging physical or virtual environment can lead to more transparency from the client. Planners can also use **active listening skills** to demonstrate empathy and responsivity to clients. When planners talk less and listen more, avoid focusing on their own talking points, show curiosity about what clients are saying, and allow for more silence in the exchange for information processing, clients tend to relax and open up more.

DEVELOPING CULTURAL HUMILITY

Theories can provide frameworks from which financial planners can build awareness about factors that impact the financial planning process. Counseling theory introduces the concept of **cultural humility**. Someone's culture is not just about someone's ethnicity, race, religion, or region of the world they grew up in but also how they were socialized around people and other social factors (including money). Cultural humility is the concept of self-reflection and self-critique, where one learns more about themselves and their culture through the lens of another's culture.

When planners develop cultural humility, they can gain a better awareness and understanding of clients' values and goals, create connections to clients that can build trust and create transparency, and provide guidance on the best ways to help clients transition through change. Planners must avoid stereotyping clients or assuming that clients "think just like me." Developing cultural humility is a lifelong process of evolvement as one becomes increasingly aware of the various factors of cultural humility. Planners can use the acronym **ADDRESSING** to help them remember that cultural factors can stem from people's **a**ge and generation, **d**evelopmental disability, **d**isability (physical), **r**eligion, **e**thnicity/race, **s**ocioeconomic status, **s**exual orientation, **n**ational origin/language, and **g**ender.

TRUST

Trust is the cornerstone of the financial planning relationship. Without trust, clients will likely lack transparency and openness and be less likely to commit to the process. Studies have shown that planners often have an inflated sense of how much trust they have established with a client. To build trust, planners must demonstrate credibility through competence and give clients a sense that the planner will act in the client's best interest. The **Commitment-Trust Theory** highlights the concept that planners can increase their efficiency, productivity, and effectiveness for their clients by focusing on activities that promote commitment and trust, building a foundation for long-term planner-client relationships.

When trust is broken, it will need to be repaired for the relationship to continue. Planners can break trust when they appear to be focused more on their agenda and recommendations than on listening to or engaging with a client, as well as not keeping clients' information confidential, being late or canceling appointments, not being timely with promised information, or taking sides in a joint client relationship. To try to repair trust, planners must reflect on the action(s) that may have caused the breakdown of trust and respond promptly and benevolently.

GENERAL PRINCIPLES OF EFFECTIVE COMMUNICATION
MULTIFACETED COMMUNICATION TECHNIQUES

Communication is an exchange of information to build a mutual understanding between parties. While planner-client communication is usually deliberate and purposeful, planners must be aware of nonverbal cues that could alter the verbal message the client is receiving. Both the planner and client can send nonverbal messages through eye contact (or lack thereof), spatial distance, and the tone, rate, and volume of speech.

By maintaining eye contact with a client, a planner can improve a client's willingness to be open and disclose information. Planners can use spatial distance to show respect appropriate to the relationship; more distance (about 3 ft.) with new clients versus closer spacing, appropriate to the length and familiarity of the relationship, with other clients. A client's tone, rate, and volume of speech can indicate to a planner a client's receptiveness to the communication process. Whether a client is speaking loudly, quickly, with an "edge" to their tone, or slowly and softly, planners can respond empathetically and attentively to communicate understanding and interest in the client's concerns. When planners develop an awareness of multifaceted communication, they can use it to deepen their exchanges with clients and improve their effectiveness.

COMMUNICATION PROCESS AND ALTERING AN INTENDED MESSAGE

Communication is processed along a channel that can change the message as it travels. The five components of the communication channel are the sender, message, form, receiver, and effect. When a sender sends a message, they must consider the form of the communication, who the receiver is, and how to use each component to ensure the effect of the message is unambiguous. How the receiver interprets the message will provide feedback. Depending on the form, a planner may not have access to verbal or nonverbal cues to effectively interpret the feedback, which is the receiver's responding message. Planners should consider carefully what message they wish to send, how they wish to send it, who is receiving it, and how the message will be interpreted to most effectively communicate with clients.

The environment in which the receiver receives the message can also impact the intended message. If a meeting is in a loud or non-private setting or disturbed by other sense-arresting activity (e.g., smells, temperature, humidity), the message can be lost through lack of hearing, distraction, or discomfort. When the environment is distracting, the message is diluted or lost completely, and the quality of the communication is greatly diminished.

CHOOSING A COMMUNICATION METHOD

How a financial planner communicates with clients can make the difference between long-term and short-term relationships. Whether they realize it or not, planners are communicating with their clients even when they aren't speaking. Clients notice the tone and cadence of speech, environment, presentation, questioning, attentiveness, responsiveness, and accuracy and usefulness of information, to name a few factors.

The communication process can also be impacted by cultural expectations, biases, and moods. Cultural norms and biases can set expectations for how a person expects an interaction to go. People from different cultures may have different ideas about greetings, such as who extends a hand first for a handshake or how far apart they stand or sit from others. Planners should also consider how specific they should make their message, whether they should use formal language, and the nature of words they choose. Women tend to prefer more specificity, formal language, and accurate descriptions, while men tend to focus on the broader message and prefer less formality, image-charged descriptors, and visual aids. Planners who successfully consider factors that can positively or negatively impact the communication process can help clients settle into a psychologically perceived comfort zone from which to safely communicate their concerns and vulnerabilities.

CRISIS EVENTS WITH SEVERE CONSEQUENCES

Crisis events with severe consequences are events that have a direct impact on clients' emotional and financial well-being. Financial planners are often one of the first advisers called when a client is experiencing a crisis event. A crisis event can be an unexpected medical diagnosis, a death of a loved one, a job loss, a natural disaster, or any other crisis that has a financial and emotional impact on a client's well-being. These events may require navigating insurance policies, investment portfolio adjustment or liquidation, cash flow disruptions, sale of property, and other emotionally charged financial transactions. They can also have an impact on the short- and long-term goals a client is working toward.

Given the mix of finances and emotions, decision-making can be impacted. During these events, planners must show empathy and support and employ effective communication skills that encourage clients to be transparent about their feelings and needs. Planners also need to be able to recognize when components of a client's crisis event are out of the scope of the planner's skill and experience and make appropriate referrals. Planners that help clients navigate crises successfully help their clients build resiliency and confidence for handling future crises.

FEAR RESPONSES

When clients are going through a crisis event with severe consequences, they will often experience physiological arousal, which is our bodies' adaptive response to stressors. These **fear responses** to uncertainty can fill our bodies with hormones that may lead us to flight, fight, or freeze. These response modes can create barriers to the decision-making process, which can impact navigation through the crisis and impact the achievement of short- and long-term goals.

Planners who are aware of these potential responses can look for nonverbal cues to help them identify a particular response in a client. A client who is in flight mode may avoid the issue. They will lack transparency or try to change the subject. A client who is in fight mode may speak aggressively, debate each recommendation, and object to referrals to other service providers. A client who is in freeze mode may be noticeably quiet, stare blankly, or say "everything is fine." Planners who recognize a fear response in a client can demonstrate empathy by tabling the meeting agenda and focusing on the client and their need to process their challenge. In these moments a planner may need to shift from financial expert to financial counselor.

CAPITAL AND RESOURCE SCAFFOLDING

While financial planners are trained in the ways of money, they can also help clients identify resources other than money to navigate a crisis event. This can effectively help clients build resiliency and confidence that will help them through future crises. Clients often aren't able to envision solutions outside of monetary resources. Planners have the unique perspective of witnessing clients go through crisis events and having access to the shared perspectives of other planners. Planners can use this information to help clients identify their own nonmonetary resources to find alternative solutions.

Capital can be broken down into the three categories of financial, social, and human capital. **Social capital** is the buildup of exchangeable value that comes from social interactions and building relationships. After a natural or personal disaster, our social networks can help us with emotional and physical support and provide access to opportunities that make the crisis more navigable. **Human capital** is the store of value that comes from education, training, experience, and innate abilities. People can use their human capital to build social capital by contributing their abilities to the well-being of others. People can also use their human capital to grow their financial capital by improving income-earning skills.

EMPATHY

For financial planners to meet their fiduciary obligation, they must be empathetic to their clients and their individual situations. To be truly empathetic, planners need to be empathetic with themselves and show self-compassion. Empathy is the ability to feel what someone else is feeling and imagine what it could be like to "be in their shoes." Planners need to practice self-reflection and self-compassion to understand how a client may feel. Only by becoming aware of people's differences, and how those differences can impact personal and financial outcomes, can planners help clients transition to well-being. Practicing empathy helps planners reduce their own biases and truly see the client and the client's needs and values.

As a planner you can use your **e**ye contact, **m**uscles of facial expression, **p**osture, **a**ffect, **t**one of voice, **h**earing, and **y**our response to demonstrate your **empathy** to a client. By maintaining appropriate eye contact, smiling, sitting in an open and receptive posture, moderating your verbal and nonverbal responses (your affect), speaking in an understanding tone, listening actively and attentively to the client, and responding in helpful, actionable ways, you can help your client find a comfort zone from which to collaborate on achieving well-being.

BUILDING AND PRACTICING EMPATHY

Financial planners are human and have their own individual experiences and socialization, have developed their own personal biases and money scripts, and can suffer from their own crisis events. Planners must learn to build and practice empathy toward their clients to ensure that they do not create conflicts of interest with their clients. Planners must also be aware of *compassion fatigue*, which can develop over time and lead to complacency and ambivalence toward their clients. By building and practicing empathy, planners can reduce their tendency toward compassion fatigue and their own biases.

Planners must understand the difference between **sympathy** and **empathy**, and **cognitive empathy** and **emotional empathy**. Sympathy is feeling sorry for someone, which is not necessarily an effort toward understanding a person's situation. Clients who sense sympathy rather than empathy from a planner may become resistant to the financial planner and the planning process. Emotional empathy is the ability to imagine what someone is feeling, whereas cognitive empathy is imagining what they are thinking. Planners must strive to practice cognitive and emotional empathy to help build trust with clients, reduce psychological barriers to the planning process, resolve conflict, and help clients transition to well-being.

CFP Practice Test

Want to take this practice test in an online interactive format?
Check out the bonus page, which includes interactive practice questions and
much more: **http://www.mometrix.com/bonus948/cfp**

SCAN HERE

1. A married couple would like to set up 529 Plan college education accounts for their two young grandchildren. For 2022, what is the maximum amount they could have contributed in total to both 529 plans without incurring gift tax?

   a. $16,000
   b. $32,000
   c. $160,000
   d. $320,000

2. Tom owns a small golf pro shop and has started a SEP IRA for himself and his employees in 2022. He wants to make minimal contributions into his employee's SEP IRAs. If Tom uses the most restrictive requirements to determine eligible employees, which of the following employees may he consider ineligible for contributions?

   a. Laura, age 21, who has worked for Tom for 3 years and received $10,000 in compensation
   b. Mary, age 65, who has worked for Tom for 20 years and received $40,000 in compensation
   c. Jack, age 22 who has worked for Tom for 5 years and received $660 in compensation
   d. Eric, age 18, who has worked for Tom for 4 years and received $8,000 in compensation

3. If structured correctly, which type(s) of ownership(s) will avoid probate and allow assets to pass directly to a planned beneficiary at the death of the owner?

1.	IRA
2.	Individual bank account
3.	JTWROS
4.	Joint Tenancy
5.	Revocable Trust

   a. 1 only
   b. 1, 2 and 3 only
   c. 3 and 4 only
   d. 1, 3, 4 and 5 only

4. Becky is an investor with a margin account. Her brokerage firm requires 50% as the initial margin, and 40% as the maintenance margin. She purchases a stock on margin for $14,000. The stock's value later drops to $10,000. What is Becky's initial margin amount and maintenance margin amount, respectively?

   a. $7,000 and $4,000
   b. $14,000 and $4,000
   c. $7,000 and $3,000
   d. $7,000 and $10,000

5. Tina, age 35, is married. She is a homemaker and doesn't work outside the home. Her husband, Tom, is a computer engineer who makes $100,000 annually. Their income tax filing status is Married Filing Jointly. Tina would like to know if she can contribute to her own Individual Retirement Account. Which of the following statements best describe Tina's situation?

   a. Tina can contribute to an IRA because her husband is a wage earner and they file their taxes jointly
   b. Tina cannot contribute to an IRA because she does not have earned income
   c. Tina cannot contribute to an IRA because of their high tax bracket
   d. More information is needed to determine if she qualifies to contribute to an IRA

6. Virginia is meeting with an estate planning attorney to have her estate planning documents drafted. Her intention is that these documents will provide for the full and legal distribution of her possessions and assets. Which estate planning documents will ensure that her specific bequests will be met at her death?

1.	A statutory will
2.	A codicil to her will
3.	A side letter of instruction
4.	A nuncupative will

   a. 1 only
   b. 1, 2, and 3 only
   c. 1 and 2 only
   d. 1, 3 and 4 only

7. When Susan passed away, she owned these assets: a life insurance policy of $100,000 with a properly named beneficiary, a home valued at $450,000 held JTWROS, jewelry valued at $35,000, an IRA valued at $575,000 with named beneficiary, an Irrevocable Trust of $375,000 for the benefit of her granddaughter Reese, and a car valued at $8,000 held fee simple by Susan. Based on this information, what is the value of Susan's Probate Estate?

   a. $0
   b. $143,000
   c. $418,000
   d. $43,000

8. With respect to gifting, which of the following individuals are required to file Form 709 with the Internal Revenue Service by April 15th of the year following such gifting activity?

1.	Tom, who made a gift of $10,000 to his daughter Laura
2.	Jim and Judy, who made a joint gift of $25,000 to their son John
3.	Maury, who gifted $100,000 to his wife, Tina
4.	Martin, who gifted $55,000 to the Red Cross

   a. 4 only
   b. 2 only
   c. 3 and 4 only
   d. 1, 2, 3, and 4

9. According to the Internal Revenue Code, Section 170(C), which entity is not considered a Qualifying Organization for purposes of charitable contributions?

   a. A cemetery company
   b. An organization created to prevent cruelty to animals
   c. Local Chamber of Commerce
   d. A public park

10. Cars International has a dividend payout ratio of 35% and pays a dividend of $2.25 per share. What are Cars International's earnings per share?

   a. $4.28
   b. $3.46
   c. $7.88
   d. $6.43

11. Thomas is purchasing his first home for $200,000 and plans to make a 15% down payment. The lender qualifies for a 30-year fixed rate loan on the remaining amount at 4.99% APR. Thomas wants to escrow the amount needed for property tax and insurance, which he believes will be around $5,000 annually. What amount of Thomas' monthly payments will be made to principal and interest of the loan?

   a. $1,324.45
   b. $1,328.23
   c. $911.56
   d. $907.78

12. Scott purchases 125 shares of QAZ stock in February at $80 per share. QAZ pays a quarterly dividend of $1.19 per share, which he receives for three quarters until he sells his shares at $89 each Scott's holding period return is...

   a. 15.71%
   b. 11.25%
   c. 13.96%
   d. 12.21%

13. American Incorporated wants to be viewed as a stable and mature company within its industry and is concerned about having a low Price to Earnings (P/E) ratio. Which of the following would increase the company's P/E?

   a. If the company sold more shares of common stock
   b. If the company repurchased outstanding stock
   c. A lower market price per share
   d. A 2:1 stock split

14. Andrea is debating between purchasing a taxable bond yielding 6% or a municipal bond yielding 4.2%. She is in the 28% federal tax bracket and 6% state tax bracket. The municipal bond is exempt from federal and state taxes. What is the municipal bond's taxable equivalent yield based on this information?

   a. 8.84%
   b. 5.83%
   c. 6.36%
   d. 4.46%

15. A Detroit Motors Dec call has a strike price of $45. Detroit Motors is currently trading at $50 per share and there are 1,200,000 shares outstanding. The premium on the call is $5.50. The fundamental value of the call is...

a. $0
b. $500
c. $50
d. $150

16. Your client would like to know the total risk of his portfolio based on his current asset allocation model. The total return on the portfolio for the previous 12 months was 8.25% and the portfolio has a standard deviation of 12.2. The rate on a 10-year Treasury Note is 3.55%. The portfolio has a beta of 1.2. Based on the Sharpe Ratio, what is the total risk of the client's portfolio?

a. 0.462
b. 0.676
c. 3.92
d. 0.385

17. Based on the Capital Asset Pricing Model and given the following information, what is the required rate of return on investment X?

Risk free rate	3.3%
Market return	6%
Beta	1.5
Standard deviation	17

a. 12.96%
b. 7.35%
c. 8.70%
d. 5.70%

18. All of the following are true regarding an S Corporation except...

a. S Corps are limited to 100 shareholders
b. an S Corp provides limited liability for shareholders
c. any classes of stock are permitted
d. income is passed through to the shareholders

19. Kathy has decided to participate in the commercial real estate business. She purchased a building for $425,000 and paid an additional $4,000 in closing costs. She hired contractors, for $72,000, to make the old building handicap accessible per state and federal laws. For income tax purposes, Kathy's cost basis for the property is...

a. $425,000
b. $429,000
c. $497,000
d. $501,000

20. Jeffrey has a $600,000 mortgage on his California home. He additionally takes out two home equity loans, one for $50,000 to fund his son's college education and another for $110,000 to add on to his home. What is the total principal from these loans on which he can deduct interest expenses?

a. $600,000
b. $710,000
c. $750,000
d. $760,000

21. Ann, age 71, works part-time, has both a Traditional IRA and a Roth IRA, and is concerned that her tax liability this year will be high, especially with any IRA distributions. Which of the following actions should Ann take to minimize her tax liability?

a. Make a contribution to her Roth IRA
b. Make a contribution to her Traditional IRA
c. Take her required minimum distribution (RMD) from her Traditional IRA, but no more
d. Convert part of her Traditional IRA balance to a Roth IRA

22. Rebecca, a stay-at-home mother with three dependent children, lost her husband Andrew in a car accident last month. Andrew was the sole breadwinner and maintained the family's health insurance coverage through his employer. All of the following are true regarding the family's COBRA benefits except...

a. under COBRA, Rebecca may be responsible to pay up to 102% of the cost of premiums on the plan
b. the three children will qualify for COBRA benefits for up to 36 months
c. Rebecca will qualify for COBRA benefits for up to 18 months
d. if Rebecca elects COBRA and fails to pay the necessary premiums, her family could lose coverage

23. Your client Jerry, age 25, would like to purchase life insurance to protect his young family in the event of his premature death. Based on the family's tight cash flow, he would like to keep the cost of his insurance minimal. However, Jerry has certain health conditions and is concerned about being denied coverage. The underwriter informs you that Jerry is eligible for coverage at his current age, but if his condition worsens he may become uninsurable in the near future. Which of the following policies is most appropriate for Jerry's situation?

a. 30-year term policy
b. Whole life insurance policy
c. Term insurance with conversion feature
d. Apply for a policy with more coverage than necessary since he may be uninsurable in the future

24. Which of the following expenses is not a qualified distribution of 529 plan funds?

a. Tuition at a private religious elementary school
b. Computers and internet access at college
c. Student loans
d. College application fees

25. Union Bank is working on a loan for your client, Dana. They inform Dana that the PITI of her home loan cannot exceed 28% of her income. Dana currently makes $67,000 per year. Taxes for the home are $3,500 per year and insurance is $1,000 per year. Dana is interested in a 30-year loan with an annual interest rate of 5.5%. Based on this information, what is the maximum loan amount Dana will qualify for?

   a. $275,337
   b. $209,291
   c. $212,240
   d. $269,000

26. If the Federal Reserve is said to have an expansionary monetary policy, which of the following is true?

1.	The supply of money will increase
2.	More money will circulate in the economy
3.	Banks will tighten lending
4.	Interest rates will decline

   a. 1 and 2 only
   b. 3 and 4 only
   c. 1, 2 and 4 only
   d. 1, 2, 3 and 4

27. Which is not a characteristic of a recession?

   a. Business inventories decrease
   b. Interest rates fall
   c. Commodity prices fall
   d. Capital investment falls

28. Which statement is inaccurate regarding elasticity of demand?

   a. When demand is price inelastic, a price decrease reduces total revenue
   b. When demand is price elastic, a price decrease reduces total revenue
   c. When demand is unit elastic, a price decrease leads to no change in total revenue
   d. Elasticity of demand measures the responsiveness in price to a change in demand

29. Which is considered an advantage of a 529 Plan college savings program?

   a. Both parents can be listed as owners of their child's 529 account
   b. Funds may be accessed without penalties or taxes to pay for any qualified educational facility
   c. 529 plan contributions are tax-deductible
   d. The plan can be invested in a variety of alternative investments including real estate and commodities

30. Which statement regarding a bond's price fluctuation is not true?

   a. The higher the coupon, the smaller the price fluctuation
   b. The smaller the coupon, the greater the price fluctuation
   c. The shorter the term to maturity, the smaller the price fluctuation
   d. The lower the market interest rate, the less the relative price fluctuation

31. Municipal bonds may be insured by which of the following?

1.	SIPC
2.	FDIC
3.	AMBAC
4.	MBIA

   a. Municipal bonds are not insurable
   b. 1, 2, 3 and 4
   c. 3 and 4 only
   d. 1, 3, and 4 only

32. Tiffany purchased a diamond ring many years ago, paying $2,000 at the time. Based on gold and diamond price estimates, the ring has appreciated by around 4% per year. She is now going to sell the ring, currently worth $7,000. How many years did Tiffany own the ring?

   a. 25 years
   b. 29 years
   c. 32 years
   d. 35 years

33. Your client Tom, age 45, is getting nervous about the market. He's a moderate investor and estimates he will earn around 6% per year on his investments. His IRA currently has $100,000. Tom is considering lowering his risk tolerance to a more conservative model, which he estimates will earn him only 4% annually. If Tom decides to lower his risk tolerance from now until he retires at age 65, how much less money is he expected to have than if he kept a moderate risk tolerance?

   a. $212,112
   b. $101,601
   c. $320,713
   d. $157,800

34. Your client Gabe has a required rate of return of 10%. He recently purchased 2,000 shares of Strong Company International because of its strong earnings and reported dividends. Today, Strong Company International reported a share price of $42, and an increase in dividend to $3.75 per share. In order to see if the investment still meets Gabe's requirements, he wants to know the implied growth rate of dividends for Strong Company International based on the Constant Growth Dividend Model. This model estimates the company's dividend would grow at a constant rate of...

   a. 0%
   b. .98%
   c. 2.2%
   d. 3.4%

35. Place the following sources of tax regulations in order; from the highest authority with full force and effect of the law, to that with no full force and effect of the law and only serving taxpayers with insight into tax law.

1.	Private letter rulings
2.	Revenue rulings and procedure
3.	Internal Revenue Code
4.	Treasury regulations

    a.   3,4,2,1
    b.   3,2,4,1
    c.   4,3,2,1
    d.   4,2,3,1

36. Paul and Jane, ages 30 and 34, are a young couple on a budget. They have two dependent children and have very little saved for retirement. Paul makes $65,000 per year and is the sole breadwinner of the family. He has group life insurance coverage of $250,000 but no disability insurance coverage or long-term care insurance. Jane has a whole life policy which provides benefits of $10,000, but also has no disability insurance coverage or long-term care.

Paul and Jane are concerned about their future long-term care needs. Due to their cash flow, they're only able to purchase one of the following insurance policies. As their planner, which do you recommend they purchase based on their current coverage and anticipated needs?

    a.   A long-term care policy on Jane and Paul
    b.   Individual disability insurance on Paul
    c.   Additional life insurance coverage on Jane
    d.   Additional life insurance coverage on Paul

37. Jeff is a participant in his company's 401(k) plan. The plan has a two- to six-year graduated vesting schedule. The current balance is $15,000, of which the employer contributed $5,000 and Jeff contributed $5,000. After three years with the company, Jeff is resigning. What amount of his 401(k) is Jeff permitted to take with him?

    a. $10,000
    b. $6,000
    c. $12,000
    d. $10,500

38. Your clients, ages 70 and 72, are discussing their estate planning needs with you. They've been married only to each other and have no children. They would like to leave any remaining assets at the end of their lives to charity. Currently, their estate is worth about $500,000. What do you suggest?

    a.   They should meet with an attorney to create a QTIP trust
    b.   They should begin a large annual gifting program to charity now, rather than wait until death
    c.   Because of their age, it's unnecessary to have their attorney draft living wills for each of them
    d.   Their attorney should discuss creating, or updating, their durable powers of attorney

39. In which of the following retirement plans are employers' contributions in any given year considered entirely discretionary?

1.	Defined benefit plan
2.	SIMPLE Plan
3.	Profit Sharing plan
4.	SEP

    a.   1 and 2 only
    b.   2 and 4 only
    c.   3 and 4 only
    d.   1, 2, 3 and 4

40. Max's short-term disability insurance is through a group policy provided by his employer who pays 50% of the premiums. Max's annual income is $70,000. In January, he gets injured and files for short-term disability benefits. There is a 0-day waiting period and the policy provides benefits of 65% of his salary for six months. How much of Max's benefits will be included in his gross income for federal income tax purposes?

    a. $0
    b. $14,788
    c. $11,375
    d. $22,750

41. The Kaelins have $20,000 invested in ABC mutual fund. The fund has a standard deviation of 7% and a mean return of 12%. They want to know the probability of receiving a return of 5% or greater. The likelihood of the Kaelins' return being less than or equal to 5% is…

    a.   34%
    b.   64%
    c.   72%
    d.   84%

42. Nancy has owned QWE mutual fund for over 20 years and has accumulated additional shares over these years. She is now ready to sell the fund, though her accountant suggests she gradually sell shares over a few years, for tax purposes. Which method would not help Nancy determine which shares of QWE are sold?

    a.   Random share method
    b.   FIFO
    c.   Specific Identification
    d.   Average cost method

43. Which statement regarding involuntary liquidation as part of Chapter 7 bankruptcy is true?

    a.   Creditors may file a petition for secured claims in the amount of $5,000 or more
    b.   Creditors may file a petition for unsecured claims of any amount
    c.   If there are more than 12 creditors, at least half of them must join in the petition
    d.   If there are fewer than 12 creditors, only one must file the petition

44. Which are not nondischargeable debts in Chapter 7 bankruptcy?

1.	Back taxes
2.	Alimony
3.	Child support
4.	Student loans

   a.   1 only
   b.   2 and 3 only
   c.   1, 2, and 3 only
   d.   1, 2, 3, and 4

45. Linda has recently gotten divorced and is short on cash. She wants to borrow money from her current 401(k). Linda has worked with the company for 10 years. Her balance is $80,000, of which $60,000 is her contributions, $10,000 is the company's contributions and $10,000 is earnings. The maximum amount Linda can borrow from her account is...

   a. $40,000
   b. $50,000
   c. $60,000
   d. $80,000

46. Melinda's company provides her with great benefits beyond her regular salary, bonuses, and profit sharing contribution. Which of the following fringe benefits provided by Melinda's employer will not be included in Melinda's gross income?

1.	Membership in an on-premises gym operated by her employer used by employees and their families
2.	Her sales group's weekly off-site lunch meetings to discuss sales goals
3.	5-, 10-, 15-, and 20 years of service awards (non-cash) provided to employees on their anniversary date of employment
4.	A parking spot in the garage located one block from the employer's building

   a.   2 and 3 only
   b.   1, 2 and 4
   c.   1, 3, and 4
   d.   1, 2, 3 and 4

47. Jackie, age 44, has a group life insurance policy in which her employer provides coverage of 2.5 times her salary. Jackie makes $80,000 annually. Based on Internal Revenue Service tables for cost of life insurance premiums, the cost for Jackie for one month of coverage per each $1,000 of coverage is $0.10. How much of the total cost of the insurance will be includable in Jackie's gross income over the year?

   a. $0
   b. $50
   c. $180
   d. $240

48. Dave bought TRE stock 20 years ago for $50 per share. The stock had a market value of $35 per share when Dave gifted it to his daughter Nina. When the stock falls to $25, Nina decides to sell it to purchase a new car. For tax purposes, what is the loss recognized per share for Nina?

    a. $0
    b. $10
    c. $15
    d. $35

49. Jessica received the following in the year 2009: Life insurance proceeds of $50,000, a scholarship for school of $15,000, and inheritance of $30,000. Jessica's adjusted gross income for the year is...

    a. $0
    b. $15,000
    c. $30,000
    d. $95,000

50. Currently, unemployment is at a 10-year high and continues to increase. Businesses are operating at their lowest capacity levels. The current business cycle is best described as...

    a. recession
    b. trough
    c. depression
    d. recovery

Answer Key and Explanations

1. D: $320,000. The couple could have contributed a total of $320,000 in 2022 without incurring any gift tax. While the annual gift tax exclusion amount for 2022 was $16,000, 529 plans allow donors to contribute up to five years' worth of contributions in one lump sum, allowing each grandparent to contribute $16,000 (annual contribution amount) x 5 years (lump sum provision) for a total of $80,000. Thus, $80,000 x 2 grandchildren = $160,000, the allowable contribution by each grandparent. Since both grandparents can make separate maximum contributions to each grandchild, the couple could have contributed $320,000 in total.

2. D: Eric, age 18, who has worked for Tom for 4 years and received $8,000 in compensation. Eric isn't eligible for a SEP IRA contribution due to his age. In order for an employee to be eligible, he must be at least 21 years old, worked for the employer at least three of the past five years, and received at least $650 in compensation from the employer for the year(as of 2022). Laura, Mary, and Jack all fulfill these requirements. An employer can opt to use less restrictive requirements to determine eligibility.

3. D: 1, 3, 4 and 5 only. If set up correctly, Individual Retirement Accounts, JTWROS, Joint Tenancy and Revocable Trusts can avoid probate and allow assets to be passed directly to beneficiaries. Individual bank accounts, as well as other assets titled individually, are usually included in the gross estate of the decedent and must go through the probate process. To avoid probate, individual bank and investment accounts can be held as TOD, or Transfer on Death accounts, which allow assets and securities to pass directly to beneficiaries at the owner's death.

4. A: $7,000 and $4,000. To buy on margin, Becky must abide by the firm's initial margin deposit. If it's 50%, then the initial margin amount is $7,000, or 50% of $14,000. Becky is also required to meet the maintenance margin of 40%. If the stock drops to $10,000, she has $3,000 in equity ($10,000-$7,000 = $3,000). This will not meet the required maintenance amount of $4,000 (40% of $10,000) so Becky will have to deposit another $1,000 into the account to bring her equity up to the required minimum maintenance amount.

5. A: Tina can contribute to an IRA because her husband is a wage earner and they file their taxes jointly. Although Tina herself does not earn income, she can contribute to a Spousal IRA since Tom has earned income and their tax status is Married Filing Jointly. Should they choose to file Married Filing Separately, Tina would not be permitted to make a contribution to her IRA as she has no earned income for the year. In 2022, based on their income and age, Tina and Tom could each contribute $6,000 to their IRAs for the year.

6. C: 1 and 2 only. A statutory will is generally drawn by an attorney and complies with the appropriate domiciliary laws of the state. Assuming Virginia had the legal capacity to execute such a will, a statutory will would provide for the full and legal distribution of her assets. In addition, a codicil, or attachment or supplement to the will would also be valid. A side letter of instruction has no legal standing, though it may be useful to the decedent's family. A nuncupative will is an oral will and is not valid in all states.

7. D: $43,000. Included in Susan's probate estate are jewelry valued at $35,000 and her car valued at $8,000. The life insurance and IRA, as long as they have properly named beneficiaries, pass outside the probate process as part of state contract law. The trust also avoids probate based on state trust laws. Her home is titled JTWROS and will pass outside probate. Therefore, her total probate estate is valued at $43,000.

8. B: 2 only. Only Jim and Judy are required to file Form 709, which must be filed for gifts made over the annual exclusion limit, and split gifts (even if under the annual exclusion limit). Gifts to charity, a spouse, and gifts made under the annual exclusion limit do not necessitate a Form 709.

9. C: Local Chamber of Commerce. Chambers of Commerce is usually not considered a Qualified Charitable Organization for tax purposes. According to tax code, qualifying organizations are:

- A state, possession of the United States, or any political subdivision
- A corporation, trust, community chest, fund or foundation organized in the U.S. and operated exclusively for:
    - Religious, charitable, scientific, literary or educational purposes
    - Fostering national or international amateur sports competition
    - Preventing cruelty to animals or children
    - A war veterans group, domestic fraternal society, order or association that operates under the lodge system
    - A cemetery company

10. D: $6.43. When given information on a company's dividend payout ratio and dividend per share, earnings per share can be calculated by dividing the dividend per share by the dividend payout ratio. In the case of Cars International, EPS = $2.25 (dividend per share) /.35 (dividend payout ratio) = $6.43.

11. C: $911.56. The home costs $200,000 and Thomas plans to make a 15% down payment of $30,000. Thus, the PV of the original loan is $170,000. N = 360, I = 4.99%/12 = 0.41583% = 0.0041583, and FV = 0. Therefore, his monthly payments of principal and interest are $911.56. While he may escrow additional funds to provide for property tax and insurance, these funds are not attributable to the payment of principal and interest on the loan.

12. A: 15.71%. Holding Period Return is calculated as: Current income + capital gain (or loss) / beginning investment value. Scott purchased 125 shares at $80 per share, giving him an initial investment value of $10,000. He receives 3 quarterly dividends of $1.19 per share, or $446.25. He then sells the shares for a gain of $1,125. Thus, Scott's holding period return is $446.25 + $1,125 / $10,000 = 15.71%. HPR is an appropriate return measure for periods of one year or less.

13. B: If the company repurchased outstanding stock. The price to earnings (P/E) ratio is market value per share / earnings per share (EPS). Repurchasing outstanding shares takes them out of market circulation, thus affecting an increase in the company's EPS. A higher EPS will result in a higher P/E ratio. If the company sold more shares of common stock, this would have the opposite effect and dilute the company's EPS. A lower market price would result in a lower number in the numerator and would decrease the P/E. A company's EPS should be adjusted for stock splits as to not affect the company's P/E.

14. C: 6.36%. The taxable equivalent yield for a municipal bond which is exempt from state and federal tax is: Municipal bond yield / (1 - tax rate). For Andrea's municipal bond, the taxable equivalent yield is = 4.2% / [1- (28% + 6%)] = 4.2% / 66% = 6.36%. Based on this information, the taxable bond would have to yield 6.36% return to match the after-tax return of the municipal tax-free bond.

15. B: $500. The fundamental value of a call is: (market price of the underlying stock - the strike price of the call) * 100. For Detroit Motors, the fundamental value of the call is ($50 - $45) * 100 =

$500. Neither the premium price nor the number of shares outstanding affects the fundamental value of a call or put.

16. D: 0.385. The Sharpe Ratio measures total risk of a portfolio. Sharpe = Total portfolio return - risk free rate / portfolio standard deviation. For this client, Sharpe = 8.25 - 3.55 / 12.2 = .385. A higher Sharpe Ratio is preferred to a lower ratio. The beta is not needed for the Sharpe Ratio, but it is for the Treynor Ratio. To keep Treynor and Sharpe straight, remember— Sharpe Ratio uses standard deviation.

17. B: 7.35%. The Capital Asset Pricing Model (CAPM) gives a risk-adjusted required rate of return for an investment. It is calculated as Rf + B (Rm-Rf). For Company X, required rate of return = 3.3 + 1.5 (6 - 3.3) = 7.35%. Because this measures the investment's required return on a risk-adjusted basis, beta and the risk-free rate of return are used, not standard deviation.

18. C: Any classes of stock are permitted. An S Corporation only permits one class of stock. The other statements are true: S Corps are limited to 100 shareholders, provide limited liability, and pass income through to shareholders for federal income tax purposes.

19. D: $501,000. Kathy's cost basis in the commercial property would include the sales price of $425,000, closing costs of $4,000 and contractor's fees for improvements of $72,000, equaling $501,000. The contractor's work is necessary to get the property in proper condition for renting and increases the value of the property, thus it's an allowable cost to determine cost basis.

20. B: $710,000. With the Tax Cuts and Jobs Act, a taxpayer may deduct interest on up to $750,000 in home loans, including mortgages and home equity loans whose proceeds are for buying, building, or substantially improving a home. (Prior to the TCJA, mortgage interest on principal up to $1,000,000 could be deducted, and interest on home equity loans up to $100,000 could be deducted, regardless of the purpose of the proceeds.) Since Jeffrey's $50,000 home equity loan is for his son's education expenses, interest on it would not be deductible. But since his other home equity loan is for his home, and since the sum of his mortgage and this loan are less than $750,000, all the interest on both of those loans is deductible to Jeffrey. The fact that this home equity loan principal exceeds $100,000 does not affect its deductibility.

21. B: Make a contribution to her Traditional IRA. Contributions to Traditional IRAs are tax-deductible and will reduce Ann's taxable income. Prior to the passing of the 2020 SECURE Act, this would have been disallowed; the maximum age for Traditional IRA contributions was 70.5 before that legislation. The SECURE Act repealed this requirement, allowing Traditional IRA contributions at any age, so long as one has earned income. A contribution to Ann's Roth IRA would not have affected her tax liability, and a Roth conversion (answer D) would have increased her current-year tax liability unnecessarily. Limiting her Traditional IRA distributions to the RMD amount would have incurred less tax liability than a larger distribution, but at age 71, there is no RMD for Ann in the first place. This was another change due to the SECURE Act, which increased the age for RMDs from 70.5 to 72.

22. C: Rebecca will qualify for COBRA benefits for up to 18 months. Since Rebecca is a widow with dependent children, all surviving immediate family members are eligible for benefits under COBRA for 36 months. Rebecca may be responsible for the cost of premiums, up to 102% of the insurance cost to the employer. If she fails to pay premiums, or the company ceases to maintain any group health plan, coverage may be lost.

23. C: Term insurance with conversion feature. Since cost is a factor for Jerry, a term insurance policy with a conversion feature is most suitable for him and his family. This will provide him current coverage at a low cost, with the option to convert to a permanent policy in the future if he becomes uninsurable. A 30-year term policy will not provide him coverage beyond age 55, and there are uncertainties regarding his future needs and ability to obtain the necessary coverage. A whole life policy purchase now does not take into consideration the family's current cash flow.

24. D: College application fees. 529 funds can be used for post-secondary education (college) costs that include tuition and fees, books and supplies, and 'other' expenses, which include room and board (so long as the student is enrolled at least half-time) and computer and internet access. Furthermore, the Tax Cuts & Jobs Act of 2017 permits 529 funds to be used for private K-12 tuition and fees, up to $10,000 annually per student. The SECURE Act of 2020 permits 529 funds to be used on student loans, also up to $10,000 per student (in aggregate, not annually). College application fees are not qualified 529 expenses.

25. B: $209,291. With an income of $67,000, the loan's PITI amount should not exceed $1,563.33 per month [(.28 * $67,000) / 12]. Taxes and insurance are $4,500 annually, or $375 per month, leaving principal and interest of the loan of up to $1,188.33 ($1,563.33-$375) to fit the model. Thus, FV = 0, PMT= 1,188.33, N=360, I = 5.5%/12 = 0.4583% = 0.004583. Solve for PV = $209,291.

26. C: 1, 2 and 4 only. An expansionary, or easy, monetary policy is one in which the supply of money will increase and more money will circulate in the economy. Because of this, banks have more money to lend, which typically pushes interest rates down. The Fed will have an expansionary monetary policy when it hopes to expand and improve income and employment.

27. A: Business inventories decrease. A recession is a decline in Real GDP (gross domestic product) for two or more consecutive quarters. Characteristics of a recession include a fall in interest rates, commodity prices, and capital investment. During a recession, business inventories typically increase because companies hold on to inventory that they cannot sell. In addition, consumer purchases decline, GDP falls, demand for labor falls, business profits fall, and unemployment is high.

28. B: When demand is price elastic, a price decrease reduces total revenue. Elasticity of demand measures how responsive the demand for a good is relative to changes in its price. When a product is elastic, demand changes (from slightly to substantially) relative to a change in price. Thus, a decrease in price will lead to an increase in total revenue. If demand is inelastic, a change in price will not cause as large a change in demand. Necessities are considered to be more inelastic, because people continue to buy them even when the price changes. Thus, a price decrease of an inelastic product will cause a decrease in total revenue. If a product is unit elastic, a price decrease leads to no change in total revenue.

29. B: Funds may be accessed without penalties or taxes to pay for any qualified educational facility. Prior to the Tax Cuts and Jobs Act, 529 funds could be accessed without penalties or taxes to pay for any qualified *higher* educational facility—college expenses. Post-TCJA, 529 funds can be accessed for K-12 expenses as well. There can be only one owner per 529 account, and the plan is not permitted to invest in alternative investments like real estate or commodities. While growth is tax-deferred and (qualified) distributions are tax-free, 529 contributions are not tax-deductible.

30. D: The lower the market interest rate, the less the relative price fluctuation. The smaller the coupon and the longer to maturity, the greater the bond's price fluctuations. Bonds that have larger coupons or shorter time to maturity will have smaller price fluctuations. The higher the market interest rate, the greater the relative price fluctuation of the bond.

31. C: 3 and 4 only. Municipal bonds are insurable through private insurers. Some of the larger ones include MBIA and Ambac. The Federal Guaranty Insurance Company (FGIC) also insures bonds. The insurance provides benefits to bondholders should the municipality default on payment of principal or interest.

32. C: 32 years. To determine that Tiffany has owned the ring for 32 years, PV= 2,000 FV=7,000 I= 4 PMT= 0 and solve for N, which in this case equals 32.

33. B: $101,601. If Tom kept his risk tolerance at moderate, then at retirement he would have $320,713. Calculations are N=20, I= 6, PV=100,000, PMT=0, solve for FV. If Tom lowered his risk tolerance to conservative and expected 4% earnings, he would have $219,112 at retirement. Thus, if he lowers his risk tolerance, he can expect a $101,601 difference in funds at retirement ($320,713-$212,112).

34. B: .98%. The formula for the Constant Growth Dividend Model is: V = D1 / k-g. For the case of Strong Company International, the calculation can be broken down into the following steps:

$$V = \$3.75(1 + g)/.10 - g = \$42$$
$$3.75(1 + g) = 42(.10 - g)$$
$$3.75 + 3.75g = 4.2 - 42g$$
$$42g + 3.75g = 4.2 - 3.75$$
$$45.75g = .45$$
$$g = .45/45.75$$
$$g = .98\%$$

35. A: 3,4,2,1. The Internal Revenue Code is the highest source of tax authority and carries with it the full force and effect of the law. Treasury regulations have the next highest authority and also carry the full force and effect of the law. Revenue Rulings and Procedures are said to be reliable for taxpayers, though they are less authoritative than the previous mentioned. Lastly, while Private Letter Rulings may serve taxpayers with insight into tax laws, they cannot be relied upon.

36. B: Individual disability insurance on Paul. Although subjective, it appears the biggest shortfall in their risk management plan is that Paul has no disability insurance coverage. Since Paul is the main breadwinner, Paul and Jane are dependent upon Paul to earn an income to meet cash flow and retirement needs. Long-term care and additional life insurance, though they may be needed, are not as immediate priorities as Paul's disability insurance coverage.

37. D: $10,500. The company is on a two- to six-year graduated vesting period. Since Jeff has been with the company three years, he is 40% vested in the company's contributions and earnings related to the company's contributions. In addition, Jeff is 100% vested in his own contributions and earnings. Therefore, he is permitted to take .40 * $7,500 = $3,000 of employer contribution and earnings and $7,500 of his own contributions and earnings for a total of $10,500.

38. D: Their attorney should discuss creating, or updating, their durable powers of attorney. A QTIP (Qualified Terminable Interest Property) trust is typically used for a second marriage, and this is your client's only marriage, thus a QTIP is unnecessary. Suggesting a large annual gifting program is not prudent, as the clients have provided no information about their current or future expected expenses. Without first being able to estimate their future cash flow needs, they should not be gifting. Living wills are appropriate for nearly all clients, regardless of age. They should meet with an attorney to update or draft their durable powers of attorney.

39. C: 3 and 4 only. SEP IRAs and profit sharing plans allow employer contributions to be entirely discretionary. Neither plan requires an employer make mandatory contributions each and every year. Defined benefit plan contributions are not discretionary. SIMPLE plans also require employers to make certain minimum contributions, though such a contribution may not be required in every consecutive year.

40. C: $11,375. Max will receive benefits of 65% of his salary for six months, or $22,750 [(.65 * $70,000) *6/12]. Since his employer paid one half of the premiums, 50% of his benefits will be taxable as income "in lieu of wages." Therefore, $11,375 of his short-term disability benefit payout will be included in his gross income for federal income tax purposes.

41. D: 84%. Since the mean return is 12%, half of the returns will fall above 12%. With a standard deviation of 7%, 1 standard deviation away from the mean is a 5% return (12%-7% = 5%). Thus, the probability of returns falling between 5% and 12% is 34% (1 standard deviation from the mean). 34% + 50% = 84% probability that the Kaelin's fund will return a 5% or greater return.

42. A: Random share method. Nancy and her accountant may use the FIFO, specific identification or average cost method to determine which shares of QWE are sold. There is no "random share" method available.

43. D: If there are fewer than 12 creditors, only one must file the petition. In order for a creditor to file a petition with the Bankruptcy Court, the creditor must have a non-contingent, and unsecured claim in the amount of $5,000 or more. If there are fewer than 12 creditors, only one must file the petition. However, if there are more than 12 creditors, three of them must join in the petition to the Court.

44. D: 1, 2, 3, and 4. Back taxes, alimony, child support and student loans are all examples of nondischargeable debts for a debtor filing Chapter 7 bankruptcy. This is true regardless if the bankruptcy is considered voluntary or involuntary.

45. A: $40,000. Loan amounts from qualified plans may not exceed the lesser of; (a) one half of the fair market value of the participant's vested account, or (b) $50,000. Since Linda has worked with the company for 10 years, it is assumed that the entire account is vested. Therefore, she can borrow up to $40,000, which is one half of the current market value. If Linda's vested benefit in the account had been less than $20,000, she would have been limited to the lesser of $20,000 or half the vested amount.

46. C: 1, 3, and 4. The gym benefit will not be included in gross income because it is on the employer's premises, operated by the employer, and open to all employees and their families. The years of service awards will also be excluded from gross income so long as they are not cash and do not exceed $400 in value. Qualified parking includes parking located on, or very near, the employer's premises. This would be considered an excludable benefit. The weekly sales group's meetings will be included in Melinda's gross income because they do not meet the Internal Revenue Code requirements for excludable fringe benefits. This is because they are held neither on the employer's premises nor for the convenience of the employer.

47. C: $180. Jackie makes $80,000 annually, thus her employer provides her life insurance coverage of $200,000. Under Internal Revenue Service (IRS) rules, the first $50,000 of group life insurance coverage is not taxable to the employee, leaving $150,000 of Jackie's benefit to be taxed. Based on the IRS premiums' table, for every $1,000 of coverage the cost is $.10 per month. $150,000/$1,000 = 150. 150* .10 = $15 per month. For the year, $180 will be included in her gross income for the cost of employer-provided life insurance.

48. B: $10. Under the double basis rule (for gifts below fair market value), Nina will have two bases in the stock. Her loss basis will be $35 and her gain basis will be $50. If the stock falls to $25 when she sells it, she will recognize a loss of $10 per share ($35-$25). However, for Dave, there is a permanent disallowance of his loss, as the stock was gifted below fair market value.

49. A: $0. Jessica has no taxable income for the year of 2009. The life insurance proceeds, scholarship and inheritance are all considered exclusions from her gross income.

50. B: Trough. This is best defined as a trough. In addition to high unemployment and businesses operating at their lowest capacity levels, gross domestic product (GDP) growth is at its lowest or even negative. Recession, depression and recovery, are not components of the business cycle. The business cycle points are expansion, peak, contraction and trough.

How to Overcome Test Anxiety

Just the thought of taking a test is enough to make most people a little nervous. A test is an important event that can have a long-term impact on your future, so it's important to take it seriously and it's natural to feel anxious about performing well. But just because anxiety is normal, that doesn't mean that it's helpful in test taking, or that you should simply accept it as part of your life. Anxiety can have a variety of effects. These effects can be mild, like making you feel slightly nervous, or severe, like blocking your ability to focus or remember even a simple detail.

If you experience test anxiety—whether severe or mild—it's important to know how to beat it. To discover this, first you need to understand what causes test anxiety.

Causes of Test Anxiety

While we often think of anxiety as an uncontrollable emotional state, it can actually be caused by simple, practical things. One of the most common causes of test anxiety is that a person does not feel adequately prepared for their test. This feeling can be the result of many different issues such as poor study habits or lack of organization, but the most common culprit is time management. Starting to study too late, failing to organize your study time to cover all of the material, or being distracted while you study will mean that you're not well prepared for the test. This may lead to cramming the night before, which will cause you to be physically and mentally exhausted for the test. Poor time management also contributes to feelings of stress, fear, and hopelessness as you realize you are not well prepared but don't know what to do about it.

Other times, test anxiety is not related to your preparation for the test but comes from unresolved fear. This may be a past failure on a test, or poor performance on tests in general. It may come from comparing yourself to others who seem to be performing better or from the stress of living up to expectations. Anxiety may be driven by fears of the future—how failure on this test would affect your educational and career goals. These fears are often completely irrational, but they can still negatively impact your test performance.

> **Review Video:** <u>3 Reasons You Have Test Anxiety</u>
> Visit mometrix.com/academy and enter code: 428468

Elements of Test Anxiety

As mentioned earlier, test anxiety is considered to be an emotional state, but it has physical and mental components as well. Sometimes you may not even realize that you are suffering from test anxiety until you notice the physical symptoms. These can include trembling hands, rapid heartbeat, sweating, nausea, and tense muscles. Extreme anxiety may lead to fainting or vomiting. Obviously, any of these symptoms can have a negative impact on testing. It is important to recognize them as soon as they begin to occur so that you can address the problem before it damages your performance.

> **Review Video: 3 Ways to Tell You Have Test Anxiety**
> Visit mometrix.com/academy and enter code: 927847

The mental components of test anxiety include trouble focusing and inability to remember learned information. During a test, your mind is on high alert, which can help you recall information and stay focused for an extended period of time. However, anxiety interferes with your mind's natural processes, causing you to blank out, even on the questions you know well. The strain of testing during anxiety makes it difficult to stay focused, especially on a test that may take several hours. Extreme anxiety can take a huge mental toll, making it difficult not only to recall test information but even to understand the test questions or pull your thoughts together.

> **Review Video: How Test Anxiety Affects Memory**
> Visit mometrix.com/academy and enter code: 609003

Effects of Test Anxiety

Test anxiety is like a disease—if left untreated, it will get progressively worse. Anxiety leads to poor performance, and this reinforces the feelings of fear and failure, which in turn lead to poor performances on subsequent tests. It can grow from a mild nervousness to a crippling condition. If allowed to progress, test anxiety can have a big impact on your schooling, and consequently on your future.

Test anxiety can spread to other parts of your life. Anxiety on tests can become anxiety in any stressful situation, and blanking on a test can turn into panicking in a job situation. But fortunately, you don't have to let anxiety rule your testing and determine your grades. There are a number of relatively simple steps you can take to move past anxiety and function normally on a test and in the rest of life.

> **Review Video: How Test Anxiety Impacts Your Grades**
> Visit mometrix.com/academy and enter code: 939819

Physical Steps for Beating Test Anxiety

While test anxiety is a serious problem, the good news is that it can be overcome. It doesn't have to control your ability to think and remember information. While it may take time, you can begin taking steps today to beat anxiety.

Just as your first hint that you may be struggling with anxiety comes from the physical symptoms, the first step to treating it is also physical. Rest is crucial for having a clear, strong mind. If you are tired, it is much easier to give in to anxiety. But if you establish good sleep habits, your body and mind will be ready to perform optimally, without the strain of exhaustion. Additionally, sleeping well helps you to retain information better, so you're more likely to recall the answers when you see the test questions.

Getting good sleep means more than going to bed on time. It's important to allow your brain time to relax. Take study breaks from time to time so it doesn't get overworked, and don't study right before bed. Take time to rest your mind before trying to rest your body, or you may find it difficult to fall asleep.

> **Review Video: <u>The Importance of Sleep for Your Brain</u>**
> Visit mometrix.com/academy and enter code: 319338

Along with sleep, other aspects of physical health are important in preparing for a test. Good nutrition is vital for good brain function. Sugary foods and drinks may give a burst of energy but this burst is followed by a crash, both physically and emotionally. Instead, fuel your body with protein and vitamin-rich foods.

Also, drink plenty of water. Dehydration can lead to headaches and exhaustion, especially if your brain is already under stress from the rigors of the test. Particularly if your test is a long one, drink water during the breaks. And if possible, take an energy-boosting snack to eat between sections.

> **Review Video: <u>How Diet Can Affect your Mood</u>**
> Visit mometrix.com/academy and enter code: 624317

Along with sleep and diet, a third important part of physical health is exercise. Maintaining a steady workout schedule is helpful, but even taking 5-minute study breaks to walk can help get your blood pumping faster and clear your head. Exercise also releases endorphins, which contribute to a positive feeling and can help combat test anxiety.

When you nurture your physical health, you are also contributing to your mental health. If your body is healthy, your mind is much more likely to be healthy as well. So take time to rest, nourish your body with healthy food and water, and get moving as much as possible. Taking these physical steps will make you stronger and more able to take the mental steps necessary to overcome test anxiety.

Mental Steps for Beating Test Anxiety

Working on the mental side of test anxiety can be more challenging, but as with the physical side, there are clear steps you can take to overcome it. As mentioned earlier, test anxiety often stems from lack of preparation, so the obvious solution is to prepare for the test. Effective studying may be the most important weapon you have for beating test anxiety, but you can and should employ several other mental tools to combat fear.

First, boost your confidence by reminding yourself of past success—tests or projects that you aced. If you're putting as much effort into preparing for this test as you did for those, there's no reason you should expect to fail here. Work hard to prepare; then trust your preparation.

Second, surround yourself with encouraging people. It can be helpful to find a study group, but be sure that the people you're around will encourage a positive attitude. If you spend time with others who are anxious or cynical, this will only contribute to your own anxiety. Look for others who are motivated to study hard from a desire to succeed, not from a fear of failure.

Third, reward yourself. A test is physically and mentally tiring, even without anxiety, and it can be helpful to have something to look forward to. Plan an activity following the test, regardless of the outcome, such as going to a movie or getting ice cream.

When you are taking the test, if you find yourself beginning to feel anxious, remind yourself that you know the material. Visualize successfully completing the test. Then take a few deep, relaxing breaths and return to it. Work through the questions carefully but with confidence, knowing that you are capable of succeeding.

Developing a healthy mental approach to test taking will also aid in other areas of life. Test anxiety affects more than just the actual test—it can be damaging to your mental health and even contribute to depression. It's important to beat test anxiety before it becomes a problem for more than testing.

> **Review Video: Test Anxiety and Depression**
> Visit mometrix.com/academy and enter code: 904704

181

Study Strategy

Being prepared for the test is necessary to combat anxiety, but what does being prepared look like? You may study for hours on end and still not feel prepared. What you need is a strategy for test prep. The next few pages outline our recommended steps to help you plan out and conquer the challenge of preparation.

STEP 1: SCOPE OUT THE TEST

Learn everything you can about the format (multiple choice, essay, etc.) and what will be on the test. Gather any study materials, course outlines, or sample exams that may be available. Not only will this help you to prepare, but knowing what to expect can help to alleviate test anxiety.

STEP 2: MAP OUT THE MATERIAL

Look through the textbook or study guide and make note of how many chapters or sections it has. Then divide these over the time you have. For example, if a book has 15 chapters and you have five days to study, you need to cover three chapters each day. Even better, if you have the time, leave an extra day at the end for overall review after you have gone through the material in depth.

If time is limited, you may need to prioritize the material. Look through it and make note of which sections you think you already have a good grasp on, and which need review. While you are studying, skim quickly through the familiar sections and take more time on the challenging parts. Write out your plan so you don't get lost as you go. Having a written plan also helps you feel more in control of the study, so anxiety is less likely to arise from feeling overwhelmed at the amount to cover.

STEP 3: GATHER YOUR TOOLS

Decide what study method works best for you. Do you prefer to highlight in the book as you study and then go back over the highlighted portions? Or do you type out notes of the important information? Or is it helpful to make flashcards that you can carry with you? Assemble the pens, index cards, highlighters, post-it notes, and any other materials you may need so you won't be distracted by getting up to find things while you study.

If you're having a hard time retaining the information or organizing your notes, experiment with different methods. For example, try color-coding by subject with colored pens, highlighters, or post-it notes. If you learn better by hearing, try recording yourself reading your notes so you can listen while in the car, working out, or simply sitting at your desk. Ask a friend to quiz you from your flashcards, or try teaching someone the material to solidify it in your mind.

STEP 4: CREATE YOUR ENVIRONMENT

It's important to avoid distractions while you study. This includes both the obvious distractions like visitors and the subtle distractions like an uncomfortable chair (or a too-comfortable couch that makes you want to fall asleep). Set up the best study environment possible: good lighting and a comfortable work area. If background music helps you focus, you may want to turn it on, but otherwise keep the room quiet. If you are using a computer to take notes, be sure you don't have any other windows open, especially applications like social media, games, or anything else that could distract you. Silence your phone and turn off notifications. Be sure to keep water close by so you stay hydrated while you study (but avoid unhealthy drinks and snacks).

Also, take into account the best time of day to study. Are you freshest first thing in the morning? Try to set aside some time then to work through the material. Is your mind clearer in the afternoon or evening? Schedule your study session then. Another method is to study at the same time of day that you will take the test, so that your brain gets used to working on the material at that time and will be ready to focus at test time.

STEP 5: STUDY!

Once you have done all the study preparation, it's time to settle into the actual studying. Sit down, take a few moments to settle your mind so you can focus, and begin to follow your study plan. Don't give in to distractions or let yourself procrastinate. This is your time to prepare so you'll be ready to fearlessly approach the test. Make the most of the time and stay focused.

Of course, you don't want to burn out. If you study too long you may find that you're not retaining the information very well. Take regular study breaks. For example, taking five minutes out of every hour to walk briskly, breathing deeply and swinging your arms, can help your mind stay fresh.

As you get to the end of each chapter or section, it's a good idea to do a quick review. Remind yourself of what you learned and work on any difficult parts. When you feel that you've mastered the material, move on to the next part. At the end of your study session, briefly skim through your notes again.

But while review is helpful, cramming last minute is NOT. If at all possible, work ahead so that you won't need to fit all your study into the last day. Cramming overloads your brain with more information than it can process and retain, and your tired mind may struggle to recall even previously learned information when it is overwhelmed with last-minute study. Also, the urgent nature of cramming and the stress placed on your brain contribute to anxiety. You'll be more likely to go to the test feeling unprepared and having trouble thinking clearly.

So don't cram, and don't stay up late before the test, even just to review your notes at a leisurely pace. Your brain needs rest more than it needs to go over the information again. In fact, plan to finish your studies by noon or early afternoon the day before the test. Give your brain the rest of the day to relax or focus on other things, and get a good night's sleep. Then you will be fresh for the test and better able to recall what you've studied.

STEP 6: TAKE A PRACTICE TEST

Many courses offer sample tests, either online or in the study materials. This is an excellent resource to check whether you have mastered the material, as well as to prepare for the test format and environment.

Check the test format ahead of time: the number of questions, the type (multiple choice, free response, etc.), and the time limit. Then create a plan for working through them. For example, if you have 30 minutes to take a 60-question test, your limit is 30 seconds per question. Spend less time on the questions you know well so that you can take more time on the difficult ones.

If you have time to take several practice tests, take the first one open book, with no time limit. Work through the questions at your own pace and make sure you fully understand them. Gradually work up to taking a test under test conditions: sit at a desk with all study materials put away and set a timer. Pace yourself to make sure you finish the test with time to spare and go back to check your answers if you have time.

After each test, check your answers. On the questions you missed, be sure you understand why you missed them. Did you misread the question (tests can use tricky wording)? Did you forget the information? Or was it something you hadn't learned? Go back and study any shaky areas that the practice tests reveal.

Taking these tests not only helps with your grade, but also aids in combating test anxiety. If you're already used to the test conditions, you're less likely to worry about it, and working through tests until you're scoring well gives you a confidence boost. Go through the practice tests until you feel comfortable, and then you can go into the test knowing that you're ready for it.

Test Tips

On test day, you should be confident, knowing that you've prepared well and are ready to answer the questions. But aside from preparation, there are several test day strategies you can employ to maximize your performance.

First, as stated before, get a good night's sleep the night before the test (and for several nights before that, if possible). Go into the test with a fresh, alert mind rather than staying up late to study.

Try not to change too much about your normal routine on the day of the test. It's important to eat a nutritious breakfast, but if you normally don't eat breakfast at all, consider eating just a protein bar. If you're a coffee drinker, go ahead and have your normal coffee. Just make sure you time it so that the caffeine doesn't wear off right in the middle of your test. Avoid sugary beverages, and drink enough water to stay hydrated but not so much that you need a restroom break 10 minutes into the test. If your test isn't first thing in the morning, consider going for a walk or doing a light workout before the test to get your blood flowing.

Allow yourself enough time to get ready, and leave for the test with plenty of time to spare so you won't have the anxiety of scrambling to arrive in time. Another reason to be early is to select a good seat. It's helpful to sit away from doors and windows, which can be distracting. Find a good seat, get out your supplies, and settle your mind before the test begins.

When the test begins, start by going over the instructions carefully, even if you already know what to expect. Make sure you avoid any careless mistakes by following the directions.

Then begin working through the questions, pacing yourself as you've practiced. If you're not sure on an answer, don't spend too much time on it, and don't let it shake your confidence. Either skip it and come back later, or eliminate as many wrong answers as possible and guess among the remaining ones. Don't dwell on these questions as you continue—put them out of your mind and focus on what lies ahead.

Be sure to read all of the answer choices, even if you're sure the first one is the right answer. Sometimes you'll find a better one if you keep reading. But don't second-guess yourself if you do immediately know the answer. Your gut instinct is usually right. Don't let test anxiety rob you of the information you know.

If you have time at the end of the test (and if the test format allows), go back and review your answers. Be cautious about changing any, since your first instinct tends to be correct, but make sure you didn't misread any of the questions or accidentally mark the wrong answer choice. Look over any you skipped and make an educated guess.

At the end, leave the test feeling confident. You've done your best, so don't waste time worrying about your performance or wishing you could change anything. Instead, celebrate the successful

completion of this test. And finally, use this test to learn how to deal with anxiety even better next time.

Important Qualification

Not all anxiety is created equal. If your test anxiety is causing major issues in your life beyond the classroom or testing center, or if you are experiencing troubling physical symptoms related to your anxiety, it may be a sign of a serious physiological or psychological condition. If this sounds like your situation, we strongly encourage you to seek professional help.

Thank You

We at Mometrix would like to extend our heartfelt thanks to you, our friend and patron, for allowing us to play a part in your journey. It is a privilege to serve people from all walks of life who are unified in their commitment to building the best future they can for themselves.

The preparation you devote to these important testing milestones may be the most valuable educational opportunity you have for making a real difference in your life. We encourage you to put your heart into it—that feeling of succeeding, overcoming, and yes, conquering will be well worth the hours you've invested.

We want to hear your story, your struggles and your successes, and if you see any opportunities for us to improve our materials so we can help others even more effectively in the future, please share that with us as well. **The team at Mometrix would be absolutely thrilled to hear from you!** So please, send us an email (support@mometrix.com) and let's stay in touch.

> **If you'd like some additional help, check out these other resources we offer for your exam:**
> **http://MometrixFlashcards.com/CFP**